LIVES

OF THE

IRISH MARTYRS.

BY
D. P. CONYNGHAM.
AUTHOR OF "LIVES OF THE IRISH SAINTS" AND OTHER WORKS.

"A stranger held the land and tower
 Of many a noble fugitive ;
No Popish lord had lordly power—
 The peasant scarce had leave to live.
They bribed the flock, they bribed the son
 To sell the priest and rob the sire ;
Their dogs were taught alike to run
 Upon the scent of wolf and friar."

Fredonia Books
Amsterdam. The Netherlands

Lives of the Irish Martyrs

by
D. P. Conyngham

ISBN 1-58963-257-5

Copyright © 2001 by Fredonia Books

Reprinted from the 1873 edition

Fredonia Books
Amsterdam, The Netherlands
http://www.fredoniabooks.com

All rights reserved, including the right to reproduce this book, or portions thereof, in any form.

In order to make original editions of historical works available to scholars at an economical price, this facsimile of the original edition of 1873 is reproduced from the best available copy and has been digitally enhanced to improve legibility, but the text remains unaltered to retain historical authenticity.

TO THE MEMORY

OF THE

APOSTLES OF CHRISTIANITY IN IRELAND

AND OF THAT

*ARMY OF WHITE-ROBED MARTYRS AND CONFESSORS WHO
SUBSEQUENTLY SUFFERED FOR THE FAITH
IN THAT COUNTRY*

THIS WORK

IS MOST REVERENTIALLY DEDICATED.

We beseech you, O holy Saints, Martyrs, and Confessors, who have sown the good seed, fought the good fight, and nurtured the faith with your blood, look down upon us, the children of your faith and sufferings, and intercede with the Lamb before whose throne you minister, that we may enjoy with you in heaven the beatitude of eternal bliss. Amen!

PREFACE

THE Christian zeal and devotion of the founders of the primitive Church in Ireland were only equaled by the great sacrifices and sufferings, endured alike by priests and people, during the fierce and bloody persecutions inaugurated by the Reformers under the sacred garb of religion.

The fanatical followers of Mohammed propagated the doctrines of the Koran by the sword; but the Reformers, bloodier far, prostituted the name of religion, and glorified the sacred name of God with their lips, while they butchered His faithful ministers and people, or tortured them in mockery and sport.

It is truly said, "The blood of martyrs is the seed of the Church," for in Ireland, the greater the persecution —the more blood that was shed—the stronger became the faith, and the more glorious her "white-robed army of martyrs."

From the year in which Henry VIII. plunged England into the guilt of heresy and schism, until the granting of Catholic Emancipation (a period of three centuries), the green fields of Ireland ran red with the blood of her children, and the martyr's cross and crown were the rewards of those who adhered to her faith—the glorious inheritance transmitted by the "Master of the Apostles" himself.

History has no other record of a people thus persecuted, who passed so triumphantly through the fiery ordeal; and no people could have withstood such sufferings, unless sustained by the Divine power of Him who has said to His Church, "Behold I am with you all days, even to the consummation of the world."

Even the Roman tyrants, whose hands reeked with the blood of their Christian victims, often stayed their butcheries in mercy to the brave sufferers, because they were of the same race and kindred with themselves. In Ireland, the victims were aliens in race and blood, and the love of gain imbittered the fanaticism of religious rancor, for by law the persecutor was rewarded with the property of his victim.

The persecution which commenced under Henry, in the early part of the sixteenth century, gradually increased in intensity and cruelty, until it culminated in the middle of the seventeenth, in the most bloody and exterminating scenes on record.

England readily embraced Protestantism, Ireland remained Catholic; hence, the war of supremacy and conquest carried on by the former was intensified by all the acerbity of religious hate and fanaticism; and though the roll of those who suffered death for the faith might be said to close with 1745, still the persecutions for religion's sake have come down to our own days.

Even as late as the famine years in Ireland, the land was overspread with men, aye, many of them professing to be ministers of Christ, who tempted the starving poor to sell their religion and their God for food and clothing; but the dying thousands, true to the faith and heritage of their ancestors, spurned the tempting offers, choosing rather to purchase an eternal kingdom by a death from hunger, than to sell their souls for a mess of pottage; thus, in the true spirit of martyrdom, "accounting all things as dross that they might gain Christ."

As an instance of the savage laws and enactments passed against Catholics during those centuries of persecution, it is only necessary to state that they were robbed by law of their properties; that they were prohibited from receiving a Catholic education under severe pains and penalties; and, as a reward for filial disobedience, the son of any Catholic becoming a Protestant, was empowered to disinherit his Catholic father and brothers, and deprive them of their property.

Any Catholic going abroad to be educated, was subject to the forfeiture of his estate; and any Catholic refusing to attend Protestant worship, incurred heavy fines and penalties.

These flagitious enactments were chiefly directed at the laity; but in the year 1697 a yet more wicked and cruel enactment was aimed at the clergy. This was entitled, "An act for banishing all papists exercising ecclesiastical jurisdiction in Ireland," etc., etc. It provided that all archbishops, bishops, vicars, deans, friars, and all papists exercising any ecclesiastical jurisdiction whatever in Ireland, should be for ever banished from the kingdom before the first of May, 1698, and if found there after that day, should be imprisoned during pleasure, without bail, and then transported for life. In the mean time, it provided that no archbishop, bishop, vicar, or ecclesiastic whatever, should land in Ireland from abroad, under pain of a year's incarceration, and then of perpetual banishment; also, if any archbishop, bishop, etc.

returned from banishment, he should be guilty of high treason, and die the death of a traitor. Harboring or concealing them was punishable by a fine of twenty pounds for the first offence, forty for the second, and confiscation of estate and chattels for a third; the fines to be divided equally between the informer and the Crown. A priest's head was valued at the same price as a wolf's; and no enactment left unpassed, no butchery undone, that might aid in exterminating Catholicity in Ireland, the expulsion of the Irish race, and the wholesale confiscation of their broad estates.

It is no wonder, therefore, that the country was desolated by rapine and slaughter, that the hospitable monasteries, the asylums of the sick, the poor, and the oppressed, were soon left in smouldering ruins, while their pious, simple inmates, were either driven forth houseless wanderers, or butchered to gratify the fanaticism of a rude soldiery. The stately chapel was laid in ruins, its sacred vessels became the spoil of the invader, and its faithful pastor was driven forth, to keep alive the faith in some lonely cave, some mountain fastness, or desert wild. Of the Church in Ireland, at this trying period, it might justly be said:—

> "Thy glory in a crimson tide went down
> Beneath the cloven hoof;
> Altar and priest, mitre, and cope, and crown,
> And choir and arch and roof!"

So great was this persecution, that in one year alone, of the regular clergy, one hundred and ninety were shipped from Galway, one hundred and fifty-three from Dublin, seventy-five from Cork, and twenty-six from Waterford, besides a large number of the secular clergy and bishops, who were expelled to France, Flanders, Spain, and other countries.

The sufferings and sacrifices of these noble martyrs of the Cross, are well worth preserving. Though their histories are given in the several works from which I draw my materials, still, the most of these are not accessible to the masses; and therefore, at the request of my enterprising publishers, I have prepared "The Irish Martyrs" as an addition, or rather, a companion to my "Lives of the Irish Saints."*

The one treats of the dawn, the rise, and splendor of Christianity; the other of how this pure, undefiled Faith withstood the rack, the gibbet, spoliation, and all but extermination itself; and, after all, to-day shines forth with a purity and a brilliancy that neither heresy can sully nor persecution extinguish.

Though we have a complete history of this Irish martyrology from the reign of Henry down to James, it is to be regretted that in the subsequent reigns, particularly during the Commonwealth, so bloody and relentless was the persecution that, for the most part, the history of their sufferings perished with the martyrs themselves.

When the poor priest and his faithful flock perished together in some mountain cave, not one lived to tell the tale; yet tradition has preserved it, for there is scarcely

* For the materials and subject-matter of this work, I am chiefly indebted to the able and learned works of Fleming, Wadding, Colgan, Ware, Roothe, Mooney, The Four Masters, and several other eminent old writers; and to the more modern works of Dr Moran, Brenan's valuable ecclesiastical history, Dr. Renehan, Father Meehan's valuable works and translations, and to Halpin's (Miles O'Reilly) "Memorials of those who suffered for the Catholic faith."

a townland in Ireland but reveres some lonely spot hallowed by such martyr-sacrifice.

The limits of this work will not allow me to treat in full of the army of martyrs, lay and clerical, who suffered persecution, death, or exile, for the faith. I simply confine myself to those whose ecclesiastical dignity, or whose zeal and sufferings, rendered them the most conspicuous.

I find that many of these martyrs, such as Bishops Plunkett and O'Hurley, were executed for high treason; but we must not forget that it was an offence of high treason, punishable with death, to deny the king's supremacy; and as religious persecution is ever held in detestation by all liberal minds, the very persecutors themselves preferred sacrificing their victims under the charge of disloyalty and treason than for their religious convictions.

History has done justice to these noble sufferers. The thin veil of treason that was woven round them by corrupt judges, perjured witnesses, and military tribunals, has been rent asunder, and their pure, saintly lives stand forth before us in justification of those singularly great and devoted men, whose tribulations, constancy, and triumphs earned for them the martyr's crown, and left to Irish Catholics an undying heritage of faith and good works to guide us, like a bright star, to that happy death which gave to them life eternal.

D. P. CONYNGHAM.

NEW YORK, May, 1872.

CONTENTS.

PERSECUTIONS UNDER HENRY VIII.

Remarks on the state of the Catholic Church in Ireland—Reign of Henry VIII—Causes that led to the Reformation in England and Ireland—Henry's divorce and views supported by Cranmer and Cromwell—George Brown appointed archbishop of Dublin—Great opposition to the Reformation—Suppression of religious houses—Martyrdom of their inmates—The rebellion of O'Neil—Death of Henry..Page 17

THE CHURCH IN IRELAND UNDER EDWARD AND MARY.

Reign of Edward—Characters of Brown, Staples, and Bale—The Common Prayer Book ordered to be read—Convocation of prelates—Bishop Dowdall's opposition to the Reformers—The primate expelled—Mary ascends the throne—Dowdall's return—The state of religion in Ireland—The Reform bishops deposed—Protestants protected in Ireland under Mary—Elizabeth ascends the throne—She is recognized as head of the Church—Archbishop Heath's opposition—Penal enactments—Oppression and persecutions of the Catholics—Churches plundered and destroyed—Bishops Magrath and Curwin apostatize—Persecution of Bishop Walsh—Torture and martyrdom of O'Duillian—Priests tortured and put to death in the convents of Galbally, Armagh, Elphin, and elsewhere—Father Dowd tortured and martyred—Vicar-general De Courcy marytred—Fearful persecutions commenced................................ 29

LEVEROUS AND OTHER BISHOPS PERSECUTED.

Leverous, bishop of Kildare—His bold stand—Persecution of the Bishops of Cork and Cashel—Martyrdom of Bishop O'Hely and Father O'Rorke—Drury cited to appear before the Judgment Seat—His death—Bishop Gallagher tortured to death—Bishop Macgauran

xii   CONTENTS.

massacred while hearing a confession—Bishop O'Duane martyred—
Several prelates and priests expelled—Bishop O'Herlaghy's sufferings—Several laymen, priests, and friars tortured and martyred—
Twenty-two old men martyred—Forty Cistercian monks massacred
—The convent of Nenagh—The dead monks glorifying God—Several priests and friars tortured and put to death—Sufferings and
death of Father Kinrehan, parish priest of Mullinahone—Sketches
of the different priests and friars persecuted and martyred..... Page 47

MARTRYDOM OF BISHOPS O'HURLEY AND CREAGH.

Bishop O'Hurley's persecutions—His triumph—His life and martyrdom—Archbishop Creagh—His sufferings—His death by poison—A
long list of priests hanged, quartered, and put to death—The black
catalogue—Persecution rampant—Protestant writers on the state of
the country and the sufferings of the people...................... 61

FEARFUL INCREASE OF RELIGIOUS AND POLITICAL OPPRESSION.

The Irish forced to rebel—Dissensions fostered—Irish lords, spiritual
and temporal, opposed to the Queen's supremacy—The O'Neils in
Ulster, and Desmond in Munster—The massacre of Mullaghmast—
The insurrection of Fitzmaurice—Persecutions increase—New penal
laws—Fearful state of persecution, famine, and misery in Ireland—
Extracts from Spencer—Chiefs and prelates divided—The Catholics
of the Pale and native Irish opposed—Father Kenrechtin—His capture and death—Martyrdom of Father O'Connor—Martyrdom of
Fathers Miller, Molloy, Doherty, and several others—Fathers Mau-
rice and Roche—Life and martyrdom of Archbishop Magauran, of
Armagh—Sufferings of several confessors and martyrs............ 78

THE FRANCISCANS PERSECUTED.

Penal persecutions continued—Catholics banned, outlawed, and butch-
ered—Sketch of the convents of Donegal, Multifernan, Kilconnel,
Galway, and others—Persecutions of the Franciscans—Father
Mooney's graphic account—Sufferings and constancy of Father
Donatus O'Molony—Betrayal and martyrdom of forty two priests—
Terrible torture and execution of Father Collins—End of Elizabeth's
reign, but not of the persecutions................................ 87

CONTENTS. xiii

PERSECUTIONS UNDER JAMES I.

The Catholics rejoice at the accession of James—Religious toleration expected—Their disappointment—Fresh persecutions—All bishops and priests ordered to quit the kingdom—Paul V exhorts the Irish to persevere in their faith—Several priests and ecclesiastics tortured and put to death—Martyrdom of Sir John De Burgo—His great faith and constancy.......................................Page 104

BISHOP O'DOVANY'S MARTYRDOM.

Zeal of the persecutors—Bishop O'Dovany—His arrest and imprisonment—His sufferings and starvation in prison—His release and re-arrest—His trial and sentence—His execution and martyrdom—Father Locheran's execution—Affliction of the people—The martyr's last moments—Dr. Roothe's account of their lives and sufferings... 114

CHICHESTER'S TREACHEROUS PLOTS.

New plans devised to entrap and torture priests and bishops—Chichester's plots and villainy—Sir Arthur O'Neill and others entrapped and executed—Several of the brethren of Multifernan imprisoned and put to death—The priest-hunters on the track of their prey—The spoliation of Askeaton, and martyrdom of its inmates—Martyrdom of the venerable MacGeoghegan and several other priests—The close of King James' reign—His death...................... 124

THE KING AND THE PURITANS.

Reign of Charles I.—His leaning towards Catholicity—Influence of the Puritans—Persecutions renewed—The confederation of Kilkenny—United it was powerful, disunited it soon split up—The Nuncio—Treachery of the wily Ormond—Terrible persecutions, death, and exile of the Catholics............................... 131

FRESH PERSECUTION AND TORTURE.

Persecution of the monastic orders—Cursory glance at their sufferings and fidelity—Father Francis Slingsby—His conversion and sufferings—His holy death—Bishop O'Reilly—His patriotism and death—Bishop Edmund O'Reilly—His persecution, exile, and death—Fearful picture of the persecutions in Ireland—Martyrdom of the Rev Peter Higgins—Persecution of the Jesuits—Massacre of Catholics on Island Magee—Capture of Dungarvan and execution of several priests—Martyrdom and heroic resolution of Father Mahony—Fifty old men, women, and children martyred—An old lady of eighty years martyred—Fearful persecution, both of the Franciscans and Dominicans......................................Page 139

MURROUGH, THE BURNER.

Life of Archbishop O'Queely—His standing with the Court of Rome—Joins the Confederates, and raises a regiment—The Irish troops surprised and defeated at Ballysadare—The archbishop slain—Inchiquin, or "Murrough, the burner," attacks Cashel—Heroic resolve of the garrison—Butchery of the soldiers, priests, and people—Fearful massacre—Twenty priests and three thousand persons slain—Desecration of the altars and churches—The monastery of Kilmallock attacked, and two priests martyred...................... 157

CROMWELL'S CAMPAIGN IN IRELAND.

Execution of King Charles—Arrival of Cromwell in Ireland—Sack of Drogheda—Terrible butchery of men, women, and children—A number of priests and friars put to death—Terrible massacre in Wexford—Neither age nor sex spared—Several priests martyred—Incarceration and death of Dr. Roothe—Capture of Bishop Egan—Offered his life and liberty if he would advise the garrison of Carrigodrohid to surrender—He advises them to fight to the last, and is cruelly put to death by Lord Broghill.......................... 167

THE PURITANS IN IRELAND.

Cromwell's return to England—His bloody agents in Ireland—Ireland under the Puritans—Bishop O'Brien of Emly—His trial and martyrdom—He summons Ireton to answer for his crimes before the judgment-seat of God—Sudden death of Ireton—Fearful massacre in Limerick—Several priests put to death—St. Vincent de Paul's interest in the Catholic Church in Ireland—Fearful state of suffering and persecution of the Church................................. 177

THE SWORD AND THE MITRE.

Bishop Heber MacMahon assumes the command of O'Neill's army—Brave and rash—His patriotism and execution—Coote's hostility

—Governor King's kind interference—Progress of the plantation of
Connaught—A large number of priests tortured and martyred—
Cruel treatment of the prisoners on the island of Inisbofin—Numbers sold into slavery—Unrelenting persecution continued.... Page 188

THE IRISH EXPELLED AND HANGED.

Persecution and martyrdom of several noble ladies and nuns—Father
Fogarty martyred in Holy Cross—The tomb of the O'Fogartys—
Borlase accused of the persecutions in Ireland—What Moiisson says
—Prendergast's Cromwellian settlement—Several priests persecuted
—The Irish expelled—Persecutions slacken for want of victims..... 200

IRELAND UNDER CHARLES II.

The reign of Charles II.—The persecution of the Catholics abated—
What the various orders had suffered by death, exile, and persecution—Sufferings of Dr. Lynch, bishop of Tuam—Persecution of Dr.
De Burgo and Bishop Talbot—Talbot's influence with the king—
Charles becomes a Catholic, and dies one—The Puritans fearing the
influence of Dr. Talbot, get up a strong persecution against him—
Sufferings and persecution of Dr. Forstall, bishop of Kildare, and
De Burgo, bishop of Elphin...................................... 212

NEW PLOTS AND PERSECUTIONS.

The Puritans aroused—The Titus-Oates plot—Intrigues of Lord
Shaftesbury and others—New persecutions aimed at the Catholics
—Life of Dr. Plunket—His arrest—His accuseis fail to appear
against him at Drogheda—His acquittal—His enemies succeed in
having him tried in London—The perjured witnesses—His trial and
condemnation—He declares his innocence—His death............. 220

THE DAWN OF TOLERATION.

The downfall of Dr. Plunket's enemies—Narrow escape of Bishop
Creagh—Heaven's judgment upon his perjured enemies—Persecution of Archbishop Russell—Fresh penal laws—The priest-hunters
and their bloodhounds—Spies pretending to be priests, in order to
betray their victims—A poor priest and several of his flock killed—
A cry for toleration—The Catholic churches of Dublin thrown
open by order of the Viceroy, on Patrick's Day, 1745.. 236

CONTENTS.

EXECUTION OF FATHER SHEEHY.

Persecutions in the eighteenth century—Contest between the people and the Cromwellian settlers—The Whiteboys—Their depredations—Father Nicholas Sheehy—His sympathy for the people and opposition to their oppressors—They plot his ruin—His trial and acquittal in Dublin—Arrested for the murder of John Bridge—How the Orange landlords of Tipperary managed his trial and procured perjured witnesses—His sentence and execution—Horrible fate of the jurors and witnesses—The execution of Ned Sheehy and others...Page 243

LIVES OF THE IRISH MARTYRS.

PERSECUTIONS UNDER HENRY VIII.

Remarks on the state of the Catholic Church in Ireland—Reign of Henry VIII—Causes that led to the Reformation in England and Ireland—Henry's divorce and views supported by Cranmer and Cromwell—George Brown appointed archbishop of Dublin—Great opposition to the Reformation—Suppression of religious houses—Martyrdom of their inmates—The rebellion of O'Neil—Death of Henry.

THE Catholic Church in Ireland had scarcely recovered from the effects of the barbarous atrocities perpetrated by the Danish invaders, when the English invasion again embroiled the country in war, and exposed the Church to fresh persecutions and spoliations. The Danes had no sympathy with Christianity, or regard for the faith of the people, and therefore had no remorse in plundering the monasteries of their treasury, of despoiling the altars of their sacred vessels, of leveling with the ground the monasteries and temples of God, and of butchering His servants and worshipers.

After the defeat of the Danes the Church recovered something of its ancient glory. Monasteries were again rebuilt or repaired by pious chieftains, and psalm and hymn and daily sacrifice glorified the Lord within their sacred walls.

War has ever impeded the progress of Christianity, and the English invaders, though they knelt at the same shrine and believed in the same faith as the Irish, held the latter in such abhorrence that even their churches and monasteries did not escape their ravages. But time and the associations that made these Norman chiefs "more Irish than the Irish themselves," slowly fused into one common channel the religious views of Norman and Celt, and we find a laudable rivalry between them in building and endowing churches and monasteries. This religious emulation between the rival races would have ultimately blended them into one common nationality, had not the Reformation, by its baleful influence and persecutions, overspread the land with sectarian hate, strife, and blood.

In 1509 Henry VIII. ascended the throne of England under the most favorable and promising auspices. He married, by particular dispensation, Catherine, princess of Arragon, the wife of his deceased brother, Arthur.

In the year 1512 the fifth general council of Lateran was held, which was attended by Mauritius de Portu, archbishop of Tuam, and Thomas Halsay, bishop of Leighlin, on behalf of the Irish Church. About the same time two provincial synods had been held in Dublin, and in 1523 a national synod was convened at Galway, most probably not only to consider the internal affairs and discipline of the Church in Ireland, but also to take precautions against the contagion of the heretical doctrines of Luther, which were fast gaining ground over the Continent.

Like all other heresies that have sprung up in the Church, that of Luther's may be traced to pride, disappointed ambition, and lust of worldly power and pleasures. It is remarkable that Henry, who afterwards became such a scourge to the Church, stood its champion, and published a work in opposition to Luther's noxious tenets, which gained for him, from Pope Leo, the distinguished title of DEFENDER OF THE FAITH, a title still retained by his successors on the throne of England.

Henry had now lived seventeen years with his lawful wife, when his real nature began to develop itself. Smitten with a blind passion for Anne Boleyn, he sought to procure a separation from Catherine. His time-serving sycophant, Wolsey, was opposed to the divorce, as it would thwart his own ambitious views, and therefore soon fell under the king's displeasure. Henry soon found a willing instrument in Cranmer, whom he had promoted to the See of Canterbury, and who secretly favored the doctrines of Luther. Though the Pope could not annul the marriage between Henry and Catherine, Cranmer readily did, and privately married the king to Anne Boleyn. An obsequious parliament, selected for that purpose, not only confirmed the acts of Cranmer, but also declared Henry *the supreme head on earth of the Church in England.*

In all his wicked schemes Cranmer found a ready and able ally in Thomas Cromwell, who had been secretary to Cardinal Wolsey, but who had entered so warmly into the schemes of the king that he was raised to be chancellor of England, and vicar-general, both in spiritual and temporal matters, under the new supremacy.

Henry did not so much desire the change of the religious principles of the people as to confirm his divorce and to plunder the wealth of the Church. Though the doctrines of the new Church favored his passions and licentious desires, still he had an innate reverence for the old faith, and desired only its wealth in order to satisfy his extravagance and debauchery. In all these rapacious schemes he had an able and unscrupulous ally in Cromwell, who was at heart a stern Lutheran, and who used his power for the furtherance of its doctrines as well as to gratify his own ambition and the desires of his master.

The times and circumstances were favorable for the spoliation of the wealthy and extensive Irish monasteries, and for the artful propagation of the heresy of Luther. Henry, with all his impiety and sensuality, never espoused the new religion. It was useful to him, for through its instrumentality he procured a divorce from his lawful wife, and it opened up to him a liberal supply of money and the unbridled gratification of his passions. Wealth and licentiousness were his religion. The schism which he caused gave him the full indulgence of the one, while the plunder of the monastic establishments promised him the enjoyment of the other. When he discovered that Cromwell and his agents were active propagators of the new heresy, he became indignant, and in 1539 he summoned a parliament, and caused an act to be passed by which it was made criminal to deny the real presence of Christ in the sacrament, the celibacy of the clergy, the obligation of vows of chastity, private Mass, and auricular confession. This act received the king's royal signature.

The See of Dublin having become vacant, the king, at the instigation of Cromwell, raised George Brown, an Englishman, to the dignity of archbishop of Dublin, in March, 1535. Brown was an Augustinian monk, and at the time provincial of the order in England. Though at heart a rank Lutheran, he remained at the head of his order until his ability and pliant disposition gained him the confidence of Cromwell, who recommended him to the king. He was *consecrated* in London by Cranmer, and immediately sailed for Dublin, accompanied by certain commissioners appointed by the king to enforce the doctrine of lay supremacy and the confiscation of the monasteries.

PERSECUTIONS UNDER HENRY VIII.

On their arrival in Dublin the prelates and several of the nobility were summoned to the Castle to give in their adhesion to the new doctrines and the king's supremacy. This proposition was met with scorn and contempt, and the primate, George Cromer, strongly denounced such a daring attempt at raising a schism in Ireland and the conduct of Bishop Brown.

Thus was the Reformation inaugurated in Ireland, and thus was its very advent opposed with a firm and determined opposition.

The excitement in Ireland became intense. The Irish looked upon death as preferable to apostasy, while the English inhabitants of the Pale nobly clung to the old faith. Brown's mission promised to be a perfect failure, and he would have fled to England but he dreaded the resentment of the king, who felt indignant at his want of success, and in a letter ordered him to bear in mind "*that we be as able to remove you agayn, and to put another man of more vertue and honestie in your place, as we were at the beginning to preferre you, upon hope that you would in the same do your office.*"*

In the meantime Brown informs Cromwell of the hopeless state of affairs in Ireland, and recommends the enforcement of vigorous laws. Accordingly, the deputy, Lord Grey, was instructed to summon a parliament, which met at Dublin on the 1st of May, 1536. This servile assembly, composed of dependants and agents chiefly selected from the Pale, declared Henry sole and supreme head of the Church in Ireland, while all appeals to the Pope on spiritual matters

---

* Neither Ware nor Harris has left us any account of the time or place of this time-serving prelate's death. His religion was ambition and power. After the accession of Edward he was the first to order the adoption of the English litturgy and service in his churches. His servility did not serve him to the end for he was deprived of his archbishopric under Queen Mary. An unhappy notoriety attaches to his name as an apostate clergyman.

were prohibited, and, to maintain the supremacy of the Apostolic See, rendered the offender subject to a *præmunire.*

Beside these enactments, the strongest temptations and inducements were held out to ecclesiastics who would apostatize, and it is to be regretted that some bishops and priests yielded to the temptation of riches and preferment.

Thus, by means of a corrupt parliament and bribery, did schism for the first time take a hold in the country.

Deputy Grey and Bishop Brown, having gained several adherents, and thus strengthened their power and influence, next turned their attention to plunder, and the wholesale confiscation and spoliation of Church property followed.

While the schismatics in Dublin had been enriching themselves with the spoils of the sanctuary in that city, the lord deputy was actively engaged in plundering the churches of Ulster. The splendid and venerable cathedral of Down was first robbed, and afterwards burned to the ground by this incendiary; at the same time the tombs and relics of Sts. Patrick, Bridget, and Columbkille, were demolished, and the ashes scattered with the winds of heaven. The image of the Blessed Virgin was torn from the high altar of the abbey of Trim, and profaned in the public market: the relics of the martyrs, after having been turned into mockery, were cast on the streets and thrown out on the highways; while the image of Christ crucified was brought from the abbey of Ballibogan, and the crozier of St. Patrick from Christ Church, and were both indignantly committed to the flames.* But the confiscation of the property belonging to the religious houses was that on which the plunderers had been most particularly intent. Among the abbeys which had been at this time suppressed, the most celebrated were those of Mellifont,† in the county of Louth; Jer-

* Register Eccl ; Ware's Annals of Henry VIII , p. 99.

† The abbey of Mellifont, in the barony of Ferrard and county of Louth,

point* and Graignemanagh, in the county of Kilkenny; Baltinglass, in the county of Wicklow; Dunbrody,† Tintern,

was founded for Cistercian monks in 1142, by Donogh O'Carrol, king of Oriel, and was supplied with monks by St. Bernard, from the abbey of Clairvaux. Mellifont was the most ancient monastery of the Cistercian Order in Ireland, having for its first abbot Christian O'Conarchy, afterwards bishop of Lismore and legate apostolic. In 1157 a synod was held here for the purpose of consecrating the church, and at which, besides the legate, several princes and bishops of the kingdom attended. Among other offerings made on this occasion was one from the celebrated Dervorgill, wife of O'Rouarc, prince of Breffny. She gave sixty ounces of gold, with a chalice of the same metal for the high altar, and presented furniture for nine other altars. The abbots of Mellifont sat as barons in parliament; the last of whom, Richard Conter, received on its suppression, in 1540, an annual pension of £40 for life. According to the last inquisition, the possessions consisted of one hundred acres, being the demesne land, five water-mills, eight messuages, and two hundred and fifty-five acres of land in the Sheep-Grange, together with seventy-two messuages, and two thousand acres, in the county of Louth. The property in the county of Meath amounted to one hundred and eighty-one messuages, and two thousand five hundred and ninety-six acres of arable and pasture land, besides the tithes to various rectories in both counties. These extensive possessions, belonging to the abbey, were granted to Sir Gerald Moore.

* The abbey of Jerpoint, in the barony of Knoctopher and county of Kilkenny, was founded for Cistercians in 1180, by Donald, prince of Ossory. The founder and Felix O'Dullany, bishop of Ossory, were interred in this abbey. Although this extensive foundation had been splendidly endowed by Donald and other chieftains of Ossory, it had not, however, been exempted from the illiberal enactments of the fourteenth century. In 1380 it was ordained by parliament that "no mere Irishman should be permitted to make his profession in this abbey." The abbots of Jerpoint were lords of parliament, the last of whom was Oliver Grace. By an inquisition taken in the 31st of Henry VIII., the possessions consisted of fifteen messuages and two hundred and twenty-four acres of arable and pasture land in Jerpoint, together with four water-mills, forty-three messuages, and one thousand three hundred and twenty acres of land in various parts of the county; also the rectories of Jerpoint, the Rowre, Blancherstown, and fourteen others, all situated in the county of Kilkenny. The possessions were granted to James, earl of Ormond.

† The abbey of Dunbrody (Portus Sanctæ Mariæ), in the barony of Shelburne and county of Wexford, was founded in 1182. Hervey de Monte Morisco, seneschal of the estates belonging to Strongbow, made a consid-

and Ferns, in the county of Wexford; Tracton, in the county of Cork; Abbington, in the county of Limerick; Monasterevan, in Offaly; and Trim, Duleek, and Bectiff, in the county of Meath. Among the priories may be mentioned those of St. John of Jerusalem (Kilmainham); the Holy Trinity (Christ Church), Dublin; Conal and St. Wolstan's, in the county of Kildare; Kenlis, in Ossory; St. Patrick's, in Down; All Saints, near Dublin; Athassell, in the county of Tipperary; and the priory of the Blessed Virgin, in the town of Louth. In the parliament held under St. Leger in 1541, an act was passed, granting the full and

erable grant of lands to St. Mary and to St. Benedict, and to the monks of Bildewas, in Shropshire, for the purpose of erecting an abbey here for Cistercians; Felix O'Dullany, bishop of Ossory, being one of the witnesses of the charter. Hervey, the founder of this abbey, became soon after a monk in the monastery of the Holy Trinity, in Canterbury. In 1380 it was enacted "that no mere Irishman be suffered to profess in this abbey." The abbot of Dunbrody sat as a baron in parliament Alexander Devereux, the last abbot, surrendered the establishment in 1539, after having first provided for his relations by the sacrilegious plunder of its possessions. By an inquisition taken in the 37th of Henry VIII, this abbey was found to possess sixty acres of pasture and an extensive grange in Dunbrody, one hundred and twenty acres in Battlestown, eighty acres in Duncannon, sixty acres in Clonard, and eleven hundred and thirty acres of arable and pasture land in various parts of the county of Wexford; besides immense possessions in Connaught and in the counties of Limerick and Waterford. In 1546, these possessions were granted to Osborne Itchingham. The ruins of the abbey of Dunbrody, rising in awful grandeur just at the conflux of the rivers Suir and Barrow, present a truly picturesque and magnificent appearance. These ruins, including the cloister and church, are perhaps the most complete, and at the same time the most extensive, of any in the kingdom. At the west end stood the porch, adorned with filagree work cut in stone, while the immense Gothic window which rises above it displays an amazing specimen of curious and splendid architecture. The chancel and walls of the church are entire; within it are three chapels, corbeled and groined; while the aisle is separated from the nave by a double row of arches, with a molding which reclines in beautiful consoles The tower, also, is complete, and the arch on which it rests is of a most beautiful finish.

free disposal of all the abbeys and priories to the king, who, as Ware remarks, soon after disposed of their possessions to his nobles, courtiers, and others, reserving to himself certain revenues, or annual rents. By another act of this parliament, Henry was, for the first time, solemnly proclaimed king of Ireland.

In some cases the superiors of these religious houses surrendered without opposition the charge intrusted unto them; but whenever they could not be induced by threats or promises to resign their monasteries to the crown, severer measures were resorted to; and one instance is especially recorded of Manus O'Fihily, the last Abbot of St. Mary's, Thurles, who, on a refusal to comply with the wishes of the crown, was carried a prisoner to Dublin, and subjected to a long and painful imprisonment.*

When we consider that in the abbeys and monasteries the poor were gratuitously educated, fed, and clothed, we can form some conception of the misery the suppression of so many religious houses caused to thousands. The fine old buildings, raised alike by the piety of Norman and Celt, were either razed to the ground, or converted into strongholds and castles. The poor, who lived on the charity and bounty of the monks, died of starvation, while the retainers or tenants, who lived at ease under their kind landlords, were soon expelled, to make room for the proselytes who, induced by liberal offers of land, sacrificed their religious convictions for worldly considerations.

---

* Grose, in his Antiquities of Ireland, speaking of the abbey of St. Mary's, Thurles, says: "This church is mostly in ruins, except the tower, and much of that is fallen down. It was built in the fifteenth century by the O'Meaghers, who placed Franciscans in it." We give an engraving of this fine old ruin as taken in 1793. We believe that the only building now remaining is the old castle. It possesses a historic interest, as its abbot was the first to refuse the surrender of his monastery, and to stand out in de ance of his persecutors.

As for the monks themselves, driven from their monasteries, many of them wandered up and down, seeking subsistence from the willing, but poor and oppressed Catholics; others left the country, and either joined or established religious houses on the Continent; while numbers of them were slain by a rude soldiery and by the followers of the nobles and courtiers who possessed their houses and lands. The country became convulsed with strife and rancor, and thousands had flocked to the standard of Con O'Neil, who had taken up arms in defence of his religion.*

Though the faithful underwent fearful persecutions toward the latter part of the reign of Henry, few publicly suffered martyrdom. Numbers of the monks and religious were killed at their expulsion from their houses, but the king's adhesion to many of the doctrines of Catholicity made it too hazardous for his agents in Ireland to resort to the stake or the gibbet. In fact, Henry burned at the same stake Lutherans, for denying the real presence, with Catholics, for denying his supremacy.

The Spanish writer Lopez states that in the year 1539 a large number of Trinitarian fathers were martyred in Ireland, while the "Annals of the Four Masters" state that in the year 1540 "The English, in every place throughout Ireland where they established their power, persecuted and banished the nine religious orders, and particularly they

---

* As we are not writing a civil history of those trying times, we pass over the insurrection of O'Neil. He successfully invaded the Pale, burned Navon and Atherdee, and reviewed his successful troops at Tara. His success, though, was shortlived, for he was utterly defeated by the deputy, Lord Grey, at Bellahoe, in Meath. After this the persecution against the religious houses was renewed with vigor, and a great number of them were surrendered to the king Among the abbots and priors thus despoiled were twenty-four who were lords in parliament. At the parliament held in Dublin in 1541 the title of the king as ' lord" was changed to that of "king of Ireland."

destroyed the monastery of Monaghan, and beheaded the guardian and a number of friars.*

The primate George Cromer, who had zealously opposed the reformers all through, after an incumbency imbittered by continued troubles, died in 1542. Upon his death, Henry, through the influence of the deputy, St. Leger, had George Dowdall, vicar-general to the late primate, appointed to the vacant see; while at the same time the learned Robert Waucop, though blind from his infancy, was consecrated archbishop of Armagh, by Pope Paul III.† This prelate was a native of Ireland, became a doctor of divinity at Paris, was afterwards appointed legate *a latere* from the Pope to Germany, and was present at the Council of Trent, from the first session, in 1545, to the eleventh, in 1547. By the exertions of this extraordinary man, the Jesuits had, in 1541, been introduced into Ireland. John Codur was the first of the society who had settled in this country; Alphonso Salmeron, Paschale Broet, and Francis Zapata arrived soon after. The Archbishop Waucop never returned to his see; he was employed in the management of several important commissions on the Continent until 1551, in which year he died, at Paris, and was interred in the convent of the Jesuits in that city.‡

In the year 1546, Henry VIII. was drawing near his end; during his unfortunate career on this earth he was a living sink of lust, and a wretched victim to the vilest passions. He lived a tyrant, hated and dreaded by all; and he died as he lived, on the 28th of January, 1547. He had six wives—two of whom were repudiated, two beheaded, one died in

---

* The convent of Monaghan was founded on the site of the ancient abbey of St Moeldod, in 1465, by Phelim MacMahoune, for Conventual Franciscans. It was granted at the suppression to Edward Withe.

† Hist. Cath., t. ii.; Ware's Annals.

‡ O'Sullivan, p. 79.

child-bed, and the last would have ended her days on a scaffold, had Providence permitted the monster to continue much longer on earth.

The Council of Trent had been holding its sessions since the year 1545, and, although religion and the state of society had been at that period frightfully convulsed in Ireland, there had been in attendance at the council, Thomas O'Herlihy, bishop of Ross; Donald Mac-Congall, bishop of Raphoe, and Eugene O'Hart, bishop of Achonry.*

---

* Ware's Bishops.

THE CHURCH IN IRELAND UNDER EDWARD AND MARY.

Reign of Edward—Characters of Brown, Staples, and Bale—The Common Prayer Book ordered to be read—Convocation of prelates—Bishop Dowdall's opposition to the Reformers—The primate expelled—Mary ascends the throne—Dowdall's return—The state of religion in Ireland—The Reform bishops deposed—Protestants protected in Ireland under Mary—Elizabeth ascends the throne—She is recognized as head of the Church—Archbishop Heath's opposition—Penal enactments—Oppression and persecutions of the Catholics—Churches plundered and destroyed—Bishops Magrath and Curwin apostatize—Persecution of Bishop Walsh—Torture and martyrdom of O'Duillian—Priests tortured and put to death in the convents of Galbally, Armagh, Elphin, and elsewhere—Father Dowd tortured and martyred—Vicar-general De Courcy martyred—Fearful persecutions commenced.

ENRY was succeeded by his son, Edward VI., then in the tenth year of his age.

The duke of Somerset, his maternal uncle, assumed the title of protector. Somerset was a zealous Lutheran, and an ambitious, despotic, unscrupulous man.

Few events of importance characterize the short reign of Edward. Acting under the instructions of Somerset, he encouraged the progress of the Reformation chiefly in Ireland, and Brown, Staples and Bale used their influence with the lord deputy, St. Leger, to increase the persecutions of the Catholics, and to compel them to embrace the new religion.

Dr. Staples was an Englishman, and had been appointed bishop of Meath, in 1530, at the request of Henry VIII. He had to fly to England, in 1534, from the fury of Silken

Thomas, to whom he had made himself obnoxious. He returned the following year, deeply imbued with the spirit of the Reformation. Brenan, in his ecclesiastical history, states that during the schism in Henry's reign, his orthodoxy became the subject of just suspicion, while, by his immoral conduct, he is said to have forfeited almost every mark of respect from his flock.*

On the other hand, Bale was well known to be one of those dangerous, rambling adventurers who, in times like the period of which we are treating, hawk about their conscience from one mart to another, ever ready to tender it to the highest and best bidder. He was born in the county of Suffolk, but became a Carmelite at Norwich.† Taking advantage of the general confusion which had prevailed, Bale fled from his convent, and set out by preaching sedition, first in York and afterwards in London, for which he was cast into prison. Here he would have remained, had he not abandoned his faith. Bale became an apostate; made application to Cromwell, and was set at liberty. Not meeting with much encouragement in England, he made his way into Germany; but that country having been already overstocked, he took his leave and set sail for Ireland.

Soon after the meeting already mentioned, Bale was consecrated by George Brown, and placed in the see of Ossory. The infamous conduct of this intruder, during the few months which he spent in Kilkenny, was not to be tolerated by the Catholic inhabitants of that city; for while he was in the act of reviling their religion, and of making a jest of their faith, he was assailed by the populace; five of his domestics were slain, and he himself narrowly escaped. Bale enjoyed his ill-gotten dignity but six months, when Mary ascended the throne. Dreading that vengeance would at length overtake him, and feeling no burning desire for

* Rymer, tom. xv., p. 206. † Scriptores Britan., cent. viii.

enjoying the palm of martyrdom, he suddenly disappeared, and took refuge in Switzerland. John Bale never returned to Ossory ; during the reign of Elizabeth he came back, it is said, to England, where he spent the remainder of his days in comparative obscurity, and died about the year 1563.*

Brown, Staples, and Bale may serve as excellent samples of the other reformers of the sixteenth century. These are the sort of characters that went over from England, to turn into scorn that ancient and venerable faith, by the belief and practice of which, in the days of our sainted forefathers, the name of Ireland was extolled over Europe.

In 1550 an edict was issued, commanding that the Common Prayer Book of the English Church should be read in English in all Irish churches. The viceroy, St. Leger, convoked the prelates, and notifying them of the king's command, demanded their assent. The primate, George Dowdall, peremptorily refused, and denounced the innovation in strong and earnest language. He was opposed by Brown and Staples; but so well did he maintain his point, that all the other bishops sustained him, and refused to obey the edict.

The primate refused to hold communion with Brown or Staples, and the latter, stung to the quick by the firmness and contempt of the primate, resolved to persecute him with the rancor of hate.

Sir James Crofts, a furious zealot and fanatical bigot, succeeded St. Leger as viceroy, and warmly entered into the schemes of the conspirators. They heaped all kinds of persecutions and troubles upon the primate, whose constancy and fidelity to his faith and flock caused them so much trouble and annoyance. Finally, they secured letters-patent depriving him of the primacy, as Ware states : "By reason that George Dowdall was obstinate and perverse, and that

* Rymer, tom xv , p. 563.

George Brown was the first of Irish bishops who embraced the order for establishing the English liturgy and reformation in Ireland."

The primate either fled or was expelled from the country, and, contrary to Bishop Brown's expectations—for he had all along intrigued to be created primate—Hugh Goodacre was appointed the first Protestant bishop of Armagh, on the 28th October, 1552.

After a short reign of six years, Edward died, and was succeeded by his sister Mary, who ascended the throne on the 6th of July, 1553.

The restoration of the ancient religion of the country, the return of the primate, and the removal of immoral ecclesiastics, are the principal events that characterize the reign of this princess. At the time of Edward's death, and during the administration of Crofts, the state of Catholicity in Ireland was deplorable. The clergy, in many places, were obliged to retire and conceal themselves from the fury of their pursuers; churches and places of worship were closed, the celebration of the divine mysteries was suspended, and religion appeared to have been threatened with all the horrors of sanguinary persecution. Providence, however, interfered, and on Mary's accession to the throne the clergy were again placed over their flocks, while the friends of order and of morality began to congratulate each other on the anticipated downfall of heresy, and on the happy restoration of ecclesiastical discipline and ancient truth.

The return of George Dowdall to the archiepiscopal see of Armagh, in 1553, gave reality to these expectations. No sooner had this excellent prelate been replaced in his see, than he commenced the real work of religious reform. For this purpose he convened a national synod in St. Peter's Church, at Drogheda, at which almost all the Catholic bishops of the kingdom attended. "In it," says Ware, "several decrees were made for reviving the rites that had been formerly practiced in the Church, and some decrees were also passed against ecclesiastical debauchees."

On the following April, 1554, the primate, together with William Walsh, doctor of divinity, and afterwards bishop of Meath, received a royal commission, investing them with authority to proceed against immoral ecclesiastics, and to depose those prelates who, by their recreancy, had done such mischief to the fold of Christ. Accordingly, on the 29th of June, Edward Staples, bishop of Meath, was removed from his see. Brown, archbishop of Dublin, was punished in the same manner, and immediately after, Lancaster, of Kildare, and Travers, of Leighlin, were likewise deposed.*

Hugh Curwin, chaplain to the queen, was appointed to succeed Dr. Brown in the archiepiscopal see of Dublin. He was a zealous supporter of Catholicity during the reign of Queen Mary, but, on the ascension of Elizabeth, proved to be a more worthless character even than Brown.

As soon as Mary had ascended the throne, the Catholic religion was restored, the acts confirming the king's supremacy abrogated, and communion with the Pope as supreme head of the Church sought for, and of course obtained. Protestant writers have endeavored to blacken the reign of Mary as one of persecution and religious intolerance. They designate her "Bloody Mary," in contradistinction to the "Virgin Queen." It is true that during her short reign many persons suffered capital punishment for their crimes and wicked lives, whose hands were red with the blood of bishops and priests shed in the two preceding reigns, but who had lately entered into a treasonable confederacy to dethrone Mary in the interest of her Protestant sister Elizabeth. Loyalty to the throne by Protestants meant loyalty to the sovereign who represented their intolerant views and

* Ware's Annals; Jus Primatiale.

supported their ascendancy. The same spirit of bigotry that aimed at the dethronement of Mary proved its loyalty by exiling the amiable James, to make room for a foreigner in the person of William of Orange. Though Cranmer has been lauded as a martyr, it must not be forgotten that, though privately married to the sister of the atheist Osiander, he took an oath of celibacy, in order to be consecrated Archbishop of Canterbury ; and that, in order to save himself from the stake, he signed a recantation of his errors.

Queen Mary having died after a short reign, her sister Elizabeth ascended the throne, and was proclaimed queen, November 17, 1558. Though she had previously professed the Catholic doctrine, she now threw off the mask, resolved to establish Protestantism by all the means in her power. Her well-known purpose drew around her ministers and agents, who urged her to the use of the sword, the rack, and torture for the extermination of the Catholic faith.

Elizabeth possessed a good deal of the dogged, splenetic nature of her father, and she could not forget that by the Pope and the laws of the Catholic Church she was declared illegitimate, and had she professed the Catholic doctrine, her hated rival, Mary, queen of Scots, would, by legitimate descent, have the best right to the crown.

In England a packed parliament was convened, for the purpose of recognizing the Protestant religion as the established one. Though threats, bribes, and honors were lavishly held forth to the members, the measure passed the commons only by a majority of six, while in the house of lords it received an equally strong opposition. Archbishop Heath, in his opposition speech, said :—

"In my study of the Holy Scripture, I have observed a power granted by Jesus Christ to loose and bind sins. To Peter, the chief and head governor of the Church, this power was granted in a special manner : 'To thee,' said our blessed

Saviour to him, 'will I give the keys of the kingdom of heaven.' (Matt. xvi. 19.) Now, it should be well considered by you, my lords, whether you have sufficient authority to say unto the queen, To thee we will give the keys of the kingdom of heaven. If you have, show your warrant for it from Holy Writ; but if you can produce no such warrant, be then assured that your lordships have not sufficient authority to make her highness supreme head of the Church of Christ in these realms."

A clause of this extraordinary bill, which made a woman the head of a Christian Church, read as follows:—

"Please your highness, that it may be established and enacted by the authority aforesaid, that such jurisdiction, privileges, superiorities, and pre-eminences, spiritual and ecclesiastical, as by any spiritual or ecclesiastical power or authority has heretofore been, or may lawfully be exercised or used for the visitation of the ecclesiastical state and persons, and for reformation, order, and correction of the same, and of all manner of heresies, errors, schisms, &c., shall forever, by authority of this present parliament, be united and annexed to the imperial crown of this realm."

It was also enacted that an oath, in the following form, should be taken by all who enter upon any civil or ecclesiastical office:—

"I, N. N., do utterly testify and declare, in my conscience, that the queen's highness is the only supreme governor of this realm, as well in all spiritual and ecclesiastical things and causes as in temporal."

There also was a clause, which authorized her majesty to exercise such unlimited power by commission, given either to clergymen or to a layman, as she should choose. "The thing," says Dr. Heylin, "seemed to be abhorrent even to nature and policy, that a woman should be declared supreme head on earth of the Church of England." To foreign nations it furnished matter for merry jest and ridicule. The fabled story of a Pope Joan at Rome, which had so often been the subject of much sarcastic wit, was now in sober earnest at Westminster, in the person of Queen Elizabeth. Even the gloomy Calvin, friend as he was to every sort of religious reformation, cracked his jokes at the ridiculous idea of a female head set upon the mystical body of Christ's Church.

A packed parliament was also convened in Ireland by the lord deputy, Thomas, earl of Essex. All Catholic noblemen were carefully excluded, and this obsequious body passed the first penal enactments against Roman Catholics. Terror and dismay pervaded throughout the country. Lawless ruffians, who, to screen themselves from the just punishment for their crimes, had reformed, joined the queen's agents in despoiling monasteries, tearing down and plundering churches, and in torturing and massacring Catholics, lay and secular.

"These acts of oppression filled the country with dismay. The churches became deserted; the clergy had, in most places, been obliged to fly and conceal themselves in the recesses of the mountains; while every unprincipled hypocrite was at liberty to tear down the altar, plunder the church, and pollute the sanctuary."*

"All over the kingdom," says Leland, "the people were left without any religious worship; and, under pretence of obeying the order of State, they seized all the most valuable furniture of the churches, which they exposed to sale without decency or reserve."

While the people of Ireland evinced an heroic determination to suffer death sooner than renounce the religion of their fathers, the innovators, on their part, demonstrated that blood, sacrilege, and licentiousness were the frightful

* Rev. M J. Brenan.

but favorite objects they had contemplated. That this truth may be placed before the reader in an unquestionable point of view, we shall take the liberty of briefly referring to the testimony of some of their own writers.

"Whatever disorders," says Spencer, "you see in the Established Church through England, you may finde here, and many more, namely, *grosse simony, greedy covetousness, fleshy incontinency, carelèsse sloath*, and generally *all disordered life* in the common clergyman."

"So deformed and overthrown a Churche," says Sidney, "there is not, I am sure, in any region where the name of Christ is professed. Such horrible spectacles there are to behold, as the burning of villages, the ruin of churches, yea, the view of the bones and skulls of the dead, who, partlie by murder, partlie by famyn, have died in the fields, as in troth hardlie any Christian with drie eies could beholde."

"I knew it was bad," observes Strafford, "very bad in Ireland, but that it was so stark nought, I did not believe."

"There were few churches to resort to," says Leland, "few teachers to exhort, fewer still who could be understood, and almost all, at least for the greater part of this reign, of scandalous iusufficiency."

Such are the characters who went over to Ireland in the sixteenth century, for the purpose of upsetting the ancient religion of the nation. These are the individuals, with their *gross simony, greedy covetousnes, fleshy incontinency,* and *disordered lives,* who had the barefaced impiety to pull down the altars erected and revered by the sainted fathers of the Irish Church, trample on the cross of Christ, and expose the sacred vessels of the sanctuary for sale in the public market.

Despite the persecutions of those frightful times, the Irish priesthood clung to the chair of St. Peter with the faith of the Apostles, and the fidelity of martyrs. From among the whole of the episcopal order we find but two defections, namely, Miler Magrath, bishop of Down, afterwards translated to Cashel, and Hugh Curwin, archbishop of Dublin.

Miler Magrath was a native of Fermanagh, and after receiving a liberal education on the Continent, he joined the Franciscans. Having gained the friendship and patronage of some high personages abroad, he was favorably recommended to Paul the Fifth, and by that pontiff consecrated as bishop of Down. He was an ambitious, domineering man, and soon joined the Reformation as the readiest road to preferment and gain. He was translated by Elizabeth to Clogher; thence to Cashel and Emly. He lived to the great age of one hundred years, and died at Cashel, in December, 1622, in the Catholic faith. All doubt on this head has been set aside by the recent publication of a letter, preserved in the archives of the Franciscan Convent at Wexford, from the Apostolic Nuncio to the Rev. Maurice Ultan, provincial of the Franciscan order in Ireland, approving of his action in restoring Bishop Magrath to the fold.*

In the early part of Elizabeth's reign, both State policy and the embarrassed state of the national affairs prevented her from displaying all the savage cruelty of her nature; but as she advanced in years, and felt secure upon the

---

* The following is the epitaph of Miler Magrath. It was composed by himself, and has been inscribed on his monument in the cathedral of Cashel:—

"Venerat in Dunum primo sanctissimus olim,
Patricius, nostri gloria magna Soli,
Huic ego succedens, utinam tam sanctus ut ille,
Sic Duni primo tempore Præsul eram.
Anglia, lustra decem sed post tua sceptra colebam,
Principibus placui, Marte tonanti, tuis.
Hic ubi sum positus, non sum, sum non ubi non sum,
Sum, nec in ambobus, sum sed utroque loco.
Dominus est qui me judicat. (1 Cor. iv.)
Qui stat, caveat ne cadat."

throne, her relentless, persecuting nature burst forth in all its terrible fury.

In presenting even an outline of the frightful persecution which now commenced, language becomes perfectly useless. It would appear (says an ancient writer) that the infernal pit itself had conspired with the dark and deadly passions of men, to root out the very name of Catholicity from the country.

The nation, from one extremity to the other, was filled with groups of hired informers; the clergy were pursued with more unsparing ferocity than the very beasts of prey; and of those who suffered, the names and the number can be known only in the just and eternal records of the book of life.

As we are not writing a history of the penal times, we will pass over the barbarous laws and enactments leveled at Catholics, and confine ourselves to a succinct account of the most prominent victims of the intolerance and cold-blooded persecutions enacted by the Reformers in Ireland.

WILLIAM WALSH, D. D., Bishop of Meath.

One of the first of that long line of martyrs and confessors in Ireland who spurned alike the threats and bribes of princes and rulers, who tried to seduce them from the faith of their fathers—from the faith planted by the blood of Chirst Himself, and spread broadcast over the world by his disciples and teachers—was William Walsh, bishop of Meath. Though victor, he was not glorified by the martyr's crown; but his faith and constancy entitled him to a crown of eternal glory.

In 1530, Dr. Edward Staples, an Englishman, and an apostate, was appointed by Henry VIII. bishop of Meath.

In 1554, Dr. William Walsh received a commission under Queen Mary to proceed against immoral bishops in Ireland,

and soon afterwards removed Staples, in whose place Dr. Walsh was duly appointed.

Ware says that Dr. Walsh was a native of Waterford, though, in a work called *De Cistertiensium Hibernorum Vivis Illustribus*, it is stated that he was a native of Dunboyne, county Meath, and that he was a Cistercian of the abbey of Bective.

After Dr. Walsh's consecration he applied himself with great zeal and energy to reform the numerous abuses and lack of discipline and morals during the incumbency of Bishop Staples. He had not time to carry out his needed reforms when the persecution of the Church under Elizabeth involved the rest of his life in troubles and sufferings. When called upon to acknowledge Elizabeth as head of the Church, he, feeling that he had a higher authority to obey, indignantly repudiated her pretensions, and resolved to adhere to his faith and guard his flock, even at the sacrifice of his life. Ware states that—

"After the return of the Earl of Sussex to Ireland, letters came from her majesty signifying her pleasure for a general meeting of the clergy of Ireland, and the establishment of the Protestant religion through the several dioceses of this kingdom. Among the bishops, the Bishop of Meath was very zealous for the Romish Church. Not content with what offers her majesty had proposed, but very much enraged, (after the assembly had dispersed themselves,) he fell to preach against the Common Prayer in his diocese at Trim, which was newly come over and ordered to be observed, for which the lord lieutenant confined him till he acqtuainted her majesty with it, who sent over her orders to clap him up in prison. Within a few months after, persisting in the same mind, he was deposed, and the bishopric of Meath was about two years vacant, till, by her majesty's provision, Hugh Brady became Walsh's successor."

Dr. Walsh was laden with chains and flung into Dublin Castle until the queen's pleasure should be known. As he remained firm in his faith and in his opposition to the queen's supremacy, he was consigned to a damp, loathsome cell, or, as an old writer calls it, "A subterraneous dungeon, damp and noisome. Not a ray of light penetrated thither; and for thirteen years this was his unvarying abode." He was prohibited the use of books or any occupation that might cheer the dreary hours and days and years of prison life. He continually walked up and down his loathsome cell, dragging his heavy chains after him, until the iron had corroded into the very bone. Prayer and meditation were his only solace, for he was as much shut out from the world as if he were dead.

His persecutors, overcome by his constancy, and finding his fervor in spiritual contemplation a continual reproach to their own wickedness, at length, about Christmas, 1572, connived at his escape. He says himself, "I was snatched from that place by the liberality and care of my friends, and having met with the opportunity of a ship of Brittany, I threw myself into it, not heeding my age, which was above sixty years, or my state of health, deeming it safer to trust my life to the dangers of the sea than again to experience the cruelty of the enemies of the Catholic religion." For sixteen days he was tossed on the waves by a violent storm, and was at length driven in shipwreck on the coast of France.

Weighed down with the infirmities which he had contracted in prison, and with the burden of more than sixty years, he was compelled to remain for six months unknown and abandoned in Nantes. At length, receiving aid from the Nuncio, he proceeded to Paris, and thence to Spain. The closing years of his life were spent in Alcalá. A noble Spanish lady received him into her house, and attended him as though he were an angel from heaven. The sores which yet remained from his dungeon chains she kissed as the trophies of his martyrdom. She would allow none but herself to wait on him, and on her knees she usually dressed his wounds and ministered to his wants. From this asylum of charity, thus providentially prepared for him, he passed to the convent of the Cistercian fathers in the same city, and there, on the 4th of January, 1577, he happily closed his earthly life, which, as many attested, he had never sullied by any stain of mortal sin. His remains were placed in the Collegiate Church of Saint Secundinus, and a monument erected over them by the Bishop of Grenada.

About this time the persecution of the ministers of God was carried on with savage barbarity throughout different parts of the country. The inducement held out to informers and priest-hunters, by those who coveted their possessions as well as their lives, was so great that it was almost impossible to escape the merciless sleuth-hounds thirsting for their prey. Father Mooney, in his admirable work on the persecutions of the Franciscans in the seventeenth century, says : "Though they were violently driven out of the convents into the great towns, and the convents profanely turned into dwellings, and some of the fathers suffered violence and others death, yet in the country and remote places they remained in their convents, celebrating the Divine office, preaching to the people, and fulfilling their other functions, holding it sinful to lay aside or even hide their religious habit, though for an hour, through human fear."

DANIEL O'DUILLIAN was one of the first martyrs of this order. He was an humble brother in the convent of Youghal, but by his unswerving adherence to his order and faith, he brought upon himself the vengeance of a Captain

Dowdal, then in command there. This tyrant selected the poor, zealous friar to make an example of him, to frighten other religious and ecclesiastics. With this object in view, Brother O'Duillian was subjected to the most cruel and excruciating tortures. They took him to Trinity Gate, and tied his hands behind his back, and, having fastened heavy stones to his feet, thrice pulled him up with ropes from the earth to the top of the tower, and left him hanging there for a time. At length, after many insults and tortures, he was hung with his head down and his feet in the air, at the mill near the monastery.* While he lived he never uttered an impatient word, but, like a good Christian, incessantly repeated prayers, now aloud, now in a low voice. At length the soldiers were ordered to shoot at him, as though he were a target, but yet, that his sufferings might be the longer and more cruel, they did not aim at his head or heart, but as much as they pleased at any other part of his body. Amidst insults, jeers, and ribaldry, the soldiers fired at him, vying with each other as to who would hit nearest to a vital part without killing him. All this time the feeble voice of the martyr, beseeching God to grant him mercy and grace, and pardon to his persecutors, mingled with the ribald oaths of his murderers.

At length, when they had grown tired of their savage sport,

* The Franciscan Convent of Youghal, the parent establishment of that order in Ireland, was founded by Maurice Fitz-Gerald, A. D. 1231. The founder was lord justice of Ireland in 1232, after which he retired to this convent and embraced the institute of St. Francis. He died in 1257, and was buried in his convent of Youghal. This abbey continued for many centuries the usual cemetery of the Desmond family. Provincial chapters had been held here in 1300, 1312, 1331, 1513, and 1531; while in 1460 the reformation of the Strict Observants had been received. During the terrors of Elizabeth's reign this extensive convent had been pillaged, and so completely demolished, that not even a single vestige of its ruins was allowed to remain. Those of the community who had escaped the storm fled for refuge into the mountains of the county of Waterford.

and when their victim had fainted, one, with more mercy than the rest, shot him through the heart. Thus did the noble martyr seal his devotion with his blood, and win his martyr's glorious crown, on the 22d day of April, 1569.

Among the Franciscan convents sacked about this time, was that of "Gallvaise Aharlagh."* A company of English soldiers suddenly surrounded the convent, so as to prevent any of the brethren from escaping. Father DERMOD O'MULRONEY and two of the brethren escaped to the bell-tower. The soldiers soon commenced setting fire to the church. Father O'Mulroney descended from his hiding-place to remonstrate with them, first signing himself with the cross, and invoking Divine mercy, for he knew that he had no human mercy to expect from the soldiers. The soldiers laughed at his appeals to spare the house of God, and kicked and buffeted him from one to the other in the most brutal manner, until the good priest fell senseless. They then sawed off his head, from which it is related that not a single drop of blood flowed. The soldiers perceiving this, vowed to knock blood out of the "old papist priest," and hacked his body in pieces. His two companions suffered a similar fate, but it is not stated what became of the rest of the brethren. These martyrs suffered in the year 1570.

About this time the convent of Roscrea was sacked, and Father DALY, one of its inmates, was put to death with the usual barbarity that attended such executions.†

Father FERGAL WARD, a native of Donegal, and a Franciscan priest, was put to death in Armagh with great cruelty. This good priest traveled through the whole province, visit-

* Roothe justly calls it "Monastery of Galbally, in the mountains of Aharlagh, near Tipperary." The town of Galbally is in the county of Tipperary, in the glen of Aharlow, at the foot of the Galtee mountains.

† The convent of Roscrea, in the barony of Ikerrin, county of Tipperary, was founded by Mulruany O'Carrol, A. D. 1490. By an inquisition taken in 1568, it was granted to Thomas, earl of Ormond.

ing scattered families and affording them the consolations of religion, and celebrating Mass in lonely caves and mountain retreats. At length he was betrayed (for there was a price set on a priest's head), and seized by the soldiery. They scourged him with great barbarity, repeating the flogging for days, as soon as the lacerated wounds would begin to heal. At length, finding that his strength was giving way, and that he was likely to die under the lash, they hung him with the cincture of his own habit.

Father Mooney narrates the death of Father O'Dowd, another Franciscan, who was martyred about this time (1577). He states that the event took place in the convent of Elphin, while other writers state that it took place in the convent of Moyne, county Mayo. The soldiers pressed one of the brethren, who was a captive, to reveal all he knew of the hiding-places of other members, as also of the plots which they said they were concealing against the queen. He begged to be allowed to make his confession to Father O'Dowd, which favor was granted. As soon as the confession was over they hung him, and then threatened the priest unless he revealed the confession, in addition to all he knew himself, they would hang and torture him; but if he confessed, they would grant him life and freedom.

Father O'Dowd spurned their offer, and embraced martyrdom. After torturing him for some time, they tied the cord of his habit around his forehead, and using a piece of wood for a tourniquet, they twisted it until his skull was broken in and his brains crushed through the bones, when he died.

About the same time, the convent of Elphin being attacked by the soldiers, all the brethren made their escape except Brother PHELIM O'HARA, who remained in the monastery, and was killed by the despoilers before the high altar.

Among the numerous martyrs who sealed their victory in Christ with their blood about this time (1577), was the Rev. THOMAS COURCY, vicar-general of Kinsale. While discharging his duties, he fell into the hands of that ruthless tyrant, Sir John Perrot, president of Munster, and by his orders was hung. He was first tortured and flogged, and then offered his life, on conditions that he would apostatize and acknowledge the queen's supremacy; but he, true to his religion and to the precepts of his order, spurned all such offers, and met his death with the constancy of a true martyr.

LEVEROUS AND OTHER BISHOPS PERSECUTED.

Leverous, bishop of Kildare—His bold stand—Persecution of the Bishops of Cork and Cashel—Martyrdom of Bishop O'Hely and Father O'Rorke—Drury cited to appear before the Judgment Seat—His death—Bishop Gallagher tortured to death—Bishop Macgauran massacred while hearing a confession—Bishop O'Duane martyred—Several prelates and priests expelled—Bishop O'Herlaghy's sufferings—Several laymen, priests, and friars tortured and martyred—Twenty-two old men martyred—Forty Cistercian monks massacred—The convent of Nenagh—The dead monks glorifying God—Several priests and friars tortured and put to death—Sufferings and death of Father Kinrehan, parish priest of Mullinahone—Sketches of the different priests and friars persecuted and martyred.

IN addition to the innumerable martyrs who won the priceless crown by torture and death, thousands, aye, hundreds of thousands, underwent persecutions more harrowing than even the lash and the gibbet. The sufferings and privations of many of these are preserved; but as they do not properly come under my list of martyrs, and as the narration of their trials and endurance would fill volumes, I must pass them over with a short notice of the most prominent among them.

Among these, first in rank and Christian endurance, comes the Right Rev. THOMAS LEVEROUS (Leary), bishop of Kildare. The memory of this prelate deserves special respect, not only for the example of fidelity to God he has left to posterity, but also from his friendly relation with the brave, but ill-fated Silken Thomas, and his care of the young Gerald Geraldine.

The Geraldines having been restored to rank and power, Thomas Leverous was established in the bishopric of Kildare in 1554. After the accession of Elizabeth, Bishop Leverous was summoned to take the oath of supremacy. He not only refused, but replied: "All true ecclesiastical jurisdiction must come from Christ our Lord; and, since He had not given even the smallest share of ecclesiastical power to His Mother, so glorious and so dear, so adorned with virtues and honors, how much less could such supreme jurisdiction be given to any one of the same sex! St. Paul would not allow any woman even to speak in church. And were it not that they are unfitted by nature and the condition of their sex from such exercise of authority, He who on earth raised His Mother to a dignity above all others, and above all women, and in heaven has placed her on a throne next to Himself, would not have lowered her by refusing her an honor fitted to her sex, and which others of that sex might enjoy. But since by nature it was not fitting that women should share in it, it was no dishonor to His Mother not to participate in the jurisdiction which her Son conferred. Hence it followed that Elizabeth could not lawfully take, nor her father Henry give, nor any parliament bestow on women that authority which Christ gave, and which was, as the Scripture says, 'a fountain sealed up' to those men to whom He assigned it, who bears on His shoulder the key of the house of David, and who gave to Peter His keys, by which the gate of heaven is shut and opened."

This good shepherd of the fold of Christ was driven from his cathedral see, and deprived of its revenues. Humble and poor, like Christ, he sought a strange and distant shelter in another district, rejoicing to suffer contumely for the name of Christ. As he had answered the viceroy when he threatened him with deprivation of all his goods and expulsion from his see, unless he bowed down to the queen's will,

PERSECUTION OF BISHOPS.

"What," said he, "will it avail a man to gain the whole world and lose his own soul?" Thus he esteemed all things as dross that he might gain Christ.

Thus, poor and persecuted, he traveled from place to place, instructing old and young, and keeping alive the faith among the poor and lowly. Having thus labored and suffered for years, he died at Naas, in the year 1577, in his eightieth year, and tradition assigns many miracles to his influence.

About the same time the Right Rev. MAURICE FITZGIBBON, archbishop of Cashel, died in exile, after suffering much persecution. Also the Right Rev. EDMUND TANNER, bishop of Cork, who had been persecuted and imprisoned in Dublin, and tortured, for denying the queen's supremacy, died about the same time.

BISHOP O'HELY.

The life, sufferings, and martyrdom of this holy bishop, and his companion in suffering and glory, Father CORNELIUS O'RORKE, have been written by several authors. As there is nothing new that we could add to Dr. Moran's excellent account of these noble martyrs, we prefer giving it entire.

"Dr. PATRICK O'HELY, the last bishop of Mayo, was a native of Connaught, and from his youth was adorned with every virtue. Having embraced the religious order of St. Francis, he proceeded to Spain, and there pursued his sacred studies with great applause in the University of Alcalá. In obedience to the minister-general of his order, he repaired to Rome in 1575, and, having resided for some time in the convent of Ara Cœli in that city, he was proposed for the vacant see of Mayo, in the Consistory of 4th July, the same year. Returning to Ireland, he was accompanied by Cornelius O'Rorke, a Franciscan priest, who, though the eldest son of the Prince of Breffiny, had abandoned all the pleasures of the world to embrace a life of prayer and poverty. They encountered many difficulties on their journey, but at length safely landed in Dingle, in the county Kerry. The heretical spies whom Drury, the lord-deputy, kept at this time stationed along the southern coast of Ireland, soon recognized the venerable strangers. They were, therefore, almost immediately on landing, arrested and transmitted to Limerick, to be examined by Goulden, the military commander of that district. By his orders the prelate and his chaplain were loaded with chains and cast into the public prison. Here they remained for some months, till the arrival of Sir William Drury in Kilmallock, before whom they were conducted, in the month of August, 1578.

"On being examined, Patrick O'Hely confessed that they belonged to the Franciscan order; that he himself was bishop of Mayo, sent by Gregory XIII. to guide and instruct his spiritual flock; this, he added, was the object of his mission, and the only motive of his return to Ireland. 'And do you dare,' asked Drury, 'to defend the authority of the Pope against the laws of the queen and parliament?' 'I repeat what I have said,' replied the bishop, 'and I am ready, if necessary, to die for that sacred truth.' Father O'Rorke replied in the same strain. Threats and promises were unavailing to change their resolution, and they both joyfully received sentence to be first put to the torture, and then to be hanged in the presence of the garrison.

"These orders of Drury were executed with an uncommon degree of barbarity. The two prisoners were first placed on the rack, their arms and feet were beaten with hammers, so that their thigh bones were broken,* and sharp iron points and needles were cruelly thrust under their nails, which caused an extreme agony of suffering. For a con-

* Domin. a Rosario.

siderable time they were subjected to these tortures, which the holy confessors bore patiently for the love of Christ, mutually exhorting each other to constancy and perseverance.

"At length they were taken from the rack, and hanged from the branches of a neighboring tree. Their bodies were left suspended there for fourteen days, and were used in the interim as a target by the brutal soldiery. When the martyr-prelate was being hurried to execution, he turned to Drury, and warned him that before many days he himself should appear before the tribunal of God to answer for his crimes. On the fourteenth day after, this unhappy man expired in great agony, at Waterford, of a distemper that baffled every remedy.* The 22d of August, 1578, was the day rendered illustrious by their martyrdom. By the care of the Earl of Desmond, their bodies were reverently laid in the Franciscan convent at Clonmel, whence, seventy years afterward, (in 1647,) they were translated with solemnity, and deposited, together with the implements of their torture, in the convent of Askeaton."

The reformers in Ireland directed all their fury against the hierarchy and priests, knowing full well that by striking down the shepherds the flock would become easy victims.

Among the saintly sufferers of the time were REDMOND O'GALLAHER, bishop of Derry. This pious and zealous prelate, when driven from his see, wandered through the mountains and secret places, preaching and ministering to the faithful, when he was betrayed and seized by a band of soldiers, who cruelly tortured him, literally mangling his body until he died.

* Besides the authorities quoted by Dr Moran, this fact is mentioned in the ancient MS in the Burgundian Library, which is entitled *Magna Supplicia*, &c. MS. No 2159

EDMUND MACGAURAN, bishop of Armagh, was, in like manner, hunted down, and, while hearing the confession of a dying man, he was massacred by the soldiers.

About the same time CORNELIUS O'DUANE, bishop of Down and Connor, with Father O'LAGHER, a good and holy priest, were tortured most cruelly on the rack, and then put to death.

To these might be added a lengthened catalogue of prelates and martyrs, who suffered about this time, many of whom fled the country, to return at more auspicious times, or to die in foreign lands.

Besides these we have mentioned, Archbishop SKERRET, of Tuam, was savagely flogged, and then incarcerated; he finally escaped, and died at Lisbon, in 1583. PETER POWER, bishop of Ferns, was also expelled, and died in Spain about the same time. THOMAS STRONG, bishop of Ossory, also died in exile; while MORIARTH O'BRIEN, bishop of Emly, died in prison in Dublin, in 1586; and RICHARD BRADY, bishop of Kilmore after undergoing much persecution, died at Multifernan, county Westmeath.*

Roothe gives a lengthened account of the life and sufferings of the Right Rev. THOMAS O'HERLAGHY, bishop of Ross. He was a man of remarkable piety, and was one of the three Irish prelates who took part in the Council of Trent. After being expelled from his see, and hunted from place to place, he was betrayed and brought a prisoner before Sir John Perrot, an English Protestant, who was then president of Munster. By him the bishop was cast into chains, a chain being fastened round his neck, and fetters on his legs; and after he had suffered much torment and misery in Ireland, he was sent to England.

The night previous to his being taken before the president he took good care to have his episcopal tonsure shaved, in

* O'Sullivan, Hist. Cath : Analecta Sacra in Appendix.

token of Catholic union and the faith which he professed, for he did not blush to confess Him before men from whom he hoped to receive the reward of his confession, the prize of victory, and the crown of immortality. But this tonsure, detested by them, drew upon him the scorn and insolent scoffs of the soldiers, his jailers. When taken to England, he was thrown into the Tower of London, where he was kept for three years and about seven months with the primate, Archbishop Creagh. At first he was shut up in a dark cell, without bed, fire, or light, having only one small window, which was open to the northern blasts, which froze his aged limbs.

Freedom and honors were offered to him if he would yield to the queen's will; but he would not. Many persons were sent to persuade him, by threats and fair words, to apostatize, but he adhered firmly to the rock on which he had taken his stand. After much persecution and suffering, he was released, through the influence of powerful friends.

His life was one of devotion and prayer, and several miracles are attributed to his influence. We are told that, "the holy Bishop O'Herlaghy continued unwearied in his apostolic labors up to his sixtieth year, and died in the territory of Muskerry, and was buried in the monastery of the Franciscan order in Kilchree (de Cellacrea), in the year 1579."*

Philadelphus informs us that, "Father MOORE, together with Oliver Plunket, an Irishman of gentle birth, and William Walsh, an English soldier, were seized by a troop of heretical soldiers, tied to stakes, and shot, and thus obtained the palm of martyrdom, on the 11th of November, the Feast of St. Martin, 1580;" while we learn from the same authority that "Father GELASIUS O'QUILLENAN, of the Cistercian order, abbot of the monastery of Boyle, was martyred, to-

* De Processu Martyriali, &c., T. N. Philadelpho, 1619.

gether with the priest EUGENE CRONIUS (probably Cronin), 1580."

About the same time the Rev. THADEUS DONALD and JOHN HANLY were seized in the convent of Bantry, and, being tied back to back, they were flung from a high rock into the sea.

DANIEL O'NIELAN, a laborious and zealous priest of the diocese of Cloyne, remarkable for his hospitality and humane attention to the poor, was put to death in a manner the most revolting, by two satellites, named Norris and Morgan, who had the command of the northern district of the county of Cork, under the administration of Adam Loftus. This apostolic man, filled with solicitude for the people, was in the habit of making occasional journeys to the neighboring villages, for the purpose of affording consolation to the dying and afflicted. He was at length overtaken by his pursuers, and conducted, under a strong military guard, to the town of Youghal. Norris and Morgan, already thirsting for his blood, had refused him even the opportunity of making a defence. They conducted him to the top of a high tower, then called Trinity, and, having fastened a rope around his waist and arms, they flung him headlong from the battlements. The rope, however, not being sufficiently strong to meet the violence of the shock, the suffering victim was instantly precipitated, and left a mangled corpse on the ground. Nor was the fury of his executioners yet satiated. Observing some signs of life still remaining, they caused him to be carried to a mill not far distant, and having secured him with chains to the wheel, they allowed it to revolve with increased velocity, until the body, disfigured and lacerated, retained no longer the appearance of a human form.* This holy priest suffered on the 28th of March, A. D. 1580.

* Bruodin, Passio Marty , p. 439.

PERSECUTION OF BISHOPS.

Daniel O'Hanrichan, Philip O'Shea, and Maurice Scanlan, three aged priests, natives of the county Kerry, suffered death for their faith during the same year. The labors of these missionaries had not been confined to the district of Kerry. During the lapse of thirty-three years they had been employed in preaching the Divine Word and administering the sacraments in almost every county throughout Ireland. At length, worn down with age and infirmity, they returned to their native country, and during the persecution of 1580 were prevailed upon to take shelter in the town of Lislaghton. On the 6th of April in that year, while the agents of Elizabeth had been scouring the country, these three venerable priests, two of whom were blind with age, took shelter in the sanctuary, and while in the act of offering themselves to their Maker, and of praying for their enemies, were beheaded; their bodies having been afterwards awfully mangled by the soldiery.*

John O'Lochran, Edmund Simmons, and Donatus O'Rourke, priests of the order of St. Francis, were cruelly tortured and put to death in the convent of Down, by a licentious soldiery under the command of a military commissioner named Britton. This unfeeling leader, after filling the country with dismay, had resolved to take up his quarters for the winter in this ancient town. On his approach the inhabitants fled, and took refuge in the adjacent country, while the clergy were entreated to consult their safety, and reserve themselves for better days.

The three venerable fathers above were captured in the convent, and, after being tortured, were hung from the branches of a tree in the garden.

Philadelphus gives the martyrdom of twenty-two old men, whose names are not stated. He says: "I have also seen a catalogue in which are written the names of many lay Cath-

* Passio Marty., p. 440.

olics who perished in consequence either of the fraud or calumnies of their enemies, or the hatred of the orthodox faith which they professed. . . . To these must be added, from the same catalogue, twenty-two old men (Catholics), whom, being unable to fly, the fury of the soldiers burnt to death in the village of Mohoriack, in Munster, the 26th day of June, 1580."

Dr. Moran gives, from Henriquez, an account of the martyrdom of forty Cistercian monks, in the convent of St. Mary, Nenagh,* and the miracle of their commemoration of the festival after death. He says:—

"About the same time (1580), the monastery of St. Mary of Maggio became illustrious by the martyrdom of its holy inmates. A heretical band having entered the adjoining country, spreading on every side devastation and ruin, the monks of Maggio, forty in number, were in hourly expectation of death. They resolved, however, not to fly from the monastery, choosing rather to consummate their course in the asylum which had been so long their happy abode. They therefore assembled in choir, and, having recited the morning office in silence and prayer, awaited their executioners

"The heretical soldiers did not long delay. On coming to the monastery, they first imagined that it had been abandoned, so universal was the silence that reigned around it; and they plundered it in every part. On arriving, however, at the church, they found the forty religious kneeling around the altar, unmoved, as if unconscious of the scenes of sacrilegious plunder that were perpetrated around them, and wholly absorbed in prayer. 'Like hungry wolves, the her-

---

* The convent of Nenagh, in the county of Tipperary, was erected in the reign of Henry III., by the Butler family. A provincial chapter was held there in 1344, and in the 30th of Henry VIII. it was granted to Robert Collon.

etics at once precipitated themselves upon the defenceless religious. The cruelty and ferocity of the soldiers was surpassed only by the meekness and heavenly joy of the victims,' and in a few minutes forty names were added to the long roll of our Irish saints. The vigil of the Assumption was the day consecrated by their death.

"One lay brother of the monastery, who had been absent for some time, returned that evening, and found his former happy abode reduced to a heap of smoking ruins, and, entering the church, he found the altar and choir streaming with blood. Throwing himself prostrate before the mutilated statue of Our Lady, he poured forth his lamentations that her monastery was no more, and her glorious festival, which should then be commenced, would pass in sadness and silence. He had scarcely breathed his prayer, when he heard the bells of the monastery toll, and, lifting his head, he saw his martyred brethren each taking his accustomed seat. The abbot intoned the solemn vespers, and psalms were sung as usual on their festive days. The enraptured lay brother knew not whether he had ascended to heaven or was still on earth, till, the office being completed, the vision ceased, and he once more contemplated around him the mangled and bleeding remains of the martyred religious."

Bruodin mentions several priests who were cruelly put to death about this time. Among others he narrates how the Rev. ÆNEAS PENNY, a priest of Connaught, was slain by the soldiers while saying Mass in the parish church of Killatra, as also how Father DONATUS O'RIEDY, parish priest of Coolrah, in Connaught, was hung up from the high altar, and then pierced with swords.

The Rev. MATHEW LAMPORT, of Dublin, was first tortured, then hung and quartered.

The Annals inform us that about the same time the Rev. DONATUS HEINRECHAN, PHILIP O'FEUS, and MAURICE O'SCAL-

LAN, O. S. F., were cruelly put to death in the monastery of Lesacten, county Kerry.

The same authority informs us that, "In the convent of Enniscorthy, THADDÆUS O'MERAN, father guardian of the convent, FELIX O'HARA, and HENRY LAYHODE, under the government of Henry Wallop, viceroy of Ireland, were taken prisoners in their convent by the soldiers, and for five days tortured in various ways, and then slain."

Father MAURICE KINREHAN was parish priest of Mullinahone, county Tipperary.* He rendered himself specially obnoxious to the persecuting heretics of that part of the country by the zeal and devotion with which he clung both to his faith and his flock. Outlawed, hunted, and persecuted, with a price on his head, he still clung to his people, and secreted himself, sometimes in the cabins of the poor, sometimes concealed in the woods, and at other times hiding in the mountain fastnesses of Slievenamon. With the human bloodhounds on his track, the good priest was driven from cover to cover, yet they could not compel him to forego his sense of duty and right. Though tracked, chased, and lashed, he felt that as a priest his place was with his people, to console them, to minister to them, and, if necessary, to die for them. Like a good soldier of Christ, he was resolved to teach his flock, by his example and sufferings, to withstand persecution, and even death itself, for the faith. Martyrdom has been the great heritage of the Church, and Christ him-

* Probably the name is Hanrahan, which is very common in that part of the country. The little village of Mullinahone, situated almost under the shadow of the stately Slievenamon, is a place of some historic importance. Tradition still points out the places hallowed by her martyrs and heroes. The grim old castle still stands, and frowns down upon the village, while the children point with awe at the spike on which was staked the patriot Norton's head in '98. Mullinahone is the native place of Charles Kickham, who has woven so much of her historic and legendary lore into song and story.

self sanctified Christianity with his precious blood. Our humble priest felt that he was honored by God in being thus immolated like his Divine Master. While meekly bearing his own cross, the sufferings and tribulations of his people and Church might justly make him exclaim, in the words of the poet:

> "Ruined altar and rifled fane,
> Scattered homestead and blighted hearth,
> Brethren banished and kindred slain,
> These are our trials, Lord, on earth.
> O, let our wail in Thy sight ascend,
> Poor and forlorn we turn to Thee;
> Turn to Thee as the sufferer's friend,
> For pity, Lord, in our misery."

For a time the good priest sought shelter in the abbey of Fethard, but soon found this a poor asylum.*

At length he was so closely harassed by his enemies that he had to conceal himself among the ravines and wooded dells of Slievenamon.† Here the scattered and affrighted peasantry collected around him, either to tend to his wants from their limited stores, or to hear the holy sacrifice offered up in some lonely glen or cave.

---

* The convent of Fethard, in the barony of Middlethird, county of Tipperary, was founded for eremites following the rule of St. Augustin, by Walter Mulcot, A. D. 1806, Maurice Mac-Carwill, archbishop of Cashel, under whom the land was immediately held, having given his assent. The last prior was William Burdon, and in the thirty-first of Henry III. this convent, with eleven messuages, twenty-five acres in Fethard, a water-mill, and sixty-three acres of arable land in Ballyclowan, parcel of the possessions, was granted to Sir Edmund Butler for ever, in capite, at the annual rent of five shillings four pence Irish money. [This convent is now in possession of the order —AUTHOR.]

† The names of several glens and caves in these lordly mountains are suggestive of the penal times. *Clash-an-affron* (the mass pit or cave) is still pointed out, where Father Kinrehan said Mass, surrounded by his poor, but faithful followers. Near Kilcash is *St. Borro-hawns Shrine*, which was evidently used for sacred purposes, as the stone altar, cross, and patten are still preserved there.—AUTHOR.

With such vigilance was he hunted down, that he feared to leave his hut in the mountain. However, one day word was brought him that a dying man wanted his ministrations. He hastened to his residence, near the little village of Ballypatrick, but while administering the last rites to the dying man, a body of soldiers, under command of an officer named Furrows, who were in pursuit of him, seized him. So popular was he that the poor people around began to flock together as if to rescue him. But the savage soldiers did not give them the chance, for, by orders of their officer, they clubbed him first, and then actually cut him in pieces with their swords, and scattered his members along the highway, retaining his head as a trophy, which they brought to their commander, at Clonmel, in order to secure their base reward.

MARTYRDOM OF BISHOPS O'HURLEY AND CREAGH.

Bishop O'Hurley's persecutions—His triumph—His life and martyrdom—Archbishop Creagh—His sufferings—His death by poison—A long list of priests hanged, quartered, and put to death—The black catalogue—Persecution rampant—Protestant writers on the state of the country and the sufferings of the people.

BISHOP O'HURLEY.

THE Most Rev. DERMOD O'HURLEY, archbishop of Cashel, was, perhaps, the ablest and most distinguished of the prelates who suffered under Elizabeth. His life has been so fully written, both by Dr. Roothe and Sullivan, as to leave nothing new to add. I therefore take the following sketch from their works:—

"The birthplace of this glorious martyr was a little village in the diocese of Limerick, less than three miles from that city, called Lycodoon,* where his parents lived respectably, by farming, both of tillage and cattle; they were held in good estimation by their neighbors, both rich, great, and poor, especially James Geraldine, earl of Desmond. His father's name was William Hurley, owner of the farm of

---

* Lycodunum: Lycodoon still retained in the town land—no longer a village—of Lycodoon, parish of Knockea, now the property of William Smith O'Brien, Esq.—*Renehan*, p. 351. Vicus, or village, seems, in writers of this period, often to mean only what is still called in Ireland, among the peasantry, "the town," namely, the dwelling-house of a gentleman or farmer, with its surrounding offices and laborers' cottages.

Lycodoon, and also steward or bailiff for many years to the said earl. His mother was Honor McBrien, who was descended from the celebrated family of Briens, earls of Thomond, and, before the conquest of Ireland, kings of Munster.

"By the care and liberality of his parents, he received a liberal education, and, having passed through all branches of study, received the doctor's degree in civil and canon law,* and, having made equal progress in piety and religion, he was chosen by the Holy See as a fitting man to be made the shepherd of his Catholic countrymen in Ireland, then suffering under the storm of schism.†

"Having then been raised to the episcopacy by Gregory XIII., and named Archbishop of Cashel, he took his route towards Ireland. But there was great difficulty in proceeding, from the dangers to which, in those turbulent times, Catholic merchants and sailors were exposed from the heretics.

"However, after some time, having found an opportunity of a Waterford ship in the port of Grosvico,‡ in Armorican Britain, he treated with the ship's factor for a passage to Ireland. There were in the same town, at that time, some other ecclesiastics of the same nation who were also desirous to cross to Ireland, among whom was Niel, abbot of the Cistercian Order of the Abbey of Newry,§ in the diocese of Armagh.

"The archbishop, taking advantage, as I have said, of a

---

* He gave public lectures in philosophy for four years in Louvain, and subsequently held, with great applause, the chair of canon law in Rheims.—*Elogium Eleqnac. ap. Moran, Hist. Archbishops,* i., 132.

† He was appointed by Gregory XIII., in 1580.—*Ex Act. Consist. ap. Moran.*

‡ Probably Cherbourg.

§ Abbas de Urio, Newry. One of the old and most commonly used Irish names of Newry was Uar, whence the Latin "de Urio." See an account of it in Ware.

Waterford ship, committed himself to the Divine Providence, and, after a prosperous voyage, reached the island of Skerries,* and from thence proceeded to Waterford. While he was hospitably entertained there,† it chanced that one day there was some conversation on religion. On these occasions his zeal and learning could not be restrained or concealed, and so offended a certain heretic who was present, whose name was Walter Baal, who broke out into violent language, and soon after, starting off to Dublin, denounced Dermod to the governors on suspicion. The departure of this man suggested to the archbishop the thought that it boded him no good, and his fears were confirmed by an honest citizen, who warned him and the companion, or rather guide, of his journey, Father John Dillon, of their danger, and advised them to leave that city immediately.‡ The same Father Dillon afterward paid the penalty of this companionship by a long imprisonment, and with difficulty escaped death by the favor of his elder brother, who was at that time one of the king's council, and filled the office of first president of the king's exchequer or treasury.

"They immediately departed, with their little baggage, and betook themselves to Slane, to the castle of the noble Lord Thomas Fleming, baron of Slane.§ Here, by desire of that pious heroine, Catherine Preston, wife of the afore-

* Sciretio insula; in Irish, Sciric. He landed at Drogheda. (See State Papers.)

† O'Sullivan says: "For two whole years English spies sought every opportunity to seize on his person; but their plans were frustiated by the fidelity of the Irish Catholics. In order to escape notice, he wore generally a secular dress, as indeed all bishops and priests are obliged to do in England, Ireland, and Scotland, ever since this persecution first broke out —P 124

‡ O'Sullivan gives the date of this 1583.

§ Ismay Dillon, daughter of Sir Bartholomew Dillon, of Riverstown, county Meath, and aunt to Sir Robert, was married to John Fleming, of Stephenstown, second son of James, Lord Slane, by whom she had Thomas,

said baron, they were concealed in a secret chamber. They remained here for some time, removed from society, and avoided being seen by any but friends, until the attempt of Baal to have them arrested should have wholly failed, and the rumor spread by him should have died away. When they thought that the whole matter was forgotten, they began to act a little more freely, to sit at table with the family and join in their conversation, and no longer to avoid meeting any guests that might chance to come to the house. Now, it so chanced that one day there came to that house, whether by accident or design, Robert Dillon, one of the king's council, and chief justice of the court of common pleas. At table the conversation turned on serious subjects, and the archbishop betrayed so much learning that it gave occasion to the sagacious chief justice to mark the man, to inquire who he was, whence he came, and to put many other questions, the answers to all of which he kept to himself until he had the opportunity to lay them before the governors and the council. He laid all his suspicions before the council, and proposed that he should be brought from his hiding-place, to answer for himself to the council, and that if he fled he would confirm their suspicions; and that the Baron of Slane should be summoned before the council, and held either to produce his guest or answer for him. The bishop fled, and the baron, having appeared before the council, was severely reprimanded for sheltering such a man, and threatened with heavy fine and imprisonment unless he found and produced his late guest. Terrified by these threats, the baron at once set out to pursue

---

Lord Slane. Dillon and Lord Slane were therefore cousins. Dillon was then chief justice of the court of common pleas. The wife of Lord Slane, Catherine Preston, was daughter of Jenico, the third Viscount Gormanston. She died in 1597, and was buried in the hermitage of St. Erk Slane. (See Archdall's Lodge.)

him; for, being tepid in faith, and bound up with the world, he shrank from what seemed to threaten certain destruction, especially as the persecutors were so bitter in their rage against the archbishop, and their threats against himself for having sheltered him. Loftus,* who was the colleague of Wallop, did not so thirst for the blood of the innocent, for he was more inclined to gentleness by nature and equity, as beseemed a chancellor; but his partner in the government was a man of blood, and not to be satisfied without shedding it.

"Looking more to his own safety than to the duty of friendship, the Baron of Slane pursued the archbishop, and, overtaking him at Carrick-on-Suir, just as he had returned from visiting the Blessed Cross,† a visit which, when in danger, he had vowed to make, he prayed him very civilly to accompany him to Dublin, there to appear before the council, and prove his innocence, and show that he had come to Ireland with a true ecclesiastical spirit, and to preach the faith. What was the pious bishop to do? He recked not of his own danger, but looked to the safety of the baron. At that time there was at Cork the great earl of Ormond, Thomas Butler, of devout memory, who loved Dermod, and respected his virtue and the dignity of his office, and ordered him to be supplied with food and all necessaries from his own house; and many say that he had his recently born son, James, who afterwards died young in England, privately baptized by him.

"As the bishop traveled back to Dublin with the baron, each night, when the latter put up, either in the public inn

---

* Anno 1582-3.—Lords-justices of Ireland, Adam Loftus, archbishop of Dublin and lord chancellor, with Sir Henry Wallop, treasurer of Ireland.—*Ware's Annals*.

† This would be the Abbey of Holy Cross, in Tipperary, a celebrated pilgrimage in those days. (See Haverty's History of Ireland, p. 413.)

or the house of a friend, the former was thrust into the public prison for greater security. One night he spent in Kilkenny in prison, and there a certain Catholic came to him to obtain the benefit of his ministry. Their conversation turned upon the unhappy Bishop of Ferns,* whom human weakness and the fear of men had led to desert the Catholic faith. 'Many,' said our holy martyr, 'who are lions before the battle are timid stags when the hour of trial comes. Lest this prove true of me, I daily pray to our good Lord for strength; for "let him that thinketh to stand look lest he fall."'

"When the archbishop arrived in Dublin, he was brought before the privy council for examination,† falsely accused of many crimes, and he meekly showed his innocence. The chancellor, Adam Loftus, treated him more gently, and sought by many cajolements to induce him to conform, as they call it. Sir Henry Wallop was more savage, and repeatedly broke out into violent and abusive threats, and showed that his inveterate hatred to the orthodox faith would never be satisfied with anything less than the slaughter of this innocent lamb.

* One circumstance connected with the heroic constancy of Dr. O'Hurley deserves to be specially commemorated. The Bishop of Ferns had wavered in his allegiance to the Holy See, and hence, at this period, stood high in court favor. Witnessing the triumph of Dr. O'Hurley, he was struck with remorse for his own imbecility and criminal denial of his faith, and, hastening to the lords-justices, declared that he was sorry for his past guilt, and now rejected with disdain the temporal supremacy of Elizabeth. "He too," writes the Bishop of Killaloe, in October that same year, "is now confined in a most loathsome dungeon, from which every ray of light is excluded."—*Moran*, p. 135, *Epist. cit.* (See a further account of this bishop, Dr. Power, at p. 156.

† O Sullivan says at his first examination he was asked if he were a priest; to which he answered in the affirmative, and added, moreover, that he was an archbishop. He was then thrown into a dark and loathsome prison, and kept there, bound in chains, till the Holy Thursday of the following year.

"This bloody soldier determined to have the peaceful bishop slain by military law, as he could not attain his end by the laws of his country. But he determined first to subject him to the torture, that, if he could not extort by pain any confession of guilt, he might perchance be induced by the intensity of his sufferings to abjure the Catholic faith. But the cruel tyrant was disappointed in Dermod; his flames could not overcome the flames of the love of Christ; the fire that burned without was less powerful than that which burned within his breast.

"Fortunately we have a description of his sufferings, written by a noble and learned man, a citizen of Dublin, who learned the circumstance from eye-witnesses, if indeed he were not himself in the city when our martyr suffered; wherefore I will give his words, as given in the introduction to his discussion with James Usher. (Stanihurst, pp. 29, 30.)

"'The Archbishop of Cashel met a harder fate, and the barbarous cruelty of Calvinism cannot be better shown than by it. The executioners placed the archbishop's feet and calves in tin boots filled with oil; they then fastened his feet in wooden shackles or stocks, and placed fire under them. The boiling oil so penetrated the feet and legs that morsels of the skin and even flesh fell off and left the bone bare.* The officer whose duty it was to preside over the torture, unused to such unheard-of suffering, and unable to look on such an inhuman spectacle, or to bear the piteous cries of the innocent prelate, suddenly left his seat and quitted the place. The cruel minds of the Calvinistic executioners were gratified, but not appeased, by these extraordinary torments; and a few days afterwards, wholly unexpectedly, they took out the archbishop, who, from his sufferings, was indeed suffering a daily death, yet had no reason

* O'Sullivan says he was subjected to this torture for an hour.

to expect execution, to a place a little distance from the Castle of Dublin. This was done at early dawn, lest the spectacle should excite a tumult among the people. There they hung him with a halter roughly woven of twigs, to increase his torture. This barbarous and inhuman cruelty satiated indeed their thirst for his blood, but opened for the holy prelate the fountain of eternal life ; so that, drinking of its eternal source, though cast down, he is raised up ; though conquered, he hath conquered ; slain, he lives, and by the cruelty of the Calvinists triumphs everlastingly.

"'The cries of the holy archbishop, of which I have spoken, were no murmurs of an impatient mind, but the sighs of a Christian breast feeling the bitterness of its torments ; for he was a man of sorrows and acquainted with infirmity, and from the sole of his foot to the crown of his head all was tormented. Not only his legs and feet were tortured with the boiling oil and salt, but his whole body was burnt with the heat, and bathed in the chill perspiration of exhaustion. With a loud voice he cried out, "Jesus, Son of David, have mercy upon me!" raising up his voice with his soul to Him who alone is mighty to save. No torture could wring from him aught but a profession of the orthodox faith ; he was stronger than his tortures, for neither boiling oil, nor piercing salt, nor blazing fire could shake his faith or extinguish his love of God.

"'Exhausted and, as it were, suffocated by his sufferings while fastened in the stocks, the archbishop lost all voice and sense, and when taken out lay on the ground like dead, unable to move hand or foot, or even eye or tongue. The head executioner began to fear lest he had exceeded his orders, which were only to torture and not to kill, and might be punished for having put him to death without orders. He therefore directed him to be wrapped in linen and laid on a feather bed, and poured a few drops into his mouth to see if any life yet remained in the tortured body, and if he could be recalled to his senses. The next morning, as he had a little revived, aromatic drinks were administered to him, to give him strength to endure new torments, the executioners rejoicing as they saw him swallow it from a spoon, for they feared to receive from Wallop the same punishment as Perillus from Phalaris.

"'Our martyr was gradually so far recovered as to be able to sit up* and to limp a little, when his enemies sought to make him waver in the faith, offering him dignity and office if he would resign his position as bishop, and acknowledge the queen to have a double sovereignty, ecclesiastical as well as secular. There was sent to him for this purpose, among others, Thomas Johns. But he remained unshaken. His only sister, too, Honor Hurley, was induced to go and tempt him to apostatize, and she urgently besought him to yield; but he, frowning on her, ordered her to fall at his knees and humbly beg pardon of God and absolution for so grave a crime against God, so hurtful to her own soul, and so abhorred by her brother.

"'These governors were about to quit their office, to be succeeded by Sir John Perrot, who was at this time arrived in Dublin; but, before he entered on office, as it was rumored that the Earl of Ormond was hastening to Dublin to congratulate the new viceroy, and intercede with him for Dermod, Wallop was determined first to slake his hatred in the blood of the archbishop.

"'As Perrot was to receive the sword of office on Sunday,

---

* O'Sullivan says: "A worthy priest named Charles MacMorris, of the society, skilled in medicine, found access to the archbishop, and treated his wounds with such skill that in a few days his strength began to return, and in less than a fortnight he was enabled to sit up in bed. This priest had himself been confined in prison by the English, but released on account of the skill with which he treated some noblemen when suffering from dangerous illness."

the Feast of the Holy Trinity, and his power would then cease, lest his successor might prove more merciful, on the preceding Friday,* and at early dawn, as we have mentioned, the archbishop was drawn on a hurdle through the garden gate to the place where he was hanged, Wallop himself (as it is said) going before with three or four guards ; and there he was hanged in a withey, calling on God and forgiving his torturers with all his heart.

"'He was taken out of the castle without any noise, lest there should be a tumult ; but the Catholics who were prisoners there, seeing him going, called out that he was innocent ; and, among others, a certain bishop, then a prisoner there, called out aloud that he rather deserved that fate for the scandal he feared he had formerly given, but that Hurley was an innocent and holy man. Upon which the jailer severely flogged him and the others, and so reduced them to silence.'

"The holy martyr was hanged in a wood near the city, and at evening was buried in the half-ruined church of St. Kevin ; and it is stated that many miracles had been wrought there."

ARCHBISHOP CREAGH.

RICHARD CREAGH, archbishop of Armagh, distinguished alike for sanctity and for the many learned works which proceeded from his pen, may, with justice, be numbered among the illustrious sufferers of these awful times. This venerable prelate had scarcely arrived in his native country when the storm began to collect around him. His unremitted zeal, and the high station which he occupied in the Cath-

* According to O'Sullivan, he was executed on the 7th June, 1584, William Simon, a citizen of London, removed the martyr's body in a wooden urn, and buried it secretly in consecrated ground Richard, a distinguished musician, celebrated his sufferings and death in a plaintive elegy called "The Fall of the Baron of Slane"

olic Church, inflamed still more the malice of his enemies. He was arrested in 1565, and transmitted to London, where he was put in chains, and imprisoned in the Tower. In this place of confinement he continued for five weeks; by the mediation of some friends he was unexpectedly liberated. When, at length, the fury of the persecution had broke out, in 1580, he was again arrested, and, after undergoing a lengthened series of sufferings in Ireland, he was conveyed to London, and committed a second time to the Tower. During his confinement in the dungeons of this fortress, promises of high preferment had been held out to him, provided he would abjure the Catholic faith. These promises, however, were just as ineffectual as the terrors of the prison; they had been repeatedly urged, but the prelate continued inflexible. His enemies, determined even on wounding his character, had at length contrived to institute a new series of accusation against him. They procured a female—the daughter of his jailer—whom they bribed; on her they prevailed to accuse the holy prelate of having offered violence to her person. The appointed day of trial had arrived; and that the feelings of his friends might suffer as well as the character of their prelate, a number of the Catholic nobility had been summoned on the occasion. His accuser made her appearance; the moment, however, she cast her eyes on this innocent and injured victim, the hand of an invisible power touched her soul with remorse; she declared that the charges alleged against him were all malicious and false, and that the archbishop was both an innocent and a holy man. His enemies thus discomfitted, had him now arraigned under the penal statutes of the day. In the meantime the primate, heroically persisting in his faith, was recommitted to the Tower, and sentenced to imprisonment for life. The malice of his persecutors continued unabated. While chained in the Tower, he was forced to pass through a prolonged ordeal of privations, and was at length poisoned, on the 14th of October, A. D. 1585.*

* Besides the martyrs and sufferers enumerated, Father Brenan gives a long catalogue of priests of the Franciscan Order, who became victims to the persecuting fury of the sixteenth century. Among these the most remarkable were: Roger MacComguil, of the convent of Armagh, flogged to death in 1565; Daniel Doolan, of the convent of Youghal, beheaded in 1569; Thadæus Daly, of the convent of Askeaton, hanged, boweled, and quartered, in Limerick, A D. 1579; John Connoly, of the convent of Askeaton, beheaded in 1582; William Ferrall, of the convent of Askeaton, hanged and quartered in 1582; Thadæus O'Moran, of the convent of Enniscorthy, flogged and strangled in 1582; Felix O'Hara and Henry de Layhode, of the convent of Sligo, both hanged and cut in quarters, in 1582; Roger Donnellan, Charles Goran, Peter Chillan, Patrick O'Kenna, Roger O'Henlan, and John Pillan, from various convents in the province of Leinster, incarcerated in the prison of Dublin, where they died, A D. 1582; Dermitius O'Mulrony, of the convent of Galbally, county of Limerick, beheaded, in 1588; Thadæus O'Boyle, of the county of Donegal, mangled and beheaded, in 1588; Patrick Brady, of the convent of Monaghan, tortured and beheaded, in 1588; Donatus O'Muirhily, of the convent of Irrelagh (Mucross), stoned to death, in 1589; Matthew O'Leyn, of the convent of Kilkenny, tortured and beheaded, in 1590; Terence Magennis, Magnus O'Fedling, and Oge MacLaughlin, of the convent of Multifarnam, confined in the prison of Ballybay, and afterwards in that of Dublin, where they died, A. D. 1591.—*Synop. Prov. Hib.*, p. 33 et seq.; *Wadding de Scrip.*, p. 102 et seq.

FEARFUL INCREASE OF RELIGIOUS AND POLITICAL OPPRESSION.

The Irish forced to rebel—Dissensions fostered—Irish lords, spiritual and temporal, opposed to the Queen's supremacy—The O'Neils in Ulster, and Desmond in Munster—The massacre of Mullaghmast—The insurrection of Fitzmaurice—Persecutions increase—New penal laws—Fearful state of persecution, famine, and misery in Ireland—Extracts from Spencer—Chiefs and prelates divided—The Catholics of the Pale and native Irish opposed—Father Kenrechtin—His capture and death—Martyrdom of Father O'Connor—Martyrdom of Fathers Miller, Molloy, Doherty, and several others—Fathers Maurice and Roche—Life and martyrdom of Archbishop Macgauran, of Armagh—Sufferings of several confessors and martyrs.

HE religious and political dissensions and troubles created in Ireland by the Reformation, during the reign of Elizabeth, led to much bloodshed and misery. The heretical adherents of the new doctrines and the queen's supremacy held all the executive power in their hands, and, in order to get rid of their enemies, or rather gain possession of their estates, it was only necessary to persecute them for their religious opinions in order to force them into the ranks of the disaffected, and next, to outlaw them as rebels.

During the early part of Elizabeth's reign, very few, not only of the common people, but also of the lords, spiritual and temporal, could be induced to join the Protestant religion. The lords and settlers of the Pale were as bitterly opposed to it as the Irish outside it.

In the parliament of 1560, the new form of worship and the penal statutes introduced were opposed by Thomas, earl of Ormond; Gerald, earl of Desmond; Richard, earl of Clanrickard; James Barry, lord Buttervant; Maurice Roche, lord Fermoy; Richard Butler, lord Mountgarret; Thomas Fitzmaurice, lord Lixnaw; John Power, lord Curraghnore; Birmingham, lord Athenry, and Courcy, lord Kinsale.

Thomas, earl of Ormond, was a Protestant, but he died a Catholic, in 1614.

The ill-fated Gerald Fitzgerald, the last earl of Desmond, took up arms against the Reformation, and lost not only his life, but also his broad patrimony of five hundred thousand acres in the struggle.*

Mountgarret and Lixnaw served in the Catholic army under Hugh O'Neil. The only two native Irish lords present at this parliament were Fitzpatrick, lord of Upper Ossory, and O'Brien, earl of Thomond, who reformed in 1572.

The Catholics were thus forced by religious persecution to take up arms for the defence of their property, their lives, and their religion. It is no wonder, therefore, that the persecuted people flocked to the standard of the O'Neils in Ulster, and Desmond in Munster. The violation of English faith made even their Anglo-Irish converts look upon them

* Earl Desmond could bring into the field six hundred knights of his own name, and two thousand footmen of his immediate followers. His principality extended over the greater portion of four counties of Munster, and he kept sovereign state in his castles of Mogeely and Adare. In 1569 he joined the national cause against Elizabeth. A protracted and sanguinary war of years followed, with varying success, until South Munster became a howling wilderness—without cow, or sheep, or living animal, except the wolf, and straggling, gaunt, starved clansmen. The patriot army defeated, the earl became a hunted outlaw. He was at length betrayed and murdered, near Tralee, and his head was carried to England and spiked over the gates of London.

INCREASED OPPRESSION. 75

with suspicion, particularly after the savage massacre of Mullaghmast.*

Though the persecution of the Catholics throughout the reign of Elizabeth was fierce and unrelenting, it reached its full fury after the failure of Fitzmaurice's insurrection, in 1569, and the unbridled soldiers swept over the country, desecrating and burning churches and monasteries, and butchering the unoffending peasantry.

Though Tyrone was sweeping the English garrisons out of the North, the old bane of Ireland, dissension and disunion, had divided the chieftains in Munster and elsewhere, so that they fell victims to the crafty policy of England—more so than to the force of her arms.

New penal laws were enacted, and while the tempest of persecution was sweeping over the church, the sword and famine were desolating the country.

The edict which came out in 1584 served to complete the persecution. We here present it to the reader without any commentary; it is to the following effect: "And if from henceforth any priest shall be detected within these realms, he shall, *ipso facto*, be guilty of high treason : wherefore, let him first be hanged, then cut down alive, and afterwards beheaded, bowelled, and burned. His head is to be set on a spike and exposed in the most public place. But should any person receive or entertain a priest, he shall suffer the confiscation of his property, and be hanged without the hope of mercy."

---

* In the year 1577 the English published a proclamation, inviting the friendly Irish to an interview at Mullaghmast, in the Kings county. A safe conduct was guaranteed to all. Some hundreds assembled, but they soon found themselves surrounded by the English soldiers, by whom they were treacherously attacked and cut to pieces.

> "At the feast, unarmed all,
> Priest, lord, and chieftain fall,
> In the treacherous Saxon's hall."

In this manner did the tempest, unabated, roll over the Church of Ireland; the reign of terror became general; the country, with all its loveliness, and religion, with all its blessings, appeared alike involved in the same universal wreck. Between plunder and profanation, racks and gibbets, pestilence and famine,* the blood of the people and of the Lord's anointed, what a revolting spectacle must not this unhappy land, at the close of the sixteenth century, present to the nations of the civilized world! And all this done under the pretext of religion, and in the name of that blessed and eternal Gospel of charity and peace, which the Redeemer of the world came down to establish among men!

"The miseries which the wretched Irish endured," says Leland, "were affecting even to their very enemies: thousands perished by famine, and the hideous resources sought for allaying the rage of hunger were more terrible than even such a calamity."

"The famine of Jerusalem," observes Cox, "did not exceed that among the Irish."

"Whosoever," writes Hollinshed, "should travel from one end to the other of all Munster, even from Waterford to the head of Smerwicke, which is about six-score miles, he would not meet anie man, woman, or child, saving in townes and cities, nor yet see anie beasts, but the very wolves, the foxes, and other like ravening beasts; many of these laie dead, being famished, and the residue gone elsewhere."

"Notwithstanding," says Spenser,† "that the same (Ire-

---

* In the space of a few months, upwards of three thousand died of starvation in Tyrone.—*Morrisson ap. Curry*, p. 50

† This same Spenser, immediately after this famine and plague, recommended Elizabeth to execute the abominable plan of destroying the fruits of the earth throughout the country, in order, as he observed, that the Irish might be driven to the necessity of devouring one another. "The end will, I assure you, be very short," says Spencer; "for although there should none of them fall by the sword, nor be slain by the soldier, yet

land) was a most rich and plentiful country, full of corn and cattle, that you would have thought they should have been able to stand long; yet, in one year and a half they were brought to such wretchedness, as that any stoney heart would have rued the same. Out of every corner of the woods and glens they came, creeping forth upon their hands, for their legs could not bear them; they looked like anatomies of death; they spake like ghosts crying out of their graves. *They did eat the dead carrions,* happy where they could find them; yea, *and one another soon after, insomuch as the very carcasses they spared not to scrape out of their graves;* and if they found a plot of water-cresses or shamrocks, there they flocked, as to a feast, for the time; yet, not being able long to continue therewithal, that in a short space there were none almost remaining, and *a most populous and plentiful country suddenly left void of both man and beast."*

Persons unacquainted with the state of Ireland at the time, will naturally ask how it was that the chiefs and nobles attached to the Catholic faith, together with the bishops, did not combine in opposition to the penal enactments and persecutions of the time. It must be recollected that Ireland was then composed of three parties as much opposed to each other as to the common enemy. These were the native Irish, the *degenerate* English, and the Anglo-Irish of the Pale. Their fierce animosity was even carried into the sanctuary, and by a bull of Pope Leo X., issued in 1516, native Irish were excluded from filling the See of Dublin.

The first victims of the persecution were the Catholics of the Pale. The native Irish had little or no sympathy for them; while the others, in turn, complacently looked upon the persecution of their old enemies. Elizabeth's advisers

their being kept from *manurance,* and their cattle from running abroad, by this hard restraint *they would quickly consume themselves, and devour one another.* The proof whereof I saw sufficiently in the late warres of Munster."

in Ireland were too wise to arouse the whole nation by a sweeping deposition of the Catholic bishops. As Sees became gradually vacant, they were filled by royal nominees. They first carefully fostered these foolish dissensions of race, until they gradually filled up the Sees and strengthened their power, until they firmly planted Protestantism equally upon the necks of Anglo-Irish lords and Irish chiefs and princes. They had corrupted ecclesiastics by the lure of the temporalities of the despoiled churches and sees, and the nobles by the bribe of a share of the broad lands confiscated.

By bribes and dissension, Protestantism got a foothold in Ireland; by the sword, persecution, and spoliation it was maintained there.

REV. FATHER KENRECHTIN.

This holy martyr's life has been given at length by Dr. Roothe, but more condensed by Father Rochfort. Father KENRECHTIN was a native of Kilmallock, county Limerick, and officiated for some time as chaplain to Gerald, earl of Desmond. This, together with his blameless life and steadfast faith, rendered him peculiarly obnoxious to the reformers.

Roothe says of him: "His attention to prayers, his sobriety and continency of life, his gentleness of speech, proved his love of God and his neighbor. Although these qualities were recognized by all, and he was loved and respected by all the good, he had the misfortune to fall into the hands of one Maurice Sweeny,* a faithless and bloody captain of hireling soldiers, a deserter from his lord, in whose forces he had been leader of the axe-bearers—those who fight with battle-axes, a weapon much used by the Irish. It was no wonder that Father Maurice was by this

* "Suvinium," which I translate "Sweeny."

perfidious man given up a prisoner to a troop of English soldiers, and thus to Sir John Norris, president of Munster; since, notwithstanding his allegiance to him, he sold, for a wretched price, the Earl of Desmond, when unarmed and defenceless. It was then not to be expected that he would treat his chaplain better. But the fate which befell the captor showed the wickedness of the capture."

The following is Father Rochfort's account of Father Kenrechtin's capture and death:—

"I send you an account of the glorious martyrdom of a friend of mine, Maurice Kenrechtin, a pious priest, chaplain to the Earl of Desmond, whom you know. He was for this cause taken prisoner by the English, and taken to your native town of Clonmel, where he lay in prison for more than a year. On the eve of Easter, 1585, Victor White, one of the principal citizens of Clonmel and a pious Catholic, obtained from the head jailer permission for the priest to pass the night in his house; this the jailer agreed to, but secretly informed the President of Munster, an English heretic, who chanced to be in the town, that, if he wished, he might easily seize all the principal citizens while hearing Mass in the house of Mr. White at daybreak; at the same time he bargained to be paid for his perfidy. At the hour agreed on the soldiers rushed into the house and seized on Victor, but all the others, hearing the noise, tried to escape by the back doors and windows; a certain matron, trying to escape, fell and broke her arm. The soldiers found the chalice and other things for Mass; they sought everywhere for the priest (who had not yet begun the Mass), and came at length to a heap of straw, under which he lay hid, and, thrusting their swords through it, wounded him in the thigh; but he preserved silence, and, through fear of worse, concealed his suffering, and soon after escaped from the town into the country. But the intrepid Victor (who, although he had for this reason suffered much, could never be induced to attend the conventicles of the heretics) was thrown into prison because he would not give up the priest, and would, no doubt, have been put to death, had not Maurice, hearing of the danger of his friend, voluntarily surrendered himself to the president, showing a friendship truly Christian. The president upbraided him much, and, having sentenced him to death, offered him his life if he would abjure our Catholic faith, and profess the queen to be head of the church. There came to him also a preacher, and strove long, but in vain, to seduce the martyr; nor would he on any account betray any of those who had heard his Mass, or to whom he had at any time administered the sacraments. At length he was dragged at the tail of a horse to the place of execution as a traitor. Being come there, he devoutly and learnedly exhorted the people to constancy in the faith. The executioner cut him down from the gallows when yet half alive, and cut off his sacred head, and the minister struck it in the face. Then the Catholics, by prayers and bribes, obtained of the executioners that they should not lacerate his body any further, and they buried it as honorably as they could. Farewell, and peace in the Lord, and be ye imitators—if occasion offers—of the courageous Maurice Kenrechtin, and till then prepare your souls for the trial. Your devoted servant, dated from the College of St. Anthony, 1586, 20th March, ROBERT ROCHFORT."*

"REV. PATRICK O'CONNOR was descended from the royal race of O'Conor, in Connaught; but, renouncing the false joys of the world in the flower of his age, he embraced the monastic life in the celebrated Cistercian monastery in the diocese of Elphin, in the year 1562. During all the twenty-

* Roothe, De Processu Martyriali.

three years he lived in the monastery he was as a shining light to his brethren. He was assiduous in prayer, during which he shed floods of tears, and unwearied in all works of charity, especially towards the sick, and rigorous in chastising his body. During the last fifteen years of his life he never touched beer or wine; he never ate meat during all te years of his profession. Almighty God, to reward the merits of Father O'Conor, suffered him, together with Father Malachy OKelly, a monk of the same monastery, remarkable alike for noble birth and virtues, to fall into the hands of the cruel satellites of Elizabeth, by whom, with barbarous torture, he was first partially hung, and then cut into four parts, near the same monastery, the 19th May, 1585." *

"MAURCE EUSTACE, a youth of great promise, entered the Society of Jesus, at Bruges, in Flanders, and being called home by his father, Sir John Eutace, a noble and influential man, he returned to Ireland, by the permission of the father (as is mentioned by the author of the *Theatre*), before he had taken his vows. He had not long enjoyed his gentle native air when he was seized by the ungentle heretics in Dublin, and examined on the suspicion of holding correspondence with the Catholic nobles who had been driven by the cruelty of Elizabeth to defend the Catholic faith by arms. Maurice, who was an intrepid young man, boldly answered the accusation and proved his innocence, adding, that he had only lately returned from Belgium (where he was enrolled among the novices of the Society of Jesus), in order to satisfy the ardent desire of his parents, and that his object was not to excite rebellion, but only to satisfy his parents' request, and return as soon as possible to take his vows. On this the chief judge answered, 'Out of your own mouth I judge you; for, as you say you are one of the

* Bruodin, lib. iii , cap. xx.

Jesuits, who are born to excite trouble and sedition, any one must see you are guilty of the crimes you are accused of.' And on this he sentenced Maurice to die. The youth was then dragged from the court to the place of execution, and there hung, and cut in four parts ; and so gloriously triumphed for Christ, 9th June, 1588." *

Rev. PETER MILLER, of Wexford, and bachelor of theology, after receiving his education and ordination in Spain, returned to Ireland to preach the faith. He had scarcely landed at Wexford, when he was captured. He was subjected to the most cruel tortures ; and when his persecutors found that they could not shake his faith, they hung him, and, before life was extinct, quartered him, on the 4th of October, 1588.

In the same year, PETER MEYLER, a Catholic student, was put to death at Galway.

In the same year, Fathers JOHN MOLLOY, CORNELIUS DOHERTY, and WALFRED FARRLAL, O. S. F., fell victims to their faith and zeal in ministering to the spiritual wants of the Catholics. These intrepid martyrs spent eight years administering religious consolation to the poor Catholics who were compelled to fly to the mountainous districts of Leinster. These faithful priests shared all their perils and hardships, visiting the sick, consoling the dying, and offering up the sacrifice of the Mass. At length they were captured by a party of cavalry, in a remote district in the Queen's county, bound hand and foot, and conducted, with every species of insult, to the garrison of Abbeyleix. Here they were repeatedly flogged ; but, as they would neither give up their faith nor betray their flock, they were put on the rack and cruelly tortured. The suffering martyrs were still unshaken, when they were half strangled, and, before life had left the body, they were embowelled and quartered.

* Bruodin, lib. iii., cap. xx.

Father Mooney tells us that, "In the convent of Clonmel is interred the Rev. Father MAURICE, a priest who suffered martyrdom at the hands of the heretics in the same Clonmel, about the year 1589, and whose relics were placed behind the high altar."*

"Father CHRISTOPHER ROCHE was born of a respectable family, in Wexford. He had nearly completed his studies at Louvain, when he was compelled by sickness to return home, but was arrested at Bristol, in England, examined, and called upon to take the oath of supremacy. He refused resolutely to stain his soul with such a perjury, and, in consequence, was sent to London, where he was flogged through the streets. Then, after having endured the horrors of Newgate prison for four months, he was put to the torture of '*the scavenger's daughter*,' and gave up his soul to God, under this torture, the 13th December, 1590.†

ARCHBISHOP MACGAURAN.

The Most Rev. EDWARD MACGAURAN was the immediate successor of Primate Creagh. In 1594, Pope Clement VIII. employed this fearless prelate as his envoy in Ireland, to encourage and strengthen the faithful there, as well as to keep alive the faith under its trying persecutions. A new edict had been published, enjoining upon all faithful subjects, under certain pains and penalties, to hunt up and discover all priests, particularly the Jesuits and Seminarists.

For the past fifty years the Irish princes had frequently implored the holy Father, either personally, or through the

○ The convent of Clonmel was founded in 1269 by Otho de Grandison, for Conventuals, and was reformed by the Observants in 1536. Robert Travers was the last guardian, when, in the thirty-fourth of Henry VIII., a moiety, consisting of four houses and twenty acres of land, was granted to the sovereign and commonalty of Clonmel; the other moiety was given to James, earl of Ormond.

† Bruodin, lib. iii., cap. xx.

Spanish or French courts, to interpose to stay the fearful persecutions in Ireland. All remonstrances having failed, Philip II. of Spain, having national wrongs as well as religious ones to gratify against England, promised to send military aid to the Irish, and commissioned Primate Macgauran to assure the Irish princes and chiefs of his intentions, and also of the speedy arrival of assistance.

Dr. Macgauran arrived in Ireland in the beginning of 1594, and lost no time in visiting the princes and chieftains of Ulster, and communicating to them the welcome intelligence. He took up his residence with Maguire, prince of Fermanagh, who had lately been in arms against the English. Lord Deputy Sussex demanded of Maguire the surrender of the primate ; but Maguire's answer was to march his forces against the English in Connaught. Sir William Guelfort, with a body of troops, marched to oppose him.

"On the 23d day of June, the two armies met at a place called Sciath-na-Feart, (The Shield of Wonders) ; the cavalry of both were before the fort, and, there being a very thick mist, they saw not each other till they met. The signal was given, and a brisk and determined action having been commenced by the cavalry, Maguire, after much fighting, fixed his eye on the opposite general, and, setting spurs to his horse, and cutting a passage for himself through the surrounding officers with his sword, he pierced Guelfort through with his lance. The English, astonished at this daring bravery, and seeing their commander slain, fled from the field. The primate was at a short distance from the engagement, administering the last sacraments, and hearing the confessions of some of the mortally wounded soldiers. (Dr. Roothe says, reconciling a dying heretic.) A party of the fugitive cavalry happened to come upon him while thus engaged, and transpierced with their lances the unarmed and inoffensive archbishop, being roused to rage by seeing him engaged in the vocation of a Catholic clergyman."*

Thus the martyr Archbishop Creagh (anno 1585) was succeeded by the martyr Dr. Macgauran (anno 1598), and at his death the headship of the Irish Church, with the title of Vice-Primate,† devolved on Dr. REDMOND, bishop of Derry, who also laid down his life for the faith (1604), when the office devolved on Dr. RICHARD BRADY, bishop of Kilmore, who was a confessor, and almost a martyr. It then passed to Dr. CORNELIUS O'DOVENEY, who also laid down his life for Christ (anno 1612). Thus, in thirty years, four martyrs and a confessor succeeded each other in the primacy of the Irish Church.

Curry, in his "Civil Wars in Ireland," gives the particulars of the sufferings and death of several confessors and martyrs who were persecuted and died for the faith, about this time. He says:

"In this reign, among many other Roman Catholic priests and bishops, were put to death, for the exercise of their functions in Ireland: John Stephens, priest, for that he said Mass to Teague McHugh, was hanged and quartered by the Lord Burroughs, in 1597 ; Thady O'Boyle, guardian of the monastery of Donegal, who was slain by the English

---

* Renehan, *Collec.* p 18, from O'Sullivan, Pet. Lombard, and Philadelph, who puts his death at 1598 ; but Dr Renehan gives strong reasons to think this arises from a confusion between two battles of Maguire, and that the true date is 1593. Sir Richard Bingham, writing to the Privy Council, on the 28th of June, 1593, describes his death. (See Moran, Hist. Archbishops of Dublin, vol. i , p 290.)

† Mooney thus explains the title of Vice-Primate : "According to the custom of the province of Armagh, which is that, when the primate is absent or the See of Armagh vacant, the oldest bishop of the province has the title of 'Vice-Primate,'....which I thought it right to hand down to remembrance, lest the custom might become obsolete by oblivion. (P. 75.)

in his own monastery; six friars were slain in the monastery of Moynihigan; John O'Calyhor and Bryan O'Trevor, of the order of St. Bernard, were slain in their own monastery, De Sancta Maria, in Ulster; as also Felimy O'Hara, a lay-brother; so was Æneas Penny, parish priest of Killagh, slain at the altar in his parish church there; Cahill McGoran; Rory O'Donnellan; Peter McQuillan; Patrick O'Kenna; George Power, vicar-general of the diocese of Ossory; Andrew Stritch, of Limerick; Bryan O'Murihirtagh, vicar-general of the diocese of Clonfert; Doroghow O'Molowny, of Thomond; John Kelly, of Louth; Stephen Patrick, of Annaly; John Pillis, friar; Rory McHenlea; Tirilagh McInisky, a lay-brother. All those that come after Æneas Penny, together with Walter Fernan, priest, died in the Castle of Dublin, either through hard usage and restraint, or the violence of torture."

THE FRANCISCANS PERSECUTED.

Penal persecutions continued—Catholics banned, outlawed, and butchered—Sketch of the convents of Donegal, Multifernan, Kilconnel, Galway, and others—Persecutions of the Franciscans—Father Mooney's graphic account—Sufferings and constancy of Father Donatus O'Molony—Betrayal and martyrdom of forty-two priests—Terrible torture and execution of Father Collins—End of Elizabeth's reign, but not of the persecutions.

ELIZABETH'S reign was fast drawing to a close, but not so the persecutions of the faithful Catholics and the spoliation and confiscation of their properties, which marked that era as one of the most bloody in history. The Irish people—banned, outlawed, and persecuted — were driven from their homes, and hunted down like wild beasts; their priests, the faithful *Soggarths Aroon*, were hunted like wolves, and forced to seek shelter and protection in gloomy dells and mountain solitudes, either to perish of cold and hunger, or, more likely, to be shot down or smothered in lonely caves while celebrating Mass.*

---

* In my travels through Ireland, I have seen several of these caves, in association with which the peasantry preserve the tradition of how they were used for the celebration of Mass. In connection with many of them the tradition also exists of how both priests and congregation were burned or smothered to death by the soldiers, who first closed the entrance with large stones, and then piled up brushwood against it, which was set on fire. In the Galtees, not far from Galbally, is one of these caves, in which it is said fifty persons were smothered together.

"Oh, that dark time of cruel wrong, when our country's breast,
A dreary load, a ruthless code, with wasting terrors prest—
Our gentry stripped of land and clan, sent exiles o'er the main,
To turn the scales on foreign fields for foreign monarchs' gain—
Our people trod like vermin down, all 'fenceless flung to sate,
Extortion, lust, and brutal whim, and rancorous bigot hate;
Our priesthood tracked from cave to hut, like felons chased and lashed,
And from their ministering hands the living chalice dashed."

It is hard to conceive how the human breast can be so far lost to all the finer feelings of humanity—to all the tender sensibilities of love and charity—as to delight in the sufferings of a fellow creature. Love your neighbor as yourself, is one of the great precepts of divine wisdom, but a still greater precept is "love your enemies," and the religion that teaches and encourages persecution and rapine, cannot have come from that pure fountain from which nothing defiled has sprung. The mantle of charity and purity throw their heavenly folds o'er the Christian soul that is warmed by the divine spark of love to all, and of peace to men of good will.

The persecutors in Ireland seemed to be sowing dragon's teeth in the blood they so freely shed. In the North, the clans of Tyrone and Tyrconnell were striking terror into the English army, and had routed them on many a bloody field, from Clontibert to the Yellow Ford; while, in Munster, the great Earl of Desmond was striking terror and dismay into their hearts; in Connaught, the sons of Clanricard, the O'Moores, and the O'Cavanaghs, and a great portion of Leinster, were up in arms against the persecutors of their creed and their country.*

* In connection with the rebellion of the Earl of Desmond, the names of Sir Walter Raleigh and Spenser, the poet, are prominently connected. The career of the former was marked by deceit and cold-blooded atrocities, unbecoming a man and a soldier. When a Spanish contingent landed near Kinsale, being closely pressed they had to surrender the forts, and were all cruelly massacred by Raleigh. Spenser, who was rewarded for

THE FRANCISCANS PERSECUTED.

Of the different religious orders in Ireland at the time, perhaps none were persecuted with greater severity than the Franciscans. Father Meehan, in his work on the Irish Franciscan monasteries, gives an elaborate account of their persecutions and sufferings. He furthermore gives the graphic account by Father Mooney, written in 1617, of the rise and fall of the most prominent of these monasteries, and the hardships and persecutions of their holy inmates. His description of the monastery of Donegal is so full of the stirring events of the time, that we take several extracts from it.

In the year 1474 Nuala O'Connor, daughter of O'Connor Faly, and wife of Hugh Roe O'Donnell, founded the monastery of Donegal. We need not follow its progressive history for the following century, but will give Father Mooney's account of the monastery during the persecutions of Elizabeth. He says:

"The monastery continued to flourish in peace and happiness, under the fostering protection of the princess of Tirconnell. In the interval countless fugitives from the Pale came with strange tidings to our friars, telling them how King Henry of England had decreed the spoliation of the religious houses, and how his immediate successor, and his wicked counsellors, had laid sacrilegious hands on the gold and silver of many a sanctuary. The Franciscans pitied their plundered brethren of the Pale, but they never thought that similar horrors were one day to overtake themselves. Wars, fierce and bloody, it is true, wasted Tirconnell, when Shane O'Neill strove to reduce all Ulster to

his loyalty by Kilcoman, with its broad acres, was a bitter enemy to the Irish, and encouraged all kinds of persecution against them Though the chivalry and sufferings of Raleigh may create a false sympathy for his fate, and the genius of Spenser may make us forget his bigotry and cruelty, we cannot forget that they had no sympathy for the sufferings of others, particularly the Irish, and are, therefore, entitled to little from Irishmen.

his sway; but although the fields of Tir-Hugh were desolated by fire and sword, and the prince and princess of Tirconnell lay fettered in the stronghold of Shane the Proud, still no faggot reached our roof-tree, and no hand profaned our altars. Nor is it to be supposed that we lacked wherewithal to tempt the cupidity of the sacrilegious, were such to be found among the clansmen of Tyrone or Tirconnell. Quite the contrary; for many years afterwards,* when I was sacristan, no monastery in the land could make a goodlier show of gold and silver than ours. During the time I held that office, I had in my custody forty suits of vestments, many of them of cloth of gold and silver—some interwoven and brocaded with gold, the remainder silk. We had also sixteen silver chalices, all of which, two excepted, were washed with gold; nor should I forget two splendid ciboriums, inlaid with precious stones, and every other requisite for the altars. This rich furniture was the gift of the princes of Tirconnell; and, as I said before, no matter what preys the Tyronians might lift off O'Donnell's lands, there was no one impious enough to desecrate or spoil our sacred treasury. We fed the poor, comforted them in their sorrows, educated the scions of the princely house to whom we owed everything, chronicled the achievements of their race, prayed for the souls of our founders and benefactors, chanted the divine offices day and night with great solemnity; and, while thus engaged, the tide of war swept harmless by our hallowed walls.

"But it was not Heaven's will that our peaceful domicile should always be exempted from outrage and invasion; for, alas! the mad dissensions of the native princes precipitated their own ruin, which involved ours. The O'Donnell who then ruled the principality had grown old and feeble, and, to add to his miseries, his eldest son, Hugh, had been cap-

A. D. 1600–1.

tured by the Deputy Perrott, and recommitted to the dungeon of Dublin castle, after an unavailing effort to baffle his pursuers. A second attempt, however, proved successful; for when the avaricious Fitzwilliams replaced his attainted predecessor, the former, for a bribe of a thousand pounds, given, as was said, by the baron of Dungannon,* connived at the flight of the illustrious captive, who, after tarrying fourteen days in the fastness of Glenmalure, spurred hard across the English Pale, and finally reached his father's castle at Ballyshannon.

"Hugh Roe had hardly been inaugurated at Kilmacrenan, when he marched, with his trusty clansmen on Donegal, and laid siege to the monastery, into which Willis and his rabble had driven three hundred head of cattle. Sensible of the straits to which he was reduced, Willis threatened to fire the buildings. But the young prince, anxious to preserve the sacred edifice, suffered him and his people to depart unharmed. The friars returned immediately afterwards.

"For fully nine years after the inauguration of Hugh Roe, the monastery of Donegal enjoyed uninterrupted happiness; for indeed the young prince—or, as he was more generally styled, 'the son of prophecy'—ever proved himself our special benefactor. After joining his forces with O'Neill's, these two great princes defeated Queen Elizabeth's armies on many a hard-fought field; nay, and so routed them, that her craftiest deputies and bravest marshals were often fain to sue for truce and peace, no matter how humiliating the conditions. Right heartily did the friars of Donegal pray for the success of their prince, for the repose of the clansmen who fell in his cause; and, oh, how their jubilant voices made vault and cloister ring, when forty throats pealed out 'Te Deum' for the defeat of Norris at Clontibret,

* Hugh O'Neill.

Bagnal, on the field of the Yellow Ford, and Clifford, in the passes of the Curlew mountains! The father of Hugh Roe always assisted at those grand solemnities; for, after resigning the name and title of O'Donnell, he lived almost constantly among us, preparing himself for the better life, and doing penance for his sins, the weightiest of which was a cruel raid on the wrecked Spaniards of the Armada, whom he slew in Innishowen, at the bidding of Deputy Fitzwilliams. He died full of years, and we buried him, clothed in our habit, in the tomb of the lords his predecessors.

"In 1601 our community consisted of forty friars; and in that same year, so memorable for calamities, the English government landed a large force of horse and foot, under the command of Docwra, on the shores of Lough Foyle. This general was instructed to sow dissensions among the Irish, by setting up chieftain against chieftain, and holding out every bribe that might induce officers and men to abandon the standard of their liege lord. The scheme prospered, and—alas that I should have to record it!—Nial Gary, our prince's brother-in-law, went over to the enemy, with a thousand of his followers. The perfidious wretch stipulated that he should have all Tirconnell as a reward for his treason, which placed Derry, Lifford, and many other strong places, in the hands of the English. O'Donnell was in Thomond when the news of the revolt reached him, and he lost not a moment in hastening homeward to inflict summary vengeance on his faithless kinsman, who combined the venom of a serpent with the impetuosity of a lion. Having had timely notice that Nial, with the revolted Irish and his English auxiliaries, were marching on Donegal, we placed all our sacred furniture in a ship, and removed it to a place of safety. I myself was the last to go on board that vessel; and, as for the rest of the brotherhood, they fled to the wooded country, where they awaited the issue of the impending contest. On the 10th of August, the Feast of St. Laurence, martyr, Nial's troops took possession of *our* monastery and of another belonging to the Franciscans of the third order, that lay close to it at Magharabeg.

"Let me draw a veil over the disasters which befell our prince, and console myself by recording that O'Dunlevy, a friar of Donegal, received his latest sigh, and that the Franciscan monastery of Valladolid holds his mortal remains.

"In the year 1602, Oliver Lambert, the English governor of Connaught, seized the entire of our sacred furniture, which he desecrated, by turning the chalices into drinking cups, and ripping up the brocaded vestments for the vilest uses. Thus perished that fair monastery, with its treasures of gold, and silver, and precious books.

"'Ergo tam doctæ nobis periere tabellæ,
Scripta quibus pariter tot periere bona!'

"Some years afterwards, Rory, the brother of O'Donnell, who had obtained a considerable portion of the wide domains of his ancestors, together with the title of earl—ah, how inferior to that with which the prince of Tirconnell used to be invested on the sacred rock of Kilmacrenan!—set about restoring the monastery of Donegal; but learning that the English were plotting against his life, he fled with the great O'Neill to Rome, where they both died, and were buried in the Franciscan monastery on the Janiculum."

Father Mooney was a friar in the Convent of Multifernan when it was despoiled. In his work, he says of it :—

"Lest, however, their names or memories should be forgotten, I would have you know that, of all our enemies, none were more cruel than Sir Dudley Loftus, Sir Richard Grear, Patrick Fox, high sheriff of Westmeath, and Sir

Oliver Lambert, formerly president of Connaught. As for Loftus, he came, accompanied by the said Grear, to Multifernan, and carried off five of our brethren to Dublin. This occurred, as well as I remember, in 1607. In 1613, Fox came stealthily on our poor friars, and arrested, among others, Father Bernard Gray, who, after a year's confinement, was suffered to seek a refuge in France, where he died of disease contracted in the dungeon of Dublin castle. In the following year, Sir Oliver Lambert came with a company of soldiers to Multifernan, seized the few friars he found there, and committed them prisoners to the jail of Mullingar. Nevertheless, as I said before, Multifernan has never lacked a community of Franciscans, for whose maintenance we are mainly indebted to the illustrious house of Nugent, and the unfailing charity of the Catholics residing in the neighborhood and throughout Westmeath." *

Among the Franciscan convents which Father Mooney

* The convent of Multifernan, in the barony of Corkery and county of Westmeath, was founded for Conventuals by William Delamar, in the year 1236 The reformation of the Strict Observants had been adopted here in 1460, and in 1529 a provincial chapter had been held in this abbey In the 8th of Henry VIII., the convent of Multifernan and its appurtenances, a water-mill and thirty acres of arable land, were granted to Edmund Field, Patrick Clynch, and Philip Pentenoy, at a fine of £80 and the annual rent of 4s. When the fury of the storm, created by Henry and Elizabeth, had somewhat subsided, this convent was again placed in the possession of the Franciscans, and continued in their hands during the reign of Charles I., until it was at length committed to the flames by the Rochfords. The walls of the cloister are still complete, while the surrounding ruins, with the steeple rising from a small arch to nearly the height of one hundred feet, and situate on the borders of a delightful lake, contribute to render the whole scene at once picturesque and magnificent. By the united exertions of a spirited public, this abbey has been lately rebuilt, and is now finished in a style altogether worthy the recollections of its former greatness. The convent of Multifernan stands, and its abbey flourishes, while the despoiler and the plunderer have disappeared, both alike laid low, and long since levelled to the dust.—*Brenan's Ecclesiastical History.*

specially mentions are those of Kilcrea and Timoleague.*
Of the former he says :

"I will now relate to you all that I have learnt concerning the monastery of Kilcrea. Of all the Irish princes, none ruled with kinglier sway than did the MacCarthys, lords of Muskerry. Their martial prowess was famed in the songs of bards, their lineage was traced to progenitors who sailed with Milesius from Spain to Ireland, and their strong castles studded the banks of the Bandon from Knocknanavon to Kinsale. Nor were they less famed for their piety and devotedness to our holy founder, St. Francis, as Kilcrea, even in its ruins, will testify to future ages. The founder of that venerable house was Cormac MacCarthy, lord of Muskerry, who erected it, under the invocation of St. Brigid, for Franciscans, A. D. 1465. The site selected for the monastery was very beautiful, away from the tumult of the world, and close to the sweet river Bride. The church was admirably constructed of the finest materials, and nothing could excel the exquisite workmanship of the nave and choir, from which springs a graceful bell-tower of considerable height. Rich marbles, finely-turned windows, and a beautiful arcade forming one side of a chapel, still show that Cormac, lord of Muskerry, was a man gifted with a high appreciation of art, and, as I have already said, with true devotedness to our order. In the chancel, and close to the grand altar, he caused a tomb to be constructed for himself, and he was interred there in 1495, having been slain by his own brother and nephews. The same tomb contains the mortal remains of many of his race, all of whom were distinguished for their

---

* The convent of Timoleague, in the barony of Ibawn and Barryroe, county of Cork, had for its founder William Barry, lord of Ibawn, about the year 1370. The Franciscans of the Strict Observance were placed here in 1400. Provincial chapters had been held in the convent of Timoleague, in 1536 and in 1563. At the suppression, this convent, with four acres of land, were granted to Lord Inchiquin.

martial prowess, but none more so than his son Cormac, who defeated the Geraldines in the celebrated battle fought near the abbey of Mourne. The inscription on the founder's tomb is worth preserving, and runs thus :—'*Hic Jacet Cormac, Filius Thadei, F. Cormac, F. Dermitii magni MacCarthy Dominus de Musgraige, ac istius conventus primus fundator.* A. D. 1495.' The Barrets and many other noble families selected Kilcrea as their burial-place, and their tombs are still there, for they spared no effort to preserve the sacred edifice from the ravages of the English troops during the wars with the Geraldines and the Ulster princes. The entire of the buildings, including the monastery, which is of no considerable magnitude, is to this day in very good condition, and lacks nothing but friars, who are not allowed to inhabit their ancient abode, since Dermot MacCarthy, who basely abjured the religion of his glorious progenitors, had a grant of the place from Sir Arthur Chichester, lord deputy, on condition that he would not suffer the Franciscans to return, or let his lands to any but Protestants. Nevertheless, some of our friars live among the people in the neighborhood, and are supported by the bounty of the Barrets and others, who, as I have already said, are very anxious to preserve the monastery and its church from dilapidation. Whilst I.was at Kilcrea, the particulars I am about to give you were related to me by trustworthy persons, and I am sure that you will think them worth recording.

"In 1584—the year after O'Moriarty had compassed the cruel murder of the great Earl of Desmond—a company of English soldiers, marauding through the district, entered the monastery and church of Kilcrea, intent on plunder. These miscreants, unawed by the sanctity of the place, demolished the statues and paintings, and laid their sacrilegious hands on the sacred utensils. At that time, the church possessed a beautiful representation of the crucifixion—a rare work of art, indeed; for, at each extremity of the cross there was a beautiful medallion of the evangelists, exquisitely wrought in gold and silver. Stimulated by a desire to seize the precious metal, the soldiers began to quarrel among themselves, and in this brawl they turned their swords against each other's breasts, till two of them fell mortally wounded, one of them dying that very night, and the other the next morning. The gold and silver glutted the impious greed of the survivors, and that noble work of art was lost to the convent for ever.

"In 1599, when the Lord Deputy Essex marched against the remnant of the Geraldines, Kilcrea was again invaded by English soldiers, who scared away the friars, and killed Father Mathew O'Leyn, at the very moment he was endeavoring to effect his escape by fording the Bride. He was a man remarkable for the holiness of his life, and had then entered on his sixty-seventh year."

The land and friary of Kilcrea had been given to Lord Broghill, for his services to the Parliamentarians. There is a tradition among the neighboring peasantry that when the hospitable monks were expelled, a colony of crows and daws took possession of the avenue and belfry.* The gloomy and neglected aisles of the monastery are covered with tombstones, covering the dust of peasants, and nobles, and chieftains alike. The old monuments bear the names of the

---

* "The Monks of Kilcrea" give a good idea of the liberal hospitality practiced in this monastery, as expressed in the following verse:

"Three monks sat by a bog-wood fire!
  Shaven their crowns, and their garments gray;
Close they sat to that bog-wood fire,
  Watching the wicket till break of day—
  Such was ever the rule at Kilcrea.
For whoever passed, be he baron or squire,
  Was free to call at that abbey and stay;
Nor guerdon nor hire for his lodging pay,
Though he tarried a week with the Holy Quire."

founders and septs of the district, such as the MacCarthys, McSwineys, Barrets, and other chiefs. This is also the last resting-place of the celebrated Roger O'Connor, the historian, and brother to Arthur O'Connor, of '98 celebrity. Here, also, rests another victim of the penal times, the brave Arthur O'Leary, who was killed in 1773; he was outlawed and shot because he would not sell a valuable race-horse to a Protestant named Morrison, for five pounds. A low altar-tomb covers his grave, with the following inscription:

> "Lo! Arthur Leary, generous, handsome, brave,
> Slain in his bloom, lies in this humble grave."

We almost feel tempted to follow Father Mooney's graphic and historical description of Timoleague, Moyne,* Rossberrick, Kilconnell,† Galway,‡ and other Franciscan monasteries, but we must not forget that we are writing the martyrology of Ireland, not its archæology, and therefore must return to our subject.

Of the many prelates and priests who suffered during the last years of Elizabeth's reign, we have to mention the Right

---

* The convent of Moyne, in the barony of Tirawley, county of Mayo, was founded for Franciscans of the Strict Observance, by McWilliam Bourk, A. D 1460. Provincial chapters had been held here in the years 1464, 1498, 1512, 1541, and 1550. In the 37th of Elizabeth, a grant was made of the convent of Moyne to Edmund Barret, to hold the same for ever, by fealty, at the annual rent of 5s

† The convent of Kilconnell, in a barony of the same name, county of Galway, derived its foundation from the family of O'Kelly, about the year 1400 The reformation of the Observants was received in this convent in 1460. In the sixteenth century this convent was granted to Charles Calthorpe

‡ The Franciscan convent of Galway was founded in St. Stephen's Island, beyond the north gate of the town, by Sir William De Burgo, A D 1296. This convent continued for many years the usual cemetery of that and of many other noble families Provincial chapters had been held here in the years 1470, 1522, and 1562. In the reign of Elizabeth it became involved in the general wreck, and reverted to the crown.

Rev. Malachy O'Mollony, bishop of Kilcrea. He was taken prisoner, buffeted, insulted, and scourged, and then flung into prison, where he lay eighteen months. Being still unshaken in his faith, he was tried, convicted, and sentenced to be first tortured, and then hung and quartered. By the aid of some influential men, and the connivance of a friend who kept sentry over him, he made his escape. Dressed as a laborer, he continued to minister to the people of Thomond until his death, in 1603.

REV. DONATUS O'MOLLONY was of a noble family, a theologian and priest, and vicar of the diocese of Killaloe. He was a truly apostolic pastor, who feared not to risk his life for his flock. He was taken in the district of Ormond, where he was visiting the parish priest, and, with his hands tied behind his back like a robber, was dragged to Dublin in the midst of the soldiers. Hardly was Donatus shut up in the Tower of Dublin, when the iron boots, the rack, the iron gauntlets, and the other instruments with which the executioners tortured the confessors of Christ, were paraded before his eyes, and he was asked by the chief judge whether he would subscribe to the queen's laws and decrees in matters of religion. Mollony, filled with the spirit of God, answered courageously *he was ready to obey the queen's commands in all things not contrary to the laws of Jesus Christ, the King of kings, and his vicar on earth.* The judge, like Pilate, answered: 'The queen in her kingdom is the only vicar of Christ, and head of the church; therefore, you must either take the oath of supremacy or die.' Mollony answered, '*Either Paul, the doctor of the Gentiles, and Christ himself in his gospels, err, or the queen is not the vicar of Christ.*' 'Then you will not acknowledge the supreme authority, after Christ, of the queen in spirituals?' '*By no means,*' said Mollony; '*a woman, who may not speak in the church, I can-*

not acknowledge as its head; nay, for the truth of the opposite I am ready, by God's help, to endure all torments, and death itself.' 'Very good,' said the judge; 'we shall see to-morrow if your deeds correspond with your words.'

"Next day, about nine o'clock, the executioners, by order of the judge, so squeezed Donatus's feet in iron boots, and his hands in like gauntlets, that blood came from all his ten fingers.'

"But the torture failed to move him, and during it Donatus more than once returned thanks to God that by His grace he was able to bear the torture for His Son's name. He was then for two hours extended on the rack, so that he was stretched out a span in length. During the cruel torture Donatus continually either prayed or exhorted the Catholics who were near to constancy in the faith, which is the only road to salvation, and for which he was ready to shed his blood. The executioners were moved to tears by the patience and constancy of the sufferer, and, by order of the judge, carried him, half dead, back to prison, where a few hours afterwards he slept piously in the Lord, on the 24th April, anno 1601."†

O'Heyn gives an account of the martyrdom of forty-two priests, who were cruelly deceived by the treachery and deceit of their enemies, to place themselves in their power. It is the old story of English faith and English treachery, which has become more remarkable in its violation than that of Carthage itself. The following is the account of the cold-blooded massacre, as related by O'Heyn:

"It was intimated in many districts of the southern province, in 1602, that such of the clergy as presented themselves to the magistrates would be allowed to take their departure from the kingdom. Two Dominican fathers, and forty others, for the most part Cistercians and secular

† Bruodin, lib iii., cap xx.

THE FRANCISCANS PERSECUTED.

priests, availed themselves of the government proposal.* They were ordered to assemble at the Island of Inniscattery, in the vicinity of Limerick; and, on the appointed day they were taken on board a vessel-of-war to sail for France. No sooner, however, had they put to sea than all were thrown overboard. When the ship returned to port, the captain and all the soldiers and sailors in her were cast into prison, and all the officers were cashiered by the queen's order, that she might seem to the world innocent of that atrocity; but, at the same time, they were privately admonished not to regard this, and after their pretended imprisonment were rewarded with a part of the goods of the abbey abandoned by those so sacrilegiously slain by them." †

About the same time, the venerable vice-primate of Ireland, the Right Rev. REDMOND O'GALLAGHER, bishop of Derry, though in his seventieth year, was cruelly butchered by some horse soldiers, who overtook him. We should also mention a gentleman of Kilkenny, named WALTER ARCHER, who was imprisoned and exiled for attempting to save the Dominican abbey from desecration.

REV. DOMINICK COLLINS, S. J., was one of the last martyrs who suffered under Elizabeth. He was a brave soldier in the service of Spain, but resigned the sword for the then no less dangerous service of the cross. He was a native of Galway, and born of a noble family. Brought up by pious parents, he went to France, and filled with the hope of aiding to free his religion and country from English heresy and misrule, he embraced a military life, and served eight years

---

* De Burgo says: "Forty-two monks, under the name of Bernardins, two fathers of ours, seven clerics of ours also, came then from the convents of Limerick and Killmallock"

† Incredible as this atrocity might appear, in 1644 another captain received the thanks of Parliament for a similar act.

both in France and Spain. Finding his bright hopes not likely to be fulfilled, he abandoned the army and became a member of the Jesuits. He was attached, as chaplain, to the Spanish troops sent to the assistance of the Irish. After their landing, he was taken prisoner at the fort of Berehaven, and though the English had guaranteed full safety to the garrison, Father Collins was thrown into prison. He was next fettered with chains, and, with his hands tied behind his back, he was sent to Cork and imprisoned. Here he lay for three months before he was brought to trial. The viceroy, Mountjoy, offered him his pardon and his favor, if he would join the queen's army, but he steadfastly refused. Threats and promises were alike unavailing; and Mountjoy, incensed at his calmness and firmness, ordered him to be tortured and then executed. He unflinchingly bore the most terrible tortures and punishment previous to his execution.

On the last day of October, 1602, at dawn, they led him out to execution, with his hands tied behind his back and a halter round his neck. He walked calmly along, with his eyes raised to heaven and his mind fixed on God, reflecting on Christ bearing his cross. When he arrived at the foot of the gallows, he fell on his knees and kissed it, commending his passage to God; then, following the example of the martyrs, he prayed for his enemies, for the queen, and for his country, and with alacrity and a cheerful countenance ascended the ladder. Turning round on the topmost step, from thence, as from a pulpit, he began more ardently than ever to exhort the Catholics to preserve the faith undaunted unto death, and disregard alike the threats and promises of the heretics. "Look up," he continued, "to Heaven, and, worthy descendants of your ancestors, who ever constantly professed it, hold fast to that faith for which I am this day to die." These words, which derived additional force from his high birth and the contempt he had shown for the goods of fortune, and the position in which he stood, were most powerful in encouraging the Catholics, and affected even those who were not Catholics. The officers, perceiving this, to prevent any further effect on the crowd, ordered him to be thrown off the ladder. Nor was he allowed to hang long on the gallows; for, while yet breathing and palpitating, the executioner, in punishment of his constant profession of his religion, cut open his breast, and, taking out his heart, held it up to the people, uttering the usual "God save the queen."

On the following night, the Catholics collected his mangled limbs with great pity, and consigned them to the earth in a chapel not far from where he suffered. Thus this last victim to God in Ireland in her reign, preceded the queen, guilty of so much innocent blood, to the judgment-seat of God.*

* Queen Elizabeth died on the 24th March, 1603; but her death brought no relaxation of the persecution.

PERSECUTIONS UNDER JAMES I.

The Catholics rejoice at the accession of James—Religious toleration expected—Their disappointment—Fresh persecutions—All bishops and priests ordered to quit the kingdom—Paul V exhorts the Irish to persevere in their faith—Several priests and ecclesiastics tortured and put to death—Martyrdom of Sir John De Burgo—His great faith and constancy.

IT was fondly hoped by the Catholics of Ireland that the accession of James would bring peace and repose to the Church in that distracted and oppressed country. A general feeling of relief and joy pervaded all classes. Many of those who had been forced into exile returned to their native country: churches were rebuilt—monasteries repaired—the sacred duties of the sanctuary were resumed, and the offices of the Church were performed with undisturbed safety throughout the kingdom. This state of comparative tranquillity was not, however, suffered to continue: the mercenary spirit of James had rendered him callous to the feelings of humanity, as well as to the dictates of religion; and whenever wealth was to be accumulated or favoritism indulged, both religion and humanity became alike disregarded.

Scarcely had this monarch been placed on the throne of England, and the hopes of the people began to revive, when the storm, with renewed fury, appeared to collect around them. It was ushered in by the publication of an edict dated the 4th of July, 1605; the enactments of

Elizabeth were to be rigorously enforced, with the following additional announcement :

" It hath seemed proper to us to proclaim, and we hereby make known to our subjects in Ireland, that no toleration shall ever be granted by us. This we do for the purpose of cutting off all hope that any other religion shall be allowed— save that which is consonant to the laws and statutes of this realm."

Thus were the hopes of the people again doomed to disappointment. The cup was held to their lips, but they found the contents to be wormwood and gall. Instead of peace and toleration, this was the warning note of fresh persecutions and massacres. The clergy were again compelled to fly to the woods and caves to conceal themselves; the nobility and people were harassed into new coalitions and outbreaks, in order to give a pretext for fresh spoliations and persecutions. A new oath, both of supremacy and allegiance was devised, and all Catholics were called on to take it.

The firm and decided stand taken by the Catholics for a time awed their enemies into a kind of passive inaction. This stillness, though, was but the prelude of the fierce storm that was so soon to sweep over the country.

In 1610, Chichester, then lord deputy, issued a proclamation embodying the edict previously published, and demanding its full enforcement. Thus was the flame rekindled, and the worst passions of tyrants and bigots evoked to oppress and massacre a suffering people. The altars and priesthood were again delivered over to the fury of fanatics, and a fresh stream of martyrs' blood soon bedewed the soil.

Knox had been sent from Scotland, and was nominated bishop of Raphoe. He was invested with unlimited powers, and before he left London he swore that he would extirpate the Catholic religion out of Ireland This Christian bishop came to preach the Gospel with the sword — to preach charity and brotherly love with the rack and the gibbet.

As an indication of the spirit of the times, we select the following from the many edicts promulgated against the Catholics:

"All bishops and priests are to quit the kingdom, under penalty of death; secondly, whoever shall harbor a priest, shall be punished by the confiscation of his property; thirdly, no papist shall send his son or relative beyond the seas for education, under the usual penalty; fourthly, no papist shall attempt to discharge the duty of schoolmaster in the kingdom; fifthly, all persons, of every age, sex, and rank, shall be present at the service of Common Prayer on the Lord's Day."

Knox and his saintly followers soon found that their pious predecessors had so robbed the sanctuaries and altars as to leave little or nothing for them. As their religion was mammon, this sorely mortified them, and the small, humble chapels were rifled, the altars demolished, vestments and sacred vessels converted to profane uses. In order to make good the deficiency, they robbed the houses of the wealthy Catholics of all the plate, under the pretence that it belonged to the churches.

The nations of Europe began to turn their attention and sympathy to the struggling Irish. Pope Paul V. addressed to them an apostolical letter, in which he compares them to the martyrs of primitive times, exhorts them to perseverance, and points out the rewards which in a better world must await them. "Ye glory in that faith," he adds, "by which your fathers procured for their country the distinguished appellation of an Island of Saints. Nor have the sufferings which ye endured been allowed to remain unpublished; your fidelity and Christian fortitude have become the subject of universal admiration, and the praise of your name has long since been loudly celebrated in every portion of the Christian world. Wherefore, be steadfast and persevere : our prayers shall be unceasing."

A supplicatory address of the Catholic prelates and nobles of Ireland, to the Catholic princes of Europe, had the effect of checking the persecution towards the close of James' reign.

Having given this cursory synopsis of the Church in Ireland during the reign of James, we will now return to the noble martyrs who suffered under him.

EUGENE O'GALLEHER, a Cistercian abbot, and an alumnus of the monastery of the Blessed Virgin of Asseroe, diocese of Raphoe, together with BERNARD O'TRUORY, his companion, a monk of the same order, were slain by some soldiers, in hatred of their religion, in the year 1606.

Bruodin states that, in the same year, the Rev. BERNARD O'CHARNEL, a priest of Leinster, of a noble family, was accused by the heretics of having administered the sacraments according to the Roman rite, and, without any more trial, was hung and quartered at Dublin.

REV. NIGEL O'BOYLE, O. S. F. of the Order of St. Francis, was cruelly tortured and beheaded in the following year.

REV. ROBERT LALOR, vicar-general of the diocese of Dublin, Kildare, and Ferns, was the next victim. Having signed a form of detraction proposed to him, in which James was recognized as supreme governor in all affairs, his friends charged him with acknowledging the king's supremacy. This he stoutly denied, and said that he had acknowledged him only in civil affairs. This reached the ear of the lord-deputy, who had him indicted, and of course convicted.

Dr. Moran, in his history of the Archbishops of Dublin, says that on his trial "he declared that there was no contradiction between the document he had signed and the declaration which he had made to his friends: he had acknowledged the king's authority in questions of social order, but he had told his friends that 'he had not acknowledged the king's supremacy in the spiritual order; and this he still affirmed to be true. This explanation was, of course, declared by the government officials to be mere 'knavery and silliness;' the sentence of the law was pronounced upon the prisoner, and in a few days another name was added to the martyrs of Dublin."

REV. DONATUS OLUIN, O. P. P., prior of Derry, in his ninetieth year was, together with several secular priests, hung and quartered by the English in the market-place of the town of Derry. His brother, WILLIAM OLUIN, another religious of the Friars Preachers, was also hung for the faith a short time before the martyrdom of the prior.

SIR JOHN DE BURGO.

The life and sufferings of this noble martyr might furnish materials for a romance. He was of noble birth, and had inherited, with the lordship of Brittas, several minor estates.* He married Grace Thornton, the daughter of Sir George Thornton, an Englishman of wealth and influence.

Sir JOHN DE BURGO, or Burke, was a sincere and devoted Catholic, and smarting from the persecution of his religion at home, he resolved to go to Spain, but was dissuaded by his father-in-law and friends. Being thus frustrated, he openly followed the Catholic faith at home, attended Mass, heard sermons, and sheltered persecuted priests and laymen. On this account, he became much hated by the Protestants, who, on account of his connections and influence, were afraid to interfere with him. On the death of Elizabeth, the Cath-

* Bruodin says he was the second son of the Baron of Castle Connel, county Limerick.

olics began openly to profess their religion, in which they were encouraged by Sir John.

On the arrival of the viceroy, Lord Mountjoy, in Limerick, charges were preferred against Sir John, the sum of which was, that he had been a leader in those tumults in the city; so they called the zeal for religion which the citizens and municipalities had shown in the interregnum which occurred on the death of Elizabeth, when it was not certain what would be the course of her legitimate successor, King James.

All the charitable and Christian acts of the good man were used as so many crimes against him; and Mountjoy gave ear to the false charges of these base informers, and he was arrested and flung into prison in Dublin. Here he remained for some time, devoting himself to his religion and pious devotions.

The plague having broken out in Dublin, the viceroy and government officials fled the city; and so great was the mortality in the prisons that the few survivors, among whom was Sir John, were set free. He now gave himself up solely to the society of ecclesiastics and holy men. He had erected an altar in the banqueting-room at Brittas, and had Mass celebrated there frequently for the Catholics around.

The president of Munster, Henry Bronkard, being incited by enemies of Sir John, resolved on his arrest; and sent a Captain Miller, with a troop of horse, for that purpose. On Sunday morning, while the priest was celebrating Mass, Captain Miller surrounded the house. The terrified congregation fled at their approach; but Sir John and the chaplain, with the sacred vessels, secured themselves in an inner tower of the castle. The captain demanded a surrender, promising not to harm him.* To this Sir John replied that he would

* Evidently the captain offered safety to Burke, but said nothing as to what would be done with the priest; and the former, well knowing what

not be admitted, unless he wanted to go to confession and become a Catholic.

The castle was regularly besieged. Despite the earnest entreaties of his wife and mother-in-law, Sir John was resolved to hold out to the last. The assailants set fire to the buildings around the castle, but could not induce him to surrender. After a few days' siege, Sir John, finding that he could not hold out, sent away his chaplain, who safely effected his escape. Having armed himself, and having wrapped up in his dress the altar-service, he and his few followers suddenly dashed through the besiegers' lines, and succeeded in making their escape. Being pursued, two of his companions fell into the hands of the enemy, but he himself succeeded in eluding the pursuit of the enemy. He wandered about for some time, but was finally arrested in Carrick-on-Suir, having been betrayed by a Protestant woman.

would be his chaplain's fate, refused the proffered terms. This is also shown by O'Sullivan's account of the transaction. He says: "Sir John held the castle until the Mass was finished. When that was over, the priest, dressed in secular habit, went out in the crowd of people, but was recognized by the Protestants and seized. Sir John, mounting his horse, with his armed retainers, rescued the priest from the Protestants. For this he was soon after besieged in the same castle by five troops. He held the castle against them for fifteen days with only five companions, and then, being pressed by hunger, he broke through his enemies by night, and having lost one of his companions, John O'Holloghan, he escaped with the other four. He was, however, taken prisoner by the Protestants a few days later in the town of Carrig-na-Suir, which is in the county of Ormond, and sent to the city of Limerick. Here he suffered much, for many days, from the darkness and filth of his dungeon, and, as he constantly refused to hear the Protestant preacher, even stopping his ears with his fingers, and preferred the Catholic religion to the title of baron and other rewards, and even to his life, he finally suffered death. It is said that two women, who were accused, the one at Carrick, the other at Waterford, of having concealed him, were burnt alive. It is also related that two other women were burnt at Limerick, the one for having said that the king's laws were unjust, the other for having concealed a priest."

While in prison, his faithful wife visited him, and consoled him as a true, loving woman only could. He advised her to be of good cheer, for though he knew that his enemies would take his life, it would be only securing him an immortal crown of eternal glory. He also urged her, as she loved him and her own salvation, to cling to the true faith, and to bring up her children in it. In order the better to strengthen and protect her, he gave her a letter to Father Edmund Halagan, beseeching him to instruct her in her religious duties, and to watch over her spiritual and temporal welfare. She set out for Waterford, to deliver this letter to Father Halagan, and not finding him there, so eager was this dutiful, loving wife to obey the will of her husband, that she at once followed him to Kilkenny.

Meantime, Sir John was sent, under the escort of a troop of horse, to Limerick, to be arraigned before the president himself. On the way he was treated with the greatest cruelty by the soldiers. They manacled his hands, and tied him on a car, and mocked and scoffed at him. He bore it all with the greatest patience, refusing even to reply to their insults and abuse.

When arraigned before the president, he also refused to reply to the charges preferred against him, but he steadfastly refused to obey the king in matters of faith, or to abandon his religious opinions.

Finding that his faith and resolution could not be shaken, he was sentenced to death.

The judge, evidently conscious of his innocence, and wishing, like Pilate, to wash his hands of his innocent blood, eagerly besought him to repent, and acknowledge the king's supremacy. Sir John fearlessly and unhesitatingly answered that he could acknowledge no king or queen against Christ, the King of heaven, and the Queen of heaven, his Mother; and that whoever sought to turn him away from the true worship and honor due to both, far from deserving to be obeyed, deserved neither honor nor assent; and that whoever would act otherwise was not a servant of God, but a slave of the devil.

He was declared guilty of high treason, and sentenced to be hanged, then beheaded, and to have his body quartered.

He met his death with wonderful firmness and serenity. On his way to the gallows, outside the city, he appeared as if going to a feast. He thanked God for the honor done him in being enrolled in the blessed choir of holy martyrs. Though he was surrounded by a crowd of mourners, who wept at his sad fate, he alone was cheerful, and besought those around him to live so that they could meet death as calmly and hopefully as he did. He was going before the Judge who judges all without favor or partiality, the Judge who reads the hearts of all men; and in Him, and Him alone, did he put his hope and trust.

When Sir John was hung, some noblemen, among others Sir Thomas Brown, entreated the president that, when taken down from the gallows, he might not be cut in pieces, and their request was granted, and his friends and relatives carried him into the city, and buried him in the church of St. John, at Limerick, about the 20th October, 1607.*

Rev. John Graves was a learned doctor of theology, who suffered martyrdom for his defence of the Pope's supremacy. Dominick, a Rosario, in his sketch of his life and sufferings, says:—

* He is mentioned also by Dominick, a Rosario; Carve, p 315; and *Hib. Dom*, p 565; but they add nothing to the facts given by Roothe and O'Sullivan Bruodin gives a long life of him, substantially agreeing with that of Roothe, which he says he took from a manuscript life of Sir John, in his possession, written by Father Matthew Crahy, his confessor, afterwards vicar-general of the diocese of Killaloe

"Have we not also the history of the martyrdom of John Graves, doctor in theology, who, being accused of having written a defence of the Pope's supremacy, was arraigned before an iniquitous tribunal? Will not the blood of this man cry aloud to Heaven till this world has grown hoary? When arraigned before his judges, and interrogated by them, here was his answer: 'See you,' said he, 'this thumb, forefinger, and middle finger? With them I wrote this writing. I do not repent of having done so, nor does it grieve me to be charged with it, nor do I blush to acknowledge it.' He was then sentenced to die, and his right hand to be burned; wonderful to relate, this hand was burned, but the three fingers remained uninjured."

About the same time, the Rev. John Lune, of Wexford, a pious and good priest, who clung to his flock, instructing them and preaching to them, was taken and sent prisoner to Dublin, where he was hung and quartered.

BISHOP O'DOVANY'S MARTYRDOM.

Zeal of the persecutors—Bishop O'Dovany—His arrest and imprisonment—His sufferings and starvation in prison—His release and re-arrest—His trial and sentence—His execution and martyrdom—Father Locheran's execution—Affliction of the people—The martyr's last moments—Dr. Roothe's account of their lives and sufferings.

BISHOP O'DOVANY.

AMONG the many who suffered persecution and death during the reign of James, none were more remarkable for their zeal and devotion in the cause of religion and for their heroic fortitude under trials and sufferings, than the venerable CORNELIUS O'DOVANY, bishop of Down and Connor, and his companion in persecution, the Rev. PATRICK LOCHERAN, a priest of Ulster.

These noble sufferers earned the martyr's crown on the same day; that is, on the 1st day of February, 1611, under the viceroyalty of Chichester. Bishop O'Dovany, having embraced the order of St. Francis when a youth, became an ornament to that order, by his piety, learning, patience, and zeal. He was raised to the Episcopal dignity as bishop of the united sees of Down and Connor in April, 1582. He was soon after cast into prison in Dublin castle, where he was detained for about three years, all the time treated with the greatest neglect and cruelty. During his imprisonment he was not supplied with a single change of clothing, and had almost perished from hunger, thirst, and the cold damp

BISHOP O'DOVANY'S MARTYRDOM.

of his miserable cell. His treatment was such that it seemed as if it was the intention to starve him in prison, or kill him by cruelty. He would have died from hunger, for he was left whole days without food, only that some poor prisoners in the cell beneath him gave him a share of their limited supply. The floor of his cell had rotted away with the damp, leaving holes in several places; through these, with a cord made out of his braces, he managed to draw up the scraps the poor prisoners, more humane and charitable than his jailers, supplied him.

Roothe, in his life of him, alluding to his sufferings in prison, says:

"We are thus reminded of the Prophet Jeremiah, who was let down by a cord into a dungeon wherein there was no water, but mire, that he might die of hunger; and had not an Ethiopian of the king's household taken of the old rags there were in the king's storehouse, and let them down by cords to Jeremiah into the dungeon, and said, 'Put these old rags and these rent and rotten things under thy arms and upon the cords,' he had not been drawn up and brought forth out of the dungeon. And, in like manner, had not the holy bishop received these crusts of bread and furtive drops of beer, he had surely perished of famine.

"At length, by divine Providence, he was released, God so disposing that his freedom of body should bring freedom to the souls of many. But a very short time passed, however, when the royal councillors repented them that they had let him go, and they sought by every art to get him again into their power. He always preferred the salvation of others to his own safety; and at length, after several years' labors, he fell into the hands of those who deemed they would do the king a great service by apprehending him.

"He was seized in the month of June,* while he was occupied putting an end to quarrels and confirming the servants of Christ.† The priest Patrick was taken prisoner the same month in the port of Cork, whither he had lately returned from Belgium, and he confessed to this provincial council that he had been a companion in their travels, and had administered the rites of the Church to those lords whom fear for their own safety, or love of religion, had made exiles from their wide domains."

---

* O'Sullivan says he was arrested June, 1611, and executed April, 1612; and this is probably correct, although Dr. Roothe, in his work, puts his death in 1611, because he himself addressed a letter to him, as in prison, on the 17th December, 1611, and had he been executed eight months before, he would have heard of it.

† An unpublished manuscript in the Burgundian Library, Brussels, entitled, *Compendium of the Martyrdom of the Right Rev Father Cornelius O'Dovany*, &c., &c., gives the following account of the bishop and his execution:

"During the whole time the bishop was in prison, he almost daily said Mass, making use of ornaments secretly conveyed into the prison by some Catholics. He was often seen by some of ours bathed in tears in mental prayer, and was heard by his fellow-captives in his prayer to break out into these words: 'O Lord God! through thy great mercy, grant me, thy servant, to lay down my life for thee, as thou didst lay down thy life on the cross for me, thy wretched creature; and grant me to end my days for the confession of thy name either by the sword of the heretic or in this prison.' He often said to noble Catholics who visited him that he would prefer life in prison to freedom, were it not for the good of his flock. . . . The bishop and priest were placed in two separate carts, and, as they went, the bishop frequently called out, 'Hasten, my friend, to receive your crown;' and the priest answered, 'Behold me; I will not hesitate or delay.' The people thought themselves happy if they could get near the cart to receive the bishop's blessing, which he lovingly gave. For many years his face had not been so fresh-colored nor his countenance so cheerful and amiable as it was from the door of the prison to the moment of his death. When they came to the place of execution, there were between five and six thousand people there. The place of execution was on a hill, and the two, getting down from the cart at the foot of the hill, knelt down and prayed fervently. Then, to the admiration of all, the old man, with strong and eager steps, walked up to the gallows, and embraced and kissed its beams, as did the priest. All were astonished to

BISHOP O'DOVANY'S MARTYRDOM. 117

Though the real charge against the prisoners was that they were Catholics, still his accusers endeavored to implicate the bishop with the rebellion of the Earl of Tyrone.*

The bishop endeavored, with valid reasons, to answer the principal heads of accusation ; and he answered that he was consecrated a bishop to labor for the salvation of the flock entrusted to him, and, as his bishopric of Down and Connor lay in that part of Ulster which Earl Hugh held by force of arms, it was his duty to labor as best he could to direct the inhabitants in the way of salvation ; that as to warlike matters, he neither desired to know nor knew anything ; and had he advised the earl against his will, he would not have heeded him or held his hand for any remonstrance of his. As far as he could, by word and example, he had led men from vice and to follow virtue, and had labored and watched to this end ; b t was not ashamed of

see such strength in so old a man, (he was about eighty years old,) and one worn out with pison. Then he asked that the priest might go first, (for he had a pastoral care for his companion,) but it was refused ; and the priest said, 'Go, then, before me, reverend father, and truly without delay will I follow you.' He mounted the ladder without assistance, the executioner going before him. When he had mounted four or five steps, he blessed all the Catholics, praying that liberty might be granted to them, and then prayed to God that he would forgive the injustice that was done to him, and that for his part he freely and willingly forgave it. So also did the priest. Then the bishop, taking for his text the words of St. Paul, 'Though an angel from heaven should preach to you another gospel than you have heard from us, believe it not,' began to address some words of exhortation to the people; but the councillors who stood around ordered him to be stopped and immediately thrown off Then gently smiling, he kissed the cord, and himself fitted it to his neck, and covered his face with a cloth, and held out his hands to the executioner to be bound."

* Hugh O'Neill, Earl of Tyrone. To the bishop's plea that the Act of Oblivion covered all offences, the judge answered that it could not avail him, as he had not submitted and taken the oath of allegiance and supremacy. This was, of course, to exclude all Catholics from its benefit, as they could not take the oath of supremacy.—*O'Sullivan.*

it, nor should it be brought as a crime against him. And even were these things, however unjustly, to be accounted crimes, he could defend himself by reminding them that, when King James ascended the throne, he had proclaimed by the voice of a herald, and publicly posted up in writing, a pardon for all offences and crimes before committed. He could, therefore, allege a double defence : first, that what was alleged against him was no crime ; secondly, that even were it one, it was forgiven by the king's pardon. That such was the intention of the king and his council in publishing the Act of Oblivion is clear, as otherwise, instead of an act of clemency, it would be a snare.

Suborned witnesses were produced on the trial ; and one of the jurors, who gave expression to his belief in the innocence of the prisoner, was so intimidated that he at once changed his opinion.

They were both, of course, convicted. The judge pronounced the sentence that "Cornelius O'Dovany, bishop of Down and Connor, should be taken back to prison, and then drawn in a cart to the place of execution, there hanged on the gallows, and cut down while alive, embowelled, and his heart and bowels burnt, his head cut off, and his body divided into four parts." * The like sentence was passed on the priest.

Both the prisoners were repeatedly offered their pardons

* A certain pious woman, who used to carry food to the bishop and the priest, which was supplied by the Catholics, after his sentence asked the bishop how he was in health. "I have not been better," said he, "these ten years, either in mind or body. My only wish now is that God will vouchsafe to take me to His heavenly kingdom by martyrdom, rather than permit me to be worn out in prison of old age. You, daughter, have done me many services, for which I thank you, as I may, and which God will reward. Do me this further service, I pray : when I am slain (as God grant I may be), have me buried in this (showing her the Franciscan habit) I value this frock, which I put on when I was young, more than the insignia of a bishop."—*O'Sullivan.*

if they would renounce the Roman Catholic religion; but, they replied by calling upon all present to witness that they died for the Catholic faith.* Roothe, in his account of their execution, says:

"As is the case with martyrs, his piety (the bishop's) increased with his worldly troubles, and in watching and prayer he awaited the day when he should be called to die. That happy and wished-for day at length came. The 1st of February, at four o'clock in the afternoon, he was called to mount the cart which, surrounded by guards, stood at the prison door. When the holy bishop came in sight of that triumphal chariot, he sighed and said, 'My Lord Jesus, for my sake, went on foot, bearing his cross, to the mountain where he suffered; and must I be borne in a cart, as though unwilling to die for him, when I would hasten with willing feet to that glory? Would that I might bear my cross, and hasten on my feet to meet my Lord!' Turning to his fellow-sufferer, Patrick, he said, 'Come, my brave comrade and worthy soldier of Christ, let us imitate His death as best we may, who was led to the slaughter as a sheep before the shearer.' Then bending down and kissing the cart, he mounted up into it, and sat down with his back to the horses, and was thus drawn through the paved streets to the field where the gallows was erected.

"Those Catholics who before his imprisonment and condemnation trembled at the sound of a falling leaf, who

* The viceroy sent several times councillors and others to offer the condemned life and reward, and especially to the bishop his bishopric, and to the priest a good living, if they would renounce the Catholic Church and the authority of the Roman pontiff, and acknowledge the king's supremacy. The bishop answered that it was far greater folly to try to persuade him, a man near eighty years of age, for the sake of a short term of happiness in this fleeting life, to incur eternal punishment, than to have advised the aged Eleazer, in order to avoid death, to eat swine's flesh. So also spoke the priest.—*O'Sullivan.*

feared to meet a Catholic priest, much less a bishop, and were slow to harbor one, lest they might thereby incur danger or the enmity of the rulers, now, when he was led to execution, poured out in a dense crowd from every door into the streets, and in the sight of the councillors, and to the indignation of the viceroy, fell on their knees. Men of the first rank, and the inhabitants of all the neighboring villages and castles, crowded as to a solemn sight; they saluted with reverence the bishop as he passed in the cart, and begged his pontifical benediction. As they lamented his death, he gently consoled them, and with forcible words exhorted them to fortitude and constancy in the faith and all Christian piety. Many noble matrons came and lamented the death of the bishop; and as they perceived several of the king's council accompanying the procession and showing their hostility, they boldly exclaimed in their hearing that it ill became the king's councillors to turn executioners.

"When he was come to the place of sacrifice, being solicitous for the constancy of his colleague, the bishop begged that Patrick might be put to death first; for he feared lest, by the sight of his death and the wiles of the Calvinists, Patrick might be induced to yield to human weakness. But as his wish would not be granted, Father Patrick assured the bishop he might lay aside all fear for him. 'Though,' said he, 'I would desire to die first, and be strengthened in my agony by your paternal charity, since we are given up to the will of others, go, happy father, and fear not for my constancy; aid me by your prayers with God, by whose help I am sure that neither death nor life, nor principalities nor powers, nor things present nor things to come, nor any other creature, shall separate me from the love of Christ, or from my companionship with you.' Rejoiced at these words, Cornelius threw himself on his knees, but had only breathed a hasty prayer (which yet reached God in heaven), when the councillors, the captain and guard called out to make an end quickly. The field, situated to the north of the city, which would easily hold three thousand persons, was crowded. The executioner was an Englishman and a Protestant, (for no Irishman could be found who would stain himself with the blood of the bishop,*) who was condemned to death for robbery, and was promised his life for acting as executioner on this occasion. Yet, though he had thus purchased his life, he was touched with reverence and compassion for the gray hairs of the bishop, and prayed his pardon, and with trembling hands adjusted the noose. The moment the bishop mounted the first step of the ladder, and his head was seen above the crowd, a great shout and groans burst from all the spectators.

"Then the minister, Challoner, furious at the cries of pity raised by the people, said to the bishop : 'Why delude ye the ignorant people? Why end ye your life with a lie, and a vain boast of martyrdom? Tell the multitude that ye are traitors, and that it is for treason and not for religion ye suffer.' To these unjust words the bishop answered : 'Far be it from us, who are about to appear before the tribunal of Christ, to impose upon the people. But also far be it from us to confess ourselves guilty of crimes of which our conscience tells us we are innocent. Nor yet do we vainly ambition the title of martyrs, though for us to die for Christ is gain. You know that you are yourself guilty of that prevarication of which you accuse us; for, but a few hours ago, sent, as you said, by the viceroy, you offered us life and freedom if we would subscribe to your heresy. Leave us, then, son of darkness, and calumniate not our innocence.'

"Then the minister departed, and left the martyrs in

* The regular executioner, who was an Irishman, had fled.—*O'Sullivan.*

peace. As they mounted the middle of the ladder, again there rose the cry of the people; and a third time, when he was about to be thrown off, the groans of those who beat their breasts rose louder than before. Thrice he prayed, as he stood there: once for all the bystanders; secondly, for the city of Dublin, and all the Catholics of this kingdom, that they may serve God piously, faithfully, and perseveringly; a third time he prayed for all heretics, and for his persecutors, that they might be converted from the evil of their ways.

"It is related that all the field was crowded with men, women, and children, and when the martyr was dead all struggled to carry away some relic, either a scrap of his clothes, or a drop of his blood, or a fragment of bone or skin; yet, though all crowded and struggled, no one was hurt; but he was deemed most happy who was able to carry off the head of the bishop, deemed more precious than gold or precious stones.*

"Lest their names, inscribed in heaven, be forgotten on

---

* The bishop's head was hardly cut off when an Irishman seized it, and, rushing into the centre of the crowd, was never found, although the viceroy offered a reward of forty pounds of silver. The Catholics gathered up his blood, and contended for his garments, despite the resistance of the soldiery. The priest Patrick followed the same road, singing, as he mounted the ladder, the canticle of Simeon, "Now, O Lord! dismiss thy servant in peace," and, after the example of the bishop, he prayed for the bystanders, blessed them, and forgave all his enemies. The rope being put round his neck, he hung for a short time, was then cut down half-alive, mutilated, and cut in pieces. The soldiers, warned by the loss of the bishop's head, resisted the unarmed crowd—who strove to catch the martyr's blood and other relics—and wounded many. The day after, the bodies were buried at the gallows' foot, but in the stillness of the night were removed by the Catholics to a chapel not defiled by heretical worship.—*O'Sullivan.*

Mooney says: "Their remains are deposited in the cemetery of St. James, together with those of many others whom I shall mention later, because all the churches of the city are defiled."

BISHOP O'DOVANY'S MARTYRDOM.

earth, let their epitaph be here recorded, that the reader, meeting with the record of the saints, may remember that the 1st of February, in the year of our salvation 1611, was the day on which was born to a better life the blessed martyr O'Dovany, bishop of Down and Connor, of the Order of Saint Francis, who for many years watched with pastoral care over the Catholic flock in Ireland; and, after many sufferings, was sentenced to death in the Chichestrian persecution by D. Sibthorpe,* and by martyrdom passed to his rest; as also the Rev. Patrick Locheran."

* O'Sullivan says, Dominick Sarsfield was the judge, "one most cruel to priests and Catholics," and that his colleague, though a Protestant, feigned illness, not to take part in the condemnation of the bishop, who was innocent.

CHICHESTER'S TREACHEROUS PLOTS.

New plans devised to entrap and torture priests and bishops—Chichester's plots and villainy—Sir Arthur O'Neill and others entrapped and executed—Several of the brethren of Multifernan imprisoned and put to death—The priest-hunters on the track of their prey—The spoliation of Askeaton, and martyrdom of its inmates—Martyrdom of the venerable MacGeoghegan and several other priests—The close of King James' reign—His death.

NOT content with hunting down bishops and priests, and massacreing the Catholic peasantry, the English agents in Ireland were always ready to devise the most diabolical plans in order to entrap those whom wealth or patriotism had rendered obnoxious to them.

Sir Arthur Chichester was not deficient in concocting these black schemes, in order to entrap his victims. Among those who fell under his displeasure were Sirs Bernard and Arthur O'Neill, Roderick and Godfrey O'Kahan, Alexander MacSorley, and the Rev. Lewis O'Labertag.

His plot to entrap these gentlemen was as ingenious as it was vicious and dishonorable. A poor, dissipated gambler, who lived on the above gentlemen, was seized by the viceroy and sentenced to be hanged. He was then promised his pardon and large rewards, if he would accuse them of a conspiracy. This the ungrateful wretch did, and they were immediately seized, cast into prison, and accused of high treason.

This witness swore that they had conspired to take some forts in Ulster, garrisoned by English and Scotch, and to slay the guards. The knights answered that the testimony of one man of infamous character was not enough to convict them. They were tortured, but confessed nothing. But as they were tried by twelve English and Scotch Protestants, who had also received land in Ulster, and did not wish to have Catholic neighbors, they were at once found guilty. The viceroy referred the sentence to the king, who sent back for answer that a free pardon should be granted to the knights and the priest if they would renounce the Catholic religion. But they boldly made answer they never would accept that condition. That night they mutually exhorted each other to endure death for Christ. The priest gave sacramental absolution to the others. The next day, having hung a short time, they were cut down, embowelled, their entrails burnt, their bodies cut in four parts and exposed in public places. This happened in the year of our Lord 1615. About the same time Sir Patrick O'Murry, knight, and Connor O'Kieran, priest, were put to death in like manner, on the same charge.

Father Mooney, in his account of the monastery of Multifernan, mentions several of the brethren who suffered about this time. Among them were Brother JOHN GROGAN and several others. He continues:

"At another time, Sir Dudley Loftus, son of the chancellor, and Sir Richard Graves, invaded the monastery and carried away prisoners—Brother Cormac O'Gabhun, prior of the province, who, being blind, had lived for six years in that monastery; Brother Philip Cluaine; Brother Terence Macanaspie, who died in prison in Dublin; Brother Manus Oge O'Fidy; and Brother Coghlin Oge MacAliadha. These two last they left by the way in the town of Baleathbeg; the others they took to Dublin and threw into prison, where, after a year and a half, two of them, who survived, were set at liberty on giving security to appear if called on.

"In the year 1613, Patrick Fox, viscount of Westmeath, invaded the monastery and carried off the vicar of the convent, Brother Bernard Grogan, a priest, who lay in prison in Dublin for a whole year, and at length was sent an exile into France, and died at Rheims, in Brittany, partly from the fatigue of the journey and the sea, partly from infirmities contracted in prison.

"In the year 1614, Sir Oliver Lambert took prisoner Brother James MacGrollen, a holy priest of the same convent, who was seeking alms through the country. Notwithstanding many threats and promises, he remained constant. He was sent into exile, and remained some time in Rouen, whence, returning into Ireland, he was by pirates at sea wounded in the face.

"In 1617, there was taken prisoner, while he was collecting alms for the convent, by a certain local tyrant whose name was Daniel, another brother of the same convent, whose name was Charles Crossan, a priest. So also, in like manner, was taken in this year Brother Didacus Conor, a priest, while, through obedience, he was collecting alms. So much for this theatre of persecution and unarmed and innocent endurance."

WILLIAM MEDE was a citizen of Cork, distinguished for his learning and wealth, and was patron and protector of the rights and immunities of that city. He persuaded his fellow-citizens, during the time between the death of Queen Elizabeth and the proclamation of King James, to resume the public practice of the Catholic religion, which had been long omitted, and thereby drew upon himself a most bitter persecution. He was put upon his trial for treason, but the twelve jurors acquitted him; and, to punish them for thus refusing to condemn the innocent, they were tormented in all sorts of ways, publicly paraded through the city with an inscription on their foreheads calling them perjurers, and being finally thrown into prison, where they were kept till they paid a heavy fine. Even then the hatred of his enemies was not appeased, and Mede was compelled to leave the country.

Dr. Renehen, in his collections, tells us that in a letter preserved in Stoneyhurst College, it is stated that about this time "a large reward had been offered for the head of Dr. Matthews, archbishop of Dublin, or that of Dr. Kearney, archbishop of Cashel, *dead or alive*. The chancellor, Adam Loftus, personally conducted a most rigorous search in Dublin, as Archbishop Matthews was supposed to be there." The letter continues: "But the archbishop, by God's will, was out of their way; but in the search many others were apprehended and cast into prison, both ecclesiastics and others. One regular, and another secular priest, by name William Donatus, who, though lying ill in bed, because he was thought to be the chaplain of the archbishop, was compelled to get up and accompany the others to prison."

Bruodin gives a long sketch of the Rev. DERMITIUS BRUODIN, O. S. F., who was sorely persecuted about this time. He was a native of Thomond, and born of respectable parents. After his ordination, he labored for many years among the poor Catholics in the mountainous districts of Clare. He was persecuted by the priest-hunters, a sacrilegious set of scoundrels, who, either in the pay of some bigot, or for the price they got for the capture of their victims, had trained dogs to hunt down bishops and priests as if they were wolves. The priest-hunters failing in capturing their victim, an informer was set on his track, who, having ascertained his whereabouts, the commander of the garrison at Limerick sent a squad of musketeers in pursuit of him. He was captured, brought into Limerick, and thrown into prison, where he remained for four months.

At the end of this time he was brought before the king's judges, and being asked many idle questions, Dermid boldly answered that his dress showed he was a Catholic and a Franciscan; that as to his name, profession, labors, and friends, they were abundantly known to those who had taken him when preaching; that therefore there was nothing to be done but either to set him free, or by torture to try his constancy in the profession of the Catholic faith. "Well," said the judge, "you shall have your wish." By his order the Franciscan habit was torn off him, and he was severely flogged by two executioners; then his hands were tied behind him, and he was lifted up by them off the ground. While he was thus tortured, he was asked by a certain preacher whether he felt pain. He answered, "I feel pain, indeed, but far less than my Lord and Saviour Jesus Christ, for whose cause I suffer, endured for me." Then, let down from the rack, he was taken back to prison.

The powerful Donatus O'Brien, earl of Thomond, being on friendly relations with his family, interfered, and ultimately saved him from execution.

The good friar returned to his duties among the poor Catholics of Clare, and lived among them to a good old age.

Among the laymen who suffered imprisonment and torture for the faith about this time was JAMES DOWDAL, a leading merchant of Athboy, who was several times cast into prison. Also, JAMES DOWDAL, of Drogheda, who, being a leading man there, was seized in England, where he had gone on business, and hung, for denying the king's supremacy.

PATRICK BROWN, of Dublin, a convert to Catholicity, was imprisoned twenty years, for his adherence to the faith.

Bruodin also states that "the Rev. JOHN O'HONAN was a native of Connaught, a priest, and a member of the Franciscan order. After he had spent many years in religion, and in the charge of the pastoral office among the afflicted Catholics of Leinster, he was taken by the English heretics in Dublin. After seven weeks' imprisonment, despising the honors and rewards which were offered to him in the name of the king, if he would renounce his faith, he was first cruelly tortured, and then hung and cut in four parts; and so gloriously triumphed on the 14th October, 1618."

As also how "the Rev. PATRICK O'DYRY, a native of Ulster, and a priest, received the crown of martyrdom at Derry, of St. Columbanus, for having disobeyed the iniquitous law of Elizabeth and James. He preferred to suffer tortures, the ignominy of the scaffold, and the cutting of his body in four parts, rather than deny the truth. He died, venerable for age and virtues, the 6th January, 1618, and, as we may piously trust, enjoys a crown of glory with the saints."

Father Mooney, speaking of the spoliations of Askeaton, says:

"The convent of Athskelin (Askeaton) is said to have been founded by the Earl of Desmond, and for a long time there have not been any monks there, because, during the war which the aforesaid earl waged against the English, many cruelties were practiced on the brethren of that convent, and several of them suffered martyrdom at the hands of the English soldiers under Nicholas Mally; but I could not learn their names with accuracy, except of one priest, whose name was Brother CORNELIUS, whose relics are interred in the chapter-house of the convent.*

"The venerable Father ARTHUR MACGEOGHEGAN, after he had completed his studies in Spain, and transacted with

* The convent of Askeaton, county of Limerick, was founded by James, earl of Desmond, in the year 1420, for Conventual Franciscans The Strict Observants were placed here in 1490; while in 1564, during the fury of the storm under Elizabeth, a provincial chapter was held in the convent of Askeaton. It was soon after suppressed, and in a few years became numbered among the ruins of the country.

much prudence the business of the order entrusted to him, sailed (from Lisbon, where he had remained for some time in the Dominican convent of our Blessed Lady of the Rosary,) to return to his own country; but, being taken on the road by the heretics, and thrown into prison in London, was tried, as was usual, for high treason, and also for having said in Spain that 'it would be lawful to kill the king of England;' but he proved that he had not said so, but, arguing against the heretical doctrine denying man's free will, 'that if it were true it would be an excuse for the greatest crimes, even killing a king.' Nevertheless, he was condemned and taken to the place of execution, where, having publicly proclaimed his faith, and that he was a Dominican, he was hung, and cut down while yet alive, his heart and entrails cut out and cast into the fire, and his body quartered; and thus gloriously completed his confession of Christ."

De Burgo adds that he was on his way to Ireland, to secure students for the Dominican college of Lisbon, but was taken and executed in England. The college became a great resort for Irish students at the time, and seven of those who left it within a few years, namely, Fathers Arthur MacGeoghegan, Gerald Dillon, Miler Magrath, Ambrose O'Cahill, Michael O'Cleary, Gerald Bagot, and Thaddeus Moriarty, suffered martyrdom.

We now come to the close of the reign of James I., whe died March 27, 1625, and though we have not sketched the lives of one-tenth of those who suffered persecutions and martyrdom under his and the previous reigns, we have written enough to prove that the Reformation was planted by persecution, torture, spoliation, the sword, and robbery; and also to show how a Christian people will cling to a Christian faith, despite all human torture and human agencies.

THE KING AND THE PURITANS.

Reign of Charles I.—His leaning towards Catholicity—Influence of the Puritans—Persecutions renewed—The confederation of Kilkenny—United it was powerful, disunited it soon split up—The Nuncio—Treachery of the wily Ormond—Terrible persecutions, death, and exile of the Catholics.

HAD Charles I., who ascended the throne upon the death of his father, been left to his own free will to carry out his principles of toleration, he would most likely have acted justly towards his Irish Catholic subjects. But he was carried away by the religious phrenzy for persecution, which was kept alive by interested advisers who surrounded him. It was the interest of those who had acquired large plantations in Ireland, by fraud and confiscation, that there should not be any investigation into the state of affairs in that country; while the greedy adventurers who were not yet satisfied, urged on further persecution, so as to give them the chance to acquire new possessions. Stranger still, we have it from no less authority than Ware, that the Protestant hierarchy—who, according to the spirit of the Bible, should be tolerant to their fellow Christians—were the most urgent on the king not to grant any toleration to Catholics.

Charles was liberal in his religious views, and felt kindly disposed towards the Catholics of Ireland; but he was weak and vacillating, and allowed himself to be influenced by designing advisers.

The persecutions in Ireland were renewed; and, in 1629,

we find the usual penal edicts revived, and vigorously enforced. A new field for religious discussion now opened. The king, instigated by Laud, archbishop of Canterbury, attempted, in 1637, to force the Protestant episcopalian doctrines and the liturgy of the English church on the Presbyterians of Scotland. This was the commencement of the disasters which brought Charles to the block.

The Puritans were becoming powerful in England; and similar causes to those which had bred the Reformation were now agitating the country, and soon afterwards subverted the crown.

The persecution in Ireland had not abated in the least; new confiscations were threatened; the prisons were full, and a general extermination of the Catholics seemed resolved upon. These circumstances, and a feeling of loyalty and respect towards the king, led to the confederation of the Irish Catholics and the rebellion of 1641.

Under such circumstances, it is no wonder that the Irish Catholics should combine for their preservation. In 1642, a general convention was held at Kilkenny. Besides the Catholic nobility and prelates of the kingdom, this memorable assembly was composed of a certain number of the most influential men chosen from each city, town, and county. The freedom of their religion, of their country, and of their king, being the great object for which they had confederated, they came to the resolution of recurring to the only means now in their power—their own union, their strength, and their arms; and they bound themselves by a solemn oath, never to sheathe the sword until they saw their religion free, their king constitutionally independent, and they themselves in possession of their natural and inalienable rights. At the same time the prelates and clergy were called on, as citizens and as the guardians of religion, to come forward and co-operate with their countrymen. In compliance with this demand of the nation, a synod was convened at Kilkenny early in the month of May, in which it was unanimously resolved—"That, whereas the Catholics of Ireland have taken up arms in defence of their religion, for the preservation of the king, already threatened with destruction by the Puritans, as likewise for the security of their own lives, possessions, and liberty; we, on the part of the Catholics, declare these proceedings to be most just and lawful. Nevertheless, if, in the pursuit of these objects, any person or persons should be actuated by motives of avarice, malice, or revenge, we declare such persons to be guilty of a grievous offence, and deservedly subject to the censures of the Church, unless upon advice they change their intentions, and pursue a different course. Given at Kilkenny, 12th of May, 1642." Thus animated, the Catholics of Ireland determined to insist on their rights; and that their proceedings might be conducted with order and becoming dignity, a council of twenty-four was selected out of the general body. The members comprising this tribunal were denominated the Supreme Council of the Confederated Catholics of Ireland: Richard Butler, viscount Mountgarret, was their president; and to the decision of this council the entire nation bound itself to pay implicit obedience. The success which attended their arms during this and the following year, surpassed even the hopes of the most sanguine; in a few months they found themselves in possession of Cork, Limerick, Galway, Sligo, and Duncannon, then considered the most fortified part of the kingdom; they had, in short, all Ireland in their hands, except Dublin and a few forts in the north.

The king entered into negotiations with the Irish Confederates, in order to strengthen himself against his enemies at home. The Earl of Glanmorgan, on behalf of the king, concluded a peace with them, granting them, in the name of his majesty, both the free exercise of their religion, and the perpetual possession of all the cathedrals, parish churches, and convents which the Catholics then enjoyed, together with the property appertaining to each of these establishments. The confederates, on their part, pledged to raise a force of ten thousand men, to embark forthwith for England, and assist Charles in reducing his enemies to subjection. Had Ormond allowed matters to remain in this state, Ireland would enjoy peace, the fanatics of Scotland would be compelled to submit, and England, it is probable, would not be disgraced by shedding the blood of its sovereign. But the measures agreed to by Glanmorgan were too favorable to the Catholics. Ormond declared the treaty to be null and void, and in a manner as treacherous as it was unjust, caused the earl to be cast into prison, insisting at the same time that to him alone were intrusted the proper powers of treating with the Catholics.

The wily Ormond, in order to create disunion among the members of the Confederation, drew up a new treaty consisting of thirty articles, in which the interests of the laity were more consulted than those of the clergy. This had the desired effect; and, from that forward this body, so powerful when united, became disrupted by dissension and divided councils.

Such was the critical state of affairs when the Nuncio, John Baptist Rinuccini, arrived in Ireland. In presenting his credentials to the Confederate Council, he said:

"I am well aware that persons will be found ready to circulate false rumors; endeavoring to make the public believe that I have been sent over here by his holiness, Innocent X., for the purpose of detaching the Catholic people of Ireland from the allegiance due to his most serene majesty, the king of England. How very far such an assertion is from truth, the Almighty Searcher of Hearts fully knows. I, therefore, publicly protest and solemnly call my God to witness, that I now do not, nor will I ever devise, approve of, or do any thing which is or shall be detrimental to the honor, rights, or interest of the most august King Charles. Nay, more, I now publish and make known to the Catholics of Ireland, both absent and present, that nothing on earth would give greater satisfaction to his holiness than that the Confederate Catholics, having recovered the full and free exercise of their faith, should show unto their mighty and most serene king, although a Protestant, every mark of subjection, assistance, and reverence."

Ormond's treaty was not agreeable to the Nuncio; however, it was finally agreed upon. On the other hand, the men in arms were displeased with the submission of the Supreme Council. In the midst of this dissension and excitement, a national synod of the prelates and clergy was convened at Waterford, at which the peace propositions of Ormond's thirty articles were condemned as ruinous to the country, and all the Confederate Catholics who should adhere to this treaty were declared perjurers. The decree issued by the synod stated—

"Among other particulars, we find that in these articles no mention is made of the Catholic religion, no pledge is given for its security, nor is there any guarantee for the preservation of the rights of the country. On the contrary, all these paramount objects are yielded up to the will and pleasure of the king himself, from whom, in the present disastrous state of affairs, nothing certain can be obtained. In the meantime, the army, the nation, and the Supreme Council are subjected to the caprice and dominion of the ministers and officers of state—men who have always manifested their hostility to the Catholic religion." *

* The signatures to the above decree are in the following order:
John Baptist, archbishop of Fermo, and Nuncio apostolic; Thomas

It is unnecessary to follow the disastrous results of the contentions that sprang up between the Ormond faction on the one hand, and those of the Nuncio on the other. We must confess, the fact that Owen Roe O'Neil and his victorious troops having sided with the Nuncio, strongly convinces us that he was right in his policy and honest in his views.*
From this forth the Supreme Council, instead of being a terror to the enemy, and of vigorously supporting the army in the field, frittered away its time in criminations and

Fleming, O. S. F., archbishop of Dublin, and primate of Ireland; Thomas Walsh, archbishop of Cashel; Bœtius Mac-Egan, O. S F., bishop of Elphin ; Patrick Comerford, O S. A., bishop of Waterford and Lismore ; John, bishop of Killaloe; John, bishop of Clonfert; Edmund O'Dempsey, O P , bishop of Leighlin; Richard O'Connell, bishop of Ardfert and Aghadoe; Francis Kirwan, bishop Killala; Edmund O'Dwyer, bishop of Limerick ; Emerus Matthews, bishop of Clogher ; Nicholas French, bishop of Ferns; James Conall, abbot of Bangor; Patrick Plunkett, abbot of St. Mary's, Dublin ; Laurence Fitz-Harris, abbot of de Surio; John Cantwell, abbot of Holy Cross ; James Tobin, abbot of Kilcool ; Robert Barry, vicar apostolic of Ross; Donald O'Gripha, vicar apostolic of Kilfenora : Gregory Ferrall, provincial of the Dominicans ; Denis O'Driscol, provincial of the Augustinians; Edmund O'Theige, procurator of the primate of Armagh (Hugh O'Reilly); Walter Lynch, vicar apostolic of Tuam ; William Burgat, vicar apostolic of Emly ; James Dempsey, V. G of Kildare ; Cornelius Gafney, V. G. of Ardagh ; Oliver Dease, V. G. of Meath ; Dominick Roche, V. G. of Cork; Simon O'Connory, V. G. of Cloyne ; Edmund Fitz-Gerald, V G. Clonmacnois ; Charles Coglan, V G. L——— ; Robert Nugent, superior of the Jesuits ; Anthony Mac-Geogan, procurator provincial of the Franciscans ; Barnabas Barnewell, commissary general of the Capuchins.

* It must be admitted that the hierarchy were more anxious to secure religious toleration than civil rights for the people, forgetting that the attainment of the latter would secure the former. Ormond saw this, and used it to divide the Confederacy. Born in England, he was thoroughly English in his nature and feelings. A proselyte in his youth to Protestantism, he was taught to hate and despise Catholics. Though commanding the royal army in Ireland, he was in sympathy with the Puritans of England. Able, intriguing, and unprincipled, his pretended friendship was more dangerous to the Confederation and the cause of the king in Ireland than an open avowed enemy. Had the Confederates stood aloof

THE KING AND THE PURITANS. 137

recriminations, excommunications and counter-excommunications. The spirit of discord made its way through every class, until a war of factions seemed imminent, while that union by which alone the Catholic cause could expect to triumph, was nowhere to be found. It was the old, old, sad story of Ireland's history—divide and conquer!

After much wrangling and dissension, a satisfactory treaty was concluded when too late, for in twelve days afterwards, January 30, 1649, Charles was executed, and Cromwell soon afterwards dissolved both the Council and the treaty with the sword.

Ireland was torn by contending factions, and was oppressed by two belligerents during the reign of Charles. The Catholics took up arms in defence of themselves, their religion, and their king. Charles, with the proverbial fickleness of the Stuarts, when pressed by the Puritans, persecuted the Irish, while he encouraged them when he hoped that their loyalty and devotion would be the means of establishing his royal prerogative. It is ever thus with Ireland. It has been used by England as mere state policy dictates, and not in accordance with the principles of equal justice and impartial legislation.

For eight years Ireland was the theatre of the most desolating war and implacable persecution. It will give my readers some idea of the way in which the persecution was carried on, to mention what Lord Clarendon says:

"The Parliament party had grounded their own authority and strength upon such foundations as were inconsistent with any toleration of the Roman Catholic religion, and

from all parties, king and parliamentarians alike, and struggled manfully for their country's independence, they must have succeeded. Or, even should they have failed, they would not have entailed the terrible hostility of the Cromwellian soldiery, nor incurred the regret and pity of posterity for having thus wantonly sacrificed a great cause by their foolish dissensions and blind allegiance to the worthless house of Stuart.

even with any humanity to the Irish nation, and more especially to those of the old native extraction, the whole race whereof they had upon the matter sworn to extirpate."

The Parliament of England, under their guidance, resolved, on the 24th of October, 1644, "that no quarter shall be given to any Irishman, or to *any papist born in Ireland;*" and their historian, Borlase, adds: "The orders of Parliament were excellently well executed." Leland and Warner refer to the letters of the lords-justices for the fact that the soldiers "slew all persons promiscuously, not sparing even the women." Cromwell declared, on landing in Dublin, that no mercy should be shown to the Irish, and that they should be dealt with as the Canaanites in Joshua's time.

When we consider with what relentless fury the Irish were persecuted, and the desperate efforts made to exterminate them, both in the reign of Charles and during the Commonwealth, the wonder is how either the people, or their religion, could have survived complete extinction.*

Having said so much relative to these dark times in Irish history, we will now return to our sketches of the martyrs and sufferers of this period.

* It is impossible to estimate the number of Catholics slain in the ten years from 1642 to 1652. Three bishops and more than 300 priests were put to death for the faith. Thousands of men, women, and children were sold as slaves for the West Indies; Sir W. Petty mentions that 6,000 boys and women were thus sold. A letter written in 1656, quoted by Lingard, puts the number at 60,000; as late as 1666 there were 12,000 Irish slaves scattered among the West Indian islands. Forty thousand Irish fled to the Continent, and 20,000 took shelter in the Hebrides and other Scottish islands. In 1641 the population of Ireland was 1,466,000, of whom 1,240,000 were Catholics. In 1659, the population was reduced to 500,091, so that very nearly 1,000,000 must have perished or been driven into exile in the space of eighteen years. In comparison with the population of both periods, this was even worse than the famine extermination of our own days.

FRESH PERSECUTION AND TORTURE.

Persecution of the monastic orders—Cursory glance at their sufferings and fidelity—Father Francis Slingsby—His conversion and sufferings—His holy death—Bishop O'Reilly—His patriotism and death—Bishop Edmund O'Reilly—His persecution, exile, and death—Fearful picture of the persecutions in Ireland—Martyrdom of the Rev. Peter Higgins—Persecution of the Jesuits—Massacre of Catholics on Island Magee—Capture of Dungarvan and execution of several priests—Martyrdom and heroic resolution of Father Mahony—Fifty old men, women, and children martyred—An old lady of eighty years martyred—Fearful persecution, both of the Franciscans and Dominicans.

STRANGE as it may appear, the fury of persecution was aimed more at the monastic orders in Ireland than at the secular clergy. The friars were more intimately associated with the people. Everybody knew them; everybody looked up to them for consolation and advice. They had branched out from the great monasteries, and settled among the people, and were thus, in a manner, too much identified with the peasantry to be allowed to live among them as their teachers, their guides; and, to their credit be it said, in many cases, their political and military leaders too.

These Franciscans and Dominicans were bold, fearless men. Separated from the world by their vows of poverty and chastity, they cared not for the things of the world, nor were they wedded to it by the allurements of riches or honor. Such men were to be feared; for they cared not for death, were unflinching patriots, and believed in the justice of opposition to tyrants, even with the sword.

It is no wonder, therefore, that the abbeys and monasteries of the monastic orders should be the first objects of destruction and spoliation by the fanatical Reformers. Besides the tempting inducements of confiscating their properties, they were specially hateful to the persecutors of the Catholic Church in Ireland.

At the inception of the persecution under Henry there were upwards of eighty Dominican and Franciscan convents in Ireland, besides a smaller number of Cistercian and Benedictine houses. There were nearly a thousand Franciscan and a thousand Dominican priests attached to these convents. Thirty years afterwards, in the reign of Elizabeth, the Dominican priests were reduced to *four*, and the Franciscans had suffered nearly as much.

Elizabeth tried to establish Protestantism by the sword. The ground was dug as for one national grave. The seed of Protestantism was cast into that soil, and the blood of thousands of martyrs was poured in, to warm it into life and to bring it forth. It never grew, it never bloomed! Ireland was as Catholic the day that Elizabeth died, in despair, at Hampton Court, as she was the day that Henry VIII. tried to coerce her into Protestantism.

After the death of Elizabeth, there came a short breathing spell to the nation, and in fifty years there were over one thousand Dominican and Franciscan priests again in the country. They had studied in Spain, in France, in Italy. Children of Irish parents, they had been smuggled out of the country. Their Irish fathers and mothers had freely given them up, though they knew almost to a certainty that they were devoting them to a martyr's death; but they freely gave them to God. Smuggled out of the country, when ordained they returned by stealth, and scattered themselves over the land, teaching and instructing the people in their religious duties, and strengthening them

FRESH PERSECUTION AND TORTURE. 141

in their faith. To avoid detection, they had to assume all kinds of disguises, and undergo wonderful hardships and privations.*

When Cromwell landed in Ireland, there were six hundred Dominican and nearly as many Franciscan priests before him. Ten years afterwards, only one hundred and fifty Dominicans were left, and about an equal number of Franciscans. The rest had perished—had shed their blood for their religion and their country, or had been shipped away to Barbadoes and other West India Islands, to be sold as slaves.

Thus wave after wave of persecution, confiscation, and robbery, rolled over the Irish Church, but both priests and people withstood the shock, giving up everything—even their lives—rather than renounce their glorious faith—the priceless jewel of their unsullied inheritance.

FATHER FRANCIS SLINGSBY, one of the earliest sufferers under Charles, was the eldest son of Sir Francis Slingsby, knight, an Englishman settled in Ireland, and Elizabeth Cuff. The family were all Protestants.

After leaving Oxford, in 1630, young Slingsby travelled for some time; and, having grave doubts of the purity of

* Illustrative of the disguises which the outlawed clergy were compelled to adopt, in the penal times, in order to screen themselves from their enemies, it may be mentioned that in the palace of the Most Rev. Dr. Conaty, bishop of Kilmore, there is a painting of an Irish piper, clad in the kilt and tartan of the Macdonalds. The picture is life-like, and the beholder is astonished when he learns that it is a portrait of Dr Macdonald, formerly bishop of Kilmore, who in this way travelled, in the penal times, from cabin to cabin, in order to attend to the spiritual wants of his poor, scattered flock. Beneath this minstrel garb he wore the robes of a Catholic bishop; and, though his disguise was known to thousands, not one was found to betray him. The bishop of Kilmore may well feel proud of this memorial of his predecessor that hangs in his hall, and of the people over whom he lifted his crozier.

the Protestant religion, he determined to seek the truth, and finally became a convert at Rome. His intimate friend, Father Spreul, whom he had converted, thus describes his conversion:

"It is worthy of remark that in his conversion to the Catholic faith he not only gave his whole time and attention to the prudent and sincere investigation of the truth, carefully examining the testimonies of the fathers on the controversies of our day, but sought to learn the will of God by continual and fervent prayer, frequent fasts, and abundant alms; so that he was strengthened to overcome all the allurements of the world, the hope of honors and dignity, and the indignation and loss of friendship of his friends. He was no sooner received into the church in Rome than he went through a course of the spiritual exercises of St. Ignatius, and at their conclusion, in obedience to the divine inspiration, he determined to renounce the inheritance of his father, and embrace the institute of the society, in which to live; and this resolution he adhered to unshaken, notwithstanding the greatest difficulties, during eight years that he remained in the world, and by a remarkable force of mind he strove after religious perfection by a most exact observance of our rules, while living with laics and heretics at court and at home."

His friends were naturally much annoyed at his conversion, which he did not conceal; indeed, he ever most openly professed his faith, and returned thanks to God for the grace he had received, as Father Spreul mentions:

"Our generous athlete so boldly overcame all these difficulties that he not only openly professed the Catholic religion, but gloried in the signal grace divinely granted to him, and ever gave thanks to God for it. And this is the more worthy of notice, as many after their conversion are

FRESH PERSECUTION AND TORTURE. 143

allowed to profess the Catholic religion, not openly, but in private." *

His father and friends used all their influence to change his resolution; even his mother wrote to him imploring and beseeching him not to abandon her in her old age.

The celebrated Dr. Usher, who was a warm friend of his father, used all his influence and logic to convince him of the errors of Catholicity; but with no success, as Francis was firmly attached to its doctrines, and convinced of their truth. After this he was flung into prison. After some months' incarceration, he was admitted to bail. Soon after, he converted his mother, his younger brothers, his sister, and several others. He travelled into England in 1636, to avoid being again thrown into prison for having caused the conversion of his sister. He also went to France, and thence to Rome, in connection with Father Spreul, whom he had converted.

Father Slingsby led a most austere life during his time, between prayers and good works. He made numerous converts, both in Ireland and England. In Rome, he entered the English college, to complete his studies for holy orders. In July, 1641, he was consecrated priest. His health had been failing for some time, and being ordered by his physician to Naples, he died there in the same year of his ordination.

His friend and brother convert, Father Spreul, has left some interesting letters on the sufferings, virtuous life, and holy death of Father Slingsby.

REV. JOHN O'MANNIN, O. P. P. of the convent of Derry,† was a most strict observer of the rule, always wore the habit

---

* Letters of Father Spreul.

† The convent of Derry was founded by O'Donnel, Jr., prince of Tirconnell, in 1274. In the thirty-fifth Henry VIII. this convent became a ruin.

of his order, and being recognized on a time by the heretics, he was by them taken prisoner and dragged before the tribunal. Here he despised alike the rewards which were offered to him and the torments with which he was threatened, and boldly professed the Catholic faith. He was ordered for several weeks to be tortured two or three times a week on the rack, and once, when he was hanging in that torture, he was let fall, and his back broken, so that, to his dying day, he remained humpbacked, showing clearly he lacked not the will, but the chance, to be a martyr.

The Most Rev. HUGH O'REILLY, archbishop of Armagh, was transferred from the see of Kilmore to that of Armagh in 1628. He contemplated the restoration of the fine old abbey,* but in 1637 this venerable prelate was thrown into prison in Dublin castle, where he suffered a painful captivity, for having dared to assemble his clergy in synod. His administration comprises that awful period of our history

* The priory of Sts. Peter and Paul, at Armagh, was refounded by Imar, the saintly and learned master of St. Malachy. Some authorities, however, ascribe its original foundation to Imar, and consider it as an institution altogether distinct from the ancient monastery, which had continued to flourish here since the days of St Patrick. Whatever variety of opinions may arise on the subject of its foundation, it is at all events certain that its church, having been erected by Imar, was consecrated in 1126, and that it had been the first establishment in this country into which that religious community designated *Canons Regular of St. Augustin* had been introduced. In process of time it became amazingly enriched, and, among other tokens of patronage, it received from the monarch Roderic O'Conor, an annual pension, for the purpose of having a public school attached to it. Notwithstanding the furious attacks which, on sundry occasions, it had sustained from De Courcy, Fitz-Adelm, De Lacy, and other adventurers, this venerable priory was upheld until the era of general confiscation had been ushered in under Henry VIII Its possessions, which were immense, were subjected to three formal inquisitions: the first in 1539, under Henry; the second in 1557, under Elizabeth, and the third under James I., in 1603. In May, 1612, this priory and its possessions were granted to Sir Toby Caulfield, at a rent of five pounds Irish.

which has been a bloody one, and during which the prudent forbearance and honorable consistency of this prelate tended powerfully to exalt his character in the estimation of all parties. Throughout the whole series of these numerous and complicated scenes, this prelate invariably attached himself to the principles of the Nuncio. When that functionary returned from Waterford, and formed a Supreme Council on the ruins of the former, the primate, Hugh O'Reilly, attended at Kilkenny, and was among the number of those who subscribed to the new oath of association. After this memorable reformation of the Supreme Council, the primate retired to the more agreeable duties of his diocese, until the year 1648, at which time the second treaty was concluded with Inchiquin. Guided by the honest dictates of his own judgment—a privilege to which, on matters of national policy, every man has an undoubted claim—he again appears on the side of the Nuncio, and enters his protest against the cessation. Whatever opinions may have been formed as to the conduct of the primate on these occasions, one thing is certain, that he had acted throughout with a degree of unbending consistency; he adhered to the fortunes of the Nuncio, and even to the wreck of the nation, as long as a single plank was suffered to remain; and when, at length, the meeting of James's-town was convened, the acts of that assembly, in which the perfidy of Ormond was reprobated, received the signature of this metropolitan, together with those of eleven bishops and several other ecclesiastical dignitaries. After having governed the archdiocese of Armagh during angry and perilous times, the primate, Hugh O'Reilly, died in the county of Cavan, about the year 1656.

The Most Rev. EDMUND O'REILLY was his successor in this metropolitan see of Armagh. He was a native of Dublin, and had been for some years rector of the Irish college at

Louvain. During the persecutions by Cromwell, he fled from the country, and took refuge in Lisle. He returned, but was again forced into exile; however, during the national synod of 1666, he again returned to Ireland, and took part in its deliberations. Immediately afterwards he was arrested, on the pretended charge of being an emissary preparing the way for an invasion from Spain. The effect of this ill-digested scheme on the public mind may be readily conceived; even among the court party it received but little credit. The primate was, however, hurried away from Dublin under the custody of Stanley, the town-major, and, having been conveyed to Dover, was transmitted from thence to Calais, and banished the kingdom. This persecuted exile continued but a short time in France; he removed to Louvain, where the severity of his past sufferings had so exhausted his constitution, that he lingered for a period, and died about the year 1669.

Rev. Martin O'Toole, a descendant of the noble and saintly Laurence O'Toole, sought shelter from the persecution of his enemies among the mountains of Wicklow. He had his retreat in the ruins of the celebrated abbey of Glendalough.* From his hiding-place, where he was consoled

* The venerable ruins of Glendalough, even at this day, present an awful and an interesting picture to the mind of the curious and contemplative stranger. Among these must be noticed the church of the Trinity, standing on a rising ground north of the abbey; the Seven Churches, which in former days were the pride and glory of Glendalough, and for which it will be celebrated, even when the vestiges now remaining are no more; the Cathedral Church, with its curious doors, jambs, and lintels, and its round tower, one hundred and ten feet high, rising up in its ancient grandeur amidst the prostrate ruins which surround it. Our Lady's Church, the most westward of the seven, and nearly opposite the cathedral, is in ruins; but these very ruins speak volumes, and the scattered monuments, crosses, and inscriptions refresh the memory, and fill the mind with new and painful thoughts. St Kevin's Kitchen, so called, and undoubtedly one of the Seven Churches is entire, together with its architraves, fretted arches, and round belfry, forty-five feet high The finger

FRESH PERSECUTION AND TORTURE.

by the reflection that everything around him was hallowed by his pious namesake centuries before, and that he was only following in his footsteps of suffering and persecution, he often sallied forth to attend to the spiritual wants of the poor Catholics who sought shelter and safety in the mountainous districts around. In one of these excursions he was captured by the soldiers, and, on declaring himself a Catholic and a priest, he was most inhumanly flogged, and then hanged from the limb of a tree.

TWENTY CAPUCHIN FATHERS, who were exiled towards the close of the year 1641, had a narrow escape from death. One of their number, writing to his superior in Rome, gives the following account of their sufferings. Speaking of the persecutions in Ireland, he says:

"Whithersoever the enemy penetrates, everything is destroyed by fire and sword; none are spared, not even the infant at its mother's breast, for their desire is to wholly extirpate the Irish race. In Dublin our order, as also the

---

of Time alone, and of human neglect, seem to have wrought the work of desolation in this part of the building. The Rhefeart, or the Sepulchre of Kings, is rendered famous for having seven kings interred within its walls. The Ivy Church stands to the westward, with its unroofed walls overgrown with ivy. The priory of St. Saviour is a complete ruin. Teampull-na-Skellig, in the recess of the mountain, was formerly called the Temple of the Desert, and whither the austere fathers of the abbey were wont to retire on vigils, and days of particular mortification. The celebrated bed of St. Kevin, on the south side of the lough, and hanging perpendicularly at a frightful height over the surface of the waters, is another object in which the mind of the antiquary would be much gratified; and on the same side of the mountain are to be seen the remains of a small stone building, called St Kevin's Cell. These hallowed ruins stand in the heart of a picturesque and beautiful country. The romantic mountains by which they are encompassed, the long-extended valley beneath, with its intermixture of rivulets, flowers, and ruins, and the solemn and dead silence of Nature throughout the scene, must render Glendalough a book of meditation for the stranger, of instruction for the Irishman, and of dread and terror for the despoiler and the plunderer.

other religious bodies, had a residence, and a beautifully ornamented chapel, in which we publicly, and in our habit, performed the sacred ceremonies; but no sooner had the soldiers arrived from England than they furiously rushed everywhere, profaned our chapels, overturned our altars, broke to pieces the sacred images, trampling them under foot, and destroying them by fire; our residences were plundered, the priests were everywhere sought for, and many, among them myself and companion, were captured and cast into prison.

"We were twenty in number, and the lords-justices at first resolved on our execution, but through the influence of some members of the council we were transported to France. The masters of the two vessels into which we were cast received private instructions to throw us into the sea, but they refused to commit this horrid crime. Oh! would to God that we had been worthy to be led to the scaffold, or thus drowned, for the faith." *

REV. FATHER HIGGINS, O. P. P., of the convent of Dublin, was taken prisoner at the commencement of the war of 1641, accused of no other crime but being a Catholic. He was condemned to death for his contumacy in adhering to the Catholic faith; and, previous to his execution, was subjected to the most cruel tortures, in order to shake his constancy. His prior visited him in disguise, and covertly prepared him for death, at the risk of his own life.

When led to the place of execution, his patience, humility, and resignation moved many to tears, but excited the fury of others, who vented their rage upon his body after execution. They actually fired into the body, and smashed in the skull of the corpse.

The Very Rev. PETER O'HIGGINS, O. P. P., suffered mar-

* Moran, Persec p. 11, and letter of Father Nicholas, Superior of the Capuchins of Dublin, from Poitiers, 12th July, 1642, quoted by him.*

tyrdom the same year in Dublin. He was prior of Naas,* and was charged with the crime of practicing the Catholic faith, and of trying to seduce Protestants from their religion. The lords-justices, Parsons and Borlase, before whom he was brought, finding no capital charge against him, offered him his freedom and preferments, in case he would reform. This he indignantly refused. Even at the very moment of his execution, a pardon was placed in his hand on condition that he would apostatize. He faced the crowd, with the pardon in his hand, and, addressing the Catholics present, said:

"Dear brethren, children of the Holy Roman Church, since the day I fell into the cruel hands of the heretics who stand around me, I have endured much hunger, great insults, dark and fœtid dungeons; and the doubt as to what was the cause seemed to me to render the palm of martyrdom doubtful; for it is the cause, not the death, that makes the martyr. But the omnipotent God, the protector of my innocence, and who ordereth all things sweetly, has so arranged that although I have been accused as a seducer and a criminal by the laws of the land, yet to-day in me it is the Catholic religion only that is condemned to death. Behold here an undoubted witness of my innocence—a pardon signed by the king's representatives, offering me not only life, but large gifts, if even now I renounce the Catholic religion. But I call God and men to witness how freely I reject this—how gladly I now embrace my doom in and for the profession of that faith."

Having thus spoken, and having thrown the pardon to a friend, he desired the executioner to do his office.

It would be impossible, in the space allotted to this work,

* The priory of Naas was founded in the twelfth century by a baron of Naas, for Canons Regular. This priory, with its possessions, was granted by Elizabeth to Richard Mannering.

to give a sketch of the numbers of Catholics, both lay and clerical, put to death about this time. Curry, in his "Civil Wars," gives a fearful picture of the wholesale massacres and murders committed on the Irish during the reign of Charles and the Commonwealth. The cold-blooded slaughter of the unoffending Catholics of Island McGee—set down by some writers as high as three thousand—by the Scotch and Puritan soldiers, so inflamed the Irish soldiers as to drive them to commit many excesses upon the Protestants in retaliation. But, it must be said, that while the massacre and persecution of the Catholics appeared to be a regular mania with the Protestants, the Catholics, as a body, were never guilty of such excesses; but, unfortunately, Protestants were murdered by irresponsible parties, through a spirit of retaliation.

Wherever the Scotch or Puritan soldiers passed, they wreaked their vengeance upon the peasantry for no other offence than that they were Catholics.

To return to our subject; about this time the Jesuits became a special mark for the persecutors. A work preserved in the Irish College at Rome, and quoted by Dr. Moran, says:

"We were persecuted and dispersed, and despoiled of all our goods; some, too, were cast into prison, and others were sent into exile. Among the fathers of the society was Father Henry Caghwell, renowned for his zeal and learning. Being confined to his bed by sickness, he was apprehended by the soldiers, and hurried to the public square. As he was unable to walk, or even to stand, he was placed on a chair, more for mockery than ease, and subjected to the cruel insults of the soldiery; he was then beaten with cudgels, and thrown into the ship with twenty others, for France."

FATHER FERGAL and CORNELIUS O'BRIEN, the latter called

FRESH PERSECUTION AND TORTURE.

the lord of Carrigh in Kerry, were executed together in 1642, by a pirate named Forbes, who infested the Shannon in the interest of the Puritans. They were hung from the mast-head, and the ropes being cut, their bodies were let drop into the river.

FATHER LATIN and several other priests and religious who labored to keep alive the gospel in and around Waterford, were seized and put to death.

A letter in the archives of Rome, written in 1642, by the bishop of Waterford, states that "The President of Ulster, having received reinforcements, once more took the field, together with the Earl of Cork, the Earl of Barymore, Lord Broghill, and Sir John Browne. Marching on Dungarvan, and seizing on the castle, they set fire to the town, and put to death Father Edmund Howe and Father John Clancy, both priests, together with others of the powerful citizens." Some friars of the convent were also put to death.*

REV. FRANCIS O'MAHONY, a native of Cork, was a prominent member of the order of St. Francis. He had filled various offices in the church, both on the continent and at home.

In 1642, he was guardian of the convent of Cork, but was arrested by order of the governor of the city, and thrown into prison. "A few days afterwards he was brought up for examination, when he confessed he was a Franciscan, but denied that he had sought, as was alleged, to betray the city to the Catholics. His constancy in the faith was tried by many torments, especially the following: the executioners wrapped the old priest's ten fingers in tow and pitch, and then tied them together with candles of pitch, and then set

---

* The convent of Dungarvan had Thomas, lord Offaley, for its founder, in 1295. The family of Magrath and the O'Briens, of Cummeragh, were among its principal benefactors. In the 37th of Elizabeth, it was granted, with sixty-two acres in the vicinity of Dungarvan, and various other property, to Roger Dalton.

fire to them, so that all his ten fingers burnt together. While his fingers were thus burning, Father Francis exhorted the Catholics who stood around to constancy in the faith, and the heretics to be converted. A certain preacher, wondering at the patience of the blessed martyr, asked him whether he felt pain. 'Touch my fingers with one of yours,' answered Father Francis, 'and you may judge.' When all his fingers were burnt down to the last joints, he was ordered to be executed. The man of God gave thanks to God, and went to the place of execution as to a feast; and, having exhorted the people, joyfully mounted the ladder, and, fitting the rope round his neck, with such meekness and resignation as to surprise all present, and having made all necessary dispositions for dying well, he desired the executioner to do his office. He was then pushed off the ladder, and so hung from eleven in the forenoon until five in the afternoon.

"Father Francis had in the city, besides one sister, two nephews and four grand-nephews, and as many friends as there were Catholics. Some of them, who were men of influence, went to the governor and asked that they might take down the body of the father, and bury it after the manner of the Catholics. The governor granted their request, and they carried the body to the house of his sister, and, having there laid it on a table, dressed in his habit, and placed lighted candles round it, devoutly venerated the deceased martyr of Christ.

"About the second hour of the night, while the Catholics who crowded the house were devoutly praying, Father Francis began to move, and, looking on his sister and the persons who stood around, desired them not to be afraid, but to lift him off the table. His friends soon crowded around him, and, removing the candles, perceived that Father Francis was really alive and well, and began to congratulate themselves and him that he had escaped the executioner. 'Not so, my dear friends,' said Father Francis; 'my soul, which had left my body, returns by the will of God, who desires the salvation of all in error; call therefore to me the governor of the city, that once more I may preach to him the words of salvation.' All the Catholics who were present besought him with tears to abstain from useless preaching; and, as the heretics held him for dead, to hide himself in some safe place for their spiritual good. 'It is the will of God,' he answered, 'which Christians must not oppose, that I should announce the words of life to the heretics; call, therefore, the governor and the leaders of the soldiers, or I will myself go to them.'

"The Catholics, compelled by his commands, sent to the governor, to inform him that Father Francis was alive and well. Astonished at the news, the governor hastened, with his principal officers and a strong guard of soldiers, to the house where Father Francis lay. The moment the father saw the Puritans—who were rebels alike to their God and their king—he rose to his feet, and, with his usual zeal, told how their merciful God desired their salvation, and earnestly besought them to abandon heresy and return to the bosom of their mother, the Church. The governor, hardened in evil, the more raged at this exhortation, and ordered the papist—who, as he said, must have preserved his life by magic—to be immediately hung with his own girdle. Some of the soldiers immediately turned executioners, for even the Puritan officers, not to speak of the soldiers, considered it no disgrace to hang a papist with their own hands, especially if he were a priest. They immediately fastened his girdle round his neck, and tied him up to the beam which supported the ceiling of the room, and, having broken his neck, left him hanging there all night, under a guard of Puritan soldiers. There are still living one hundred men, who were then living at Cork, and witnesses of what I write." *

It is remarkable that after the suppression of several abbeys and monasteries, the scattered brethren still clung to them, and sought shelter in the ruins, with the vain hope that the persecution would blow over, and that the Houses would be again restored to the order. As an instance of this, we find that about this time the Rev. HUGH TALBOT was seized in the abbey of Kells,† and cruelly put to death.

Rev. Father KEOGH, of the convent of Roscommon; Father STEPHEN PELITT, sub-prior of the convent of Mullingar; Brothers RAYMOND KEOGH and CORMAC EGAN, were all martyred for the faith this year (1642).

Moran, in his work on the persecution, tells us that the

* *Bruodin*, lib. iv., cap. xv. Bruodin evidently considers the revival of Father Francis miraculous, which is not necessarily so. We have on record too many extraordinary cases of suspended animation from hanging, where the parties recovered, to doubt the truth of this. We have on record well authenticated statements of men who had been suspended for hours, but whose necks were not broken, being restored to life. What we have to admire most in the case of Father Francis is the faith and zeal of the man who despised his own life in comparison with the salvation of the souls of his persecutors.

† The abbey of Kells, in the county of Meath, was founded by St. Columbkill, about 550, and was dedicated to the Blessed Virgin. This abbey is remarkable for many memorable events. In 967, a furious attack had been made on it by Sitric, the Dane, when he was routed with great slaughter by O'Neil the Great. In 1152, the famous synod was held in the abbey of Kells, at which Cardinal Paparo, the pope's legate, presided, and in which he distributed palliums to the four archbishops. The abbey of Kells was six times destroyed by fire, but was afterwards rebuilt in a style of greater magnificence, partly by the bounty of the princes of Ireland, but much more out of the immense revenues attached to it. It had the most splendid library of any monastery in the kingdom, having been celebrated for its manuscripts, among which was St. Columbkill's book of the four Gospels, adorned with gold and precious stones. Richard Plunkett was the last abbot, in 1537, when Henry VIII. held three inquisitions, and took into his own hands the extensive possessions belonging to this abbey.

FRESH PERSECUTION AND TORTURE. 155

soldiers mercilessly slew fifty old men, women, and little boys, with their swords and spears, in the town of Dunshaughlin. Mrs. Reade, then in her eightieth year, encouraged these martyrs in their faith, for which offence the Puritan soldiers set her up as a target, and riddled her body with bullets.

Rev. Cornelius O'Connor and Eugene Daly were Trinitarian fathers, and were sent into Ireland by their superiors. They remained in Ireland some time, and it is even stated that Father Cornelius recovered the convent of Adare.* They returned to Spain, to make arrangements for a college of their order in Seville or elsewhere, and, having arranged for the reception of Irish youths in the convents and colleges of Aragon, Castile, and Andalusia, embarked for Ireland; but their ship fell into the hands of a heretical pirate named John Plunkett, by whom they were thrown into the sea, either in 1643 or 1644.

In the year 1644, a large number of Franciscans were martyred and exiled. Among these was a very learned man, namely, Father Francis Mathews, of Cork, who had written several works. He was first cruelly tortured, whipped, and then hanged and quartered.

---

* It is curious, as illustrating the way in which the Catholics from time to time restored, at least partially, the possession of the convents to the religious, that although the Trinitarian convent of Adare was suppressed in the reign of Henry VIII., in a survey of the manor of Adare, dated 6th November, 1559 (second Elizabeth), it is said : "There standeth an abbey of Friars of the Trinity, which hath a crosse of redd and blewe upon their brests, of the foundation of the earl's ancestors, as the minister (that is, the father-minister) did shew, which hath, etc. And the said minister hath in Adare a small acre, with certen gardens," etc   N. B.—The lands here enumerated as belonging to the abbey and minister are only a small part of the original possessions of the abbey   In 1566, Elizabeth demised the Trinitarian Abbey to Sir Warham St Leger; yet, about 1640, "Father Cornelius had a lawsuit with some heretics about the recovery of the convent of Adare," as is stated in the letter of Father Burgatt, in Lopez.

The Dominicans were fearfully persecuted about this time. Several were put to death. The Rev. PETER COSTELLO was ran through the body while preaching. Father GERALD DILLON was flung into prison, where he was starved and tortured to death. They both belonged to the convent of Orlar, county Mayo.

The same year (1645) Father HENRY WHITE, an old, venerable man of eighty, was taken prisoner by the garrison of Dublin, and hung, by order of Sir Charles Coote, governor of the city, in the town of Rath-Connell.

FATHER DOMINICK A. NEAGREN, of the convent of Roscommon, was several times flogged, and, still persevering in the faith, was put to death by the soldiers.

About the same time, Father JOHN O'LAIGHIN, prior of Derry, was taken prisoner and put in chains. After much suffering and torture in prison, this holy and learned man was finally hung and beheaded.

MURROUGH, THE BURNER.

Life of Archbishop O'Queely—His standing with the Court of Rome—Joins the Confederates, and raises a regiment—The Irish troops surprised and defeated at Ballysadare—The archbishop slain—Inchiquin, or "Murrough, the burner," attacks Cashel—Heroic resolve of the garrison—Butchery of the soldiers, priests, and people—Fearful massacre—Twenty priests and three thousand persons slain—Desecration of the altars and churches—The monastery of Kilmallock attacked, and two priests martyred.

ARCHBISHOP O'QUEELY

THE following sketch of this pious and patriotic prelate, taken from the Rev. Father Meehen's work on the "Rise and Fall of the Irish Franciscan Monasteries," is so graphic and descriptive of the period of which it treats, that we quote it in preference to anything we could write on the subject:

"MALACHY O'QUEELY, son of Donatus, was a native of the county Clare, and lineally descended from the lords of Conmacne-mara, where they ruled as princes long before and after the Anglo-Norman invasion. A chieftain of this race marched with Brien Borumha to Clontarf in 1014, and centuries afterwards the name was famous in bardic story—

> "Over Conmacne-mara great
> Was O'Cadhla, friend of banquets."

"Malachy, when a mere youth, went to Paris, where he studied in the college of Navarre, and took the degree of doctor in divinity. On his return to Ireland, he was appointed vicar-apostolic of Killaloe, and ultimately, on October 11, 1631, was, by Thomas Walsh, archbishop of Cashel, consecrated successor to Florence Conry in the archiepiscopal see of Tuam. The prelates who assisted on this occasion were Richard Arthur, of Limerick, and Bœtius Egan, of Elphin ; and the ceremony took place at Galway.

"In 1632, the year immediately following his elevation, O'Queely presided at a synod in Galway, for removing abuses and enforcing the decrees of the Council of Trent ; and in the interval between the last-named period and the rising of 1641, he devoted himself with singular zeal to the discharge of his high office, consoling and enlightening the flock committed to his charge, then sadly harassed by the tyrannical proceedings of Lord-Deputy Strafford.

"In 1641, when the people rose to shake off the intolerable oppression under which they had so long groaned, O'Queely took his place among them, not indeed as a military chief, but rather with a view to repress tumultuary assaults, and save the Protestant portion of the community from pillage and insult. For this laudable object he raised a regiment, which was officered by the O'Flaherties and others of the Connaught gentry, whose zeal for their religion and the false-hearted Charles I. was crowned with a temporary triumph, though sadly requited by the son and successor of that unhappy monarch. In all the transactions of the Confederates, O'Queely, then president of Connaught, was regarded as a high authority, and not only by them, but by the court of Rome ; for the instructions given to Rinuccini by Innocent X. marked out the archbishop as the fittest person for his guidance. 'Although each of the four archbishops,' says the document, 'is remarkable for zeal, nevertheless he of Tuam is to be your confidant, and among the *bishops* he of Clogher.'

"The last appearance of O'Queely in the general assembly at Kilkenny was in October, 1645, the month of the Nuncio's arrival in Ireland, and the same in which the ferocious Coote was appointed by the Parliament president of Connaught, with a commission 'to extirpate the Irish by fire and sword.' Sligo, at that time, had fallen into the hands of the Scotch Covenanters; and the Supreme Council of the Confederates, wishing to possess a seaport which enabled their enemies to land men and munitions of war, resolved to recover it if possible. As a spiritual peer, O'Queely voted supplies for the undertaking, and immediately set out with the forces destined for the expedition, which was commanded by Lord Taaffe and Sir James Dillon.

"On leaving Kilkenny, the archbishop's mind was overclouded by sinister omens; and he not only removed all his baggage, but bade adieu to each of his friends, telling them that he was destined never to see them again. On crossing the Shannon, he was met by a vast concourse of the people, who came to look their last on him; for there was then rife among them an old prophecy concerning the violent death of one of St. Jarlath's successors, and it was popularly believed that the prediction was to be fulfilled in the person of O'Queely. Indeed, he himself seems to have given it credit; for, a few years before, while being punctured for a dropsical affection, he told Dr. Nicholson, his medical attendant, that *the* prophecy was to be fulfilled in him, and that he had not long to live. The Nuncio, too, in his dispatches, alludes to the prediction, remarking that the Irish were much given to the 'folly of prophesying.'

"On Sunday, 17th October, 1645, the Irish troops encamped in the vicinity of Ballysadare; and so confident were Taaffe and Dillon of the safety of their position, that they accepted on that fatal day an invitation to dine with the archbishop, who, always proverbial for hospitality, had also asked all the other officers to his table. It was during this merrymaking that Sir Charles Coote, Sir William Cole, and Sir Francis Hamilton had intelligence of the loose discipline observable in the Confederate camp; and, taking advantage of the information, they swooped down unexpectedly, with a large force, and, before the Irish could arm themselves, put them to flight, and cut them up fearfully.

"In this extremity, Dillon told the archbishop to save himself as best he could; but being *obese and of great stature*, he lacked the necessary speed. His faithful secretary, Father Thady O'Connell, of the order of Hermits of St. Augustine, and another priest, lost their lives endeavoring to protect him from the Scotch, who, ignorant of the prize they had within their grasp, hewed him to pieces with their claymores, after wounding him with a pistol shot in the loins.

"The list of prisoners made in this sad raid shows that the archbishop was accompanied by some of the foremost men in Connaught; for it mentions, among others, Murraghna-do, O'Flahertie, William O'Shaughnessy, and Captain Garrett Dillon, son to Sir Lucas Dillon, who stated that his father was shot in the thigh.

"Intelligence of this unfortunate event, which the Puritans styled 'Good News from Ireland,' was immediately forwarded to both houses of Parliament, and that very quaint bulletin tells us that 'the Irish forces amounted to one thousand foot and three hundred horse. In the pursuit,' says the writer, 'their commander and president of that province was slain, the titular archbishop of Tuam, who was a principal agent in these wars. Divers papers were found in his carriage. He had, for his own particular use, an order from the council at Kilkenny for levying the arrears of his bishopric, and the Pope's bull and letter from Rome. The Pope would not at first engage himself for the sending of a Nuncio for Ireland, until the Irish agents had fully persuaded him that the re-establishment of the Catholic religion was a thing feasible in this kingdom ; whereupon he undertook the solicitation of their cause with Florence, Venice, and other estates, and to delegate his Nuncio to attend to the affairs of this kingdom.' In the archbishop's baggage was found the private treaty which Charles I. empowered Lord Glanmorgan to negotiate with the Confederates ; and the discovery of this important document, we need hardly say, helped to exasperate the Puritans against the unfortunate king.

"As soon as the Scotch discovered the high rank of the individual whose mutilated corse was left on the roadside, they demanded a sum of thirty pounds before surrendering it ; and when the money was paid by Walter Lynch, he caused the remains to be dressed in pontifical robes, and conveyed to Tuam, where Mass for the deceased was duly celebrated in presence of a vast crowd, who bitterly lamented their well-beloved archbishop. Unfortunately, there is now no record of the place of O'Queely's interment ; but we have it, on the authority of one who was personally acquainted with him, that some years after his decease, Brigid, Lady Athenry, wife of Francis, nineteenth lord of that title, and daughter of Sir Lucas Dillon, of Lough Glynn, in the county Roscommon, caused all that remained of the archbishop to be reinterred in some place only known to herself and the pious few who were employed to perform that charitable work."

Murrough O'Brien, lord Inchiquin, was justly styled the curse of Munster. Wherever his victorious army, with fire and sword, desolated the country, priest and monk and peasant alike glutted their insatiable appetite for blood. Never was a proud name, or a noble house, so dishonored as was the house of O'Brien, by this renegade to his religion and his country. His cold-blooded, atrocious butchery of the peasantry of Clare, Limerick, and Tipperary, is only paralleled by the massacres of Cromwell himself. We do not mean to follow the career of this renegade Irishman, as it is one of the dark pages in Irish history, but will confine ourselves to his butchery of the garrison and innocent inhabitants of Cashel, lay and clerical.

This incendiary, who spared neither age nor sex, temple nor altar, still lives in the minds of the Irish people, under the sobriquet of "Murrough, the burner."

There is not on record a more appalling tragedy than his slaughter in Cashel.

In 1647, after burning the crops and massacreing the peasantry along his line of march, he attacked Cashel, which he soon converted into a very slaughter-house.

The city being poorly fortified, accepted Inchiquin's terms of surrender.

The garrison, comprising only about three hundred soldiers, together with the priests and religious, and a large number of citizens, retired to the cathedral church on the Rock, resolved to withstand a siege.* Inchiquin having gained possession of the city, set it on fire, and then attacked the garrison.

After considerable fighting and the most heroic resistance on the part of the besieged, Inchiquin offered permission to the garrison to depart with their arms and ammunition, and all the honors of war; but, making it a condition that the clergy and citizens should be abandoned to his mercy.

* The vain, arrogant, and, it is to be feared, traitorous Taaffe, who commanded the Confederate troops in Munster against Inchiquin, who commanded the Royalists, or, rather, the Puritan army, fled at the approach of the latter, scarcely offering him the slightest resistance. Early in September, Inchiquin sat down before Cashel, which Taaffe left with a feeble garrison, exposed to the mercy of the former.

The brave soldiers scorned to entertain any such proposition, vowing that they would sooner all perish than do anything so dishonorable ; adding that they chose rather to perish defending God's sanctuary, than to allow it to be profaned by such dogs. Inchiquin, having about seven thousand troops, after opening a heavy fire on the Rock, prepared to take it by storm. The assault was a fierce and bloody one. The assailants dashed through a breach, climbed over the walls, and in through the windows and doors, but were fiercely met by the brave handful of men inside. The assault was desperately met by the besieged. The garrison fought with all the desperation of despair, through the very aisles and corridors of the church and palace, until almost the last armed man had sank in death before the assailants. Inchiquin's bloodthirsty soldiers were not satisfied with the massacre of the armed defenders, but savagely butchered old men, women, and children who had sought protection and safety before the very altar in the cathedral.

> "The prattling child, the matron, and the maid,
> And hoary age, sank beneath the Saxon blade."

Twenty priests were dragged from beneath the altar, where they had fled, hoping that its sanctity would protect them, and were butchered in the most cruel manner. Within the cathedral alone, over nine hundred persons were slain. The dead bodies were strewn all round ; the altars, and chapels, and sacristy, and seats were covered with them. The slaughter throughout the city was terrible ; scarcely a human being who could be found, escaped. Old, decrepid men and women were killed in their beds ; children not able to walk were hoisted up on the tops of pikes and halberds ; the bloody carnage did not cease until, according to good authority, fully three thousand persons were slain.

One of the priests who had taken refuge in the cathedral,

Father THEOBALD STAPLETON, was remarkable for his piety; clothed with a surplice and stole, and holding a crucifix in his left hand, he sprinkled with holy water the enemy's troops as they rushed into the sacred edifice. The heretics, mad with rage, strove with each other who should pierce him with their swords; and thus he was hewn to pieces. At each wound the holy man exclaimed, "Strike this miserable sinner!" till he yielded his soul into the hands of his Creator.

Of Father BOYTON, the Jesuit, we read:

"As the enemy forced their way in, he exhorted all, with great fervor, to endure death with constancy for the Catholic religion, and was wholly occupied in administering to them the sacrament of penance. The enemy, finding him at this work, slew the father with his children. But God revenged the unworthy death of His servants, and by a manifest sign showed the cruelty of this massacre. A garrison of heretical soldiers was stationed on the rock; on a certain night an old man of venerable aspect appeared to its commander, and, taking him by the hand, led him forcibly to the top of the church tower, and then asked him how he madly dared so impiously to profane that holy place. And as he trembled and did not answer, he flung him down into the cemetery below, where he lay half dead, and with many bones broken, until the following day, when, having fully declared the divine vengeance which had overtaken him, he expired." *

Dominick a Rosario gives the following account of the death of Father RICHARD BARRY, the Dominican: †

"The colonel who led the assault, struck with his appear-

---

* Tanner, Soc. Jesu.

† He was a native of Cork, and Prior of Cashel, and had desired all his brethren to seek their safety by flight, but himself refused to leave his flock.

ance (for he was a grave and noble-looking man, and held a sword in his hand), said to him, 'I see you are a brave man, and I promise you safety if you will cast off that dress, which we hate (he was in the habit of his order); for the terms of this war allow of no mercy to those colors, which excite not our favor, but our rage.'* The father answered: 'My dress is the emblem of Christ and His passion, and the banner of my warfare. I have borne it from my youth, and will not put it off in death. Let my safety or doom be that of the emblem of my spiritual warfare.' The colonel answered: 'Be more careful of yourself. If you fear not to die, you shall soon have your way; but if you desire to live, cast away that traitor's dress; if you look for the foolish vanity of martyrdom, we will take care that you shall well earn it.' 'Since so excellent an occasion is offered me,' answered the father, 'to suffer is my joy, and to die my gain.' Provoked at this answer, the colonel gave the father over to the soldiers, who struck him and spat on him; then, tying him on a chair,† they applied a slow fire from the soles of his feet to his thighs for about two hours, until, while he looked up to heaven and the blood bubbled from his pores, the officer ordered his death to be hastened by driving a sword through him. The soldiers remained there three days plundering, for they did not think the place strong enough for a permanent garrison. During this time a certain pious woman, who was of the Third Order of St. Dominick,‡ sought out his body, and when she had found it, she informed the vicar-general. He was interred in the convent of his order." §

* It must be observed that putting off the religious habit was often looked upon as a sort of tacit apostasy.

† The "Acts of the General Chapter" say, "to a column."

‡ Third Order of St Dominick: those who lived in the world

§ Dominick a Rosario sets down the day of his death as the 15th of September, 1647, while Tanner states that it took place on the 18th.

Lord Castlehaven, in his Memoirs, says: "It (the rock) was carried by storm, so that within and without the church, there was a great massacre; and, among others, more than twenty priests and religious were killed." Rinuccini says: "They slew in the church the priests and the women who clung to the statue of the Saint."

Not content with their butchery of the garrison, priests, and citizens, Inchiquin's soldiers destroyed the altars and images and engravings in the churches. The great crucifix which stood at the entrance of the choir, as if it had been guilty of treason, was beheaded, and soon after its hands and feet were amputated. With a like fury did they rage against all the other chapels of the city. Gathering together the sacred vases and all the most precious vestments, they, through ridicule, formed a procession. They advanced through the public squares, wearing the sacred vestments and having the priests' caps on their heads, and inviting to Mass those whom they met on the way. A beautiful statue of the Immaculate Virgin, taken from the church, was borne along (the head being broken off) in mock state, with laughter and ridicule. The leader of the Puritan army had, moreover, the temerity to assume the archiepiscopal mitre, and boast that he was not only governor and lieutenant of Munster, but also Archbishop of Cashel.

About the same time, the monastery of Kilmallock was suddenly attacked by the Puritan soldiers, hoping, no doubt, to capture and slay the brethren; but, fortunately, they had escaped, all but Father Gerald Geraldine and Father David Fox, whom they found kneeling before the altar in prayer, with their rosaries around their necks. After hacking them with their swords, they blew out their brains, and then despoiled the monastery of all its valuables.

CROMWELL'S CAMPAIGN IN IRELAND.

Execution of King Charles—Arrival of Cromwell in Ireland—Sack of Drogheda—Terrible butchery of men, women, and children—A number of priests and friars put to death—Terrible massacre in Wexford—Neither age nor sex spared—Several priests martyred—Incarceration and death of Dr. Roothe—Capture of Bishop Egan—Offered his life and liberty if he would advise the garrison of Carrigodrohid to surrender—He advises them to fight to the last, and is cruelly put to death by Lord Broghill.

N the 30th of January, 1649, the unfortunate Charles ended his days on the scaffold; and thenceforth both the altar and the throne became the prey of the fanatical Puritans. In August of the same year, Cromwell landed in Ireland with a force of eight thousand foot and four thousand horse.

On his arrival in Dublin, he issued an address to his army, in which he proclaimed that no mercy should be shown to the Irish, and that they should "be dealt with as the Canaanites in Joshua's time."

Drogheda was garrisoned by three thousand troops, commanded by Sir Arthur Ashton, a Catholic nobleman. Cromwell attacked the town with two thousand. The besieged made a gallant defence, but were finally compelled to capitulate on favorable terms, which terms were grossly violated. Cromwell, writing to the Parliament, boasts that, despite the promised quarter, he gave orders that all should be put to the sword,* as a "*righteous judgment of God upon the bar-*

* "Our men were ordered by me to put them all to the sword."—*Cromwell's Letter to Lenthal-Lingard.*.

barous wretches—a great mercy vouchsafed to us—a great thing done, not by power or might, but by the spirit of God."

The slaughter of the inhabitants continued for five days, and the Puritan troops spared neither age nor sex, so much so that the Earl of Ormond, writing to the secretary of Charles II., to convey the intelligence of the loss of Drogheda, declares that "Cromwell had exceeded himself, and anything he had ever heard of, in breach of faith and bloody inhumanity;" and the Parliamentarian General Ludlow speaks of it as an *extraordinary severity*. The church of St. Peter, within the city, had been for centuries a place of popular devotion; a little while before the siege the Catholics had reobtained possession of it, and dedicated it anew to the service of God, and the Holy Sacrifice was once more celebrated there with special pomp and solemnity. Thither many of the citizens fled as to a secure asylum, and, with the clergy, prayed around the altar; but the Puritans respected no sanctuary of religion. "*In this very place,*" writes Cromwell, "*near one thousand of them were put to the sword. I believe all the friars were killed but two, the one of which was Father Peter Taaffe, brother to Lord Taaffe, whom the soldiers took the next day, and made an end of; the other was taken in the round tower; he confessed he was a friar, but that did not save him.*"

Quarter had been promised to all who should lay down their arms, but faith was only kept until they surrendered, when they were butchered. A large number of women and children took shelter in the church and its steeple; but these were soon set on fire, and, as the people rushed out from the flames, they were butchered. Among these were several Carmelite monks.

Wood, one of the Puritan officers, engaged in the massacre, relates how a multitude of the defenceless inhabitants of the city, including most of the principal ladies and their children, who were concealed in the vaults and crypts of the church, were cruelly dragged forth by the soldiers and butchered.* Lord Clarendon states that during five days the streets of Drogheda ran red with blood.† He adds: "The whole army executed all manner of cruelty, and put every man of the garrison, and all citizens who were Irish—man, woman, and child—to the sword."

Cromwell states that some thirty escaped the massacre, and these, he adds, " are in safe custody for the Barbadoes."

REV. JOHN BATHE and his brother, secular priests, were discovered by the soldiers the following day, and were borne in triumph, amidst the jeers and ribald shouts of the soldiers, to the market-place, where they were tied to a stake and cruelly flogged, and then shot.

FATHERS DOMINICK DILLON and RICHARD OVERTON and ATHY were also executed, amidst the jeers and laughter of the army.

FATHER ROBERT NETTERVILLE was another victim to their fury. He was aged, and confined to bed by his infirmities; nevertheless, he was forced away by the soldiers, and dragged along the ground, being violently knocked against each obstacle that presented itself on the way ; then they beat him with clubs, and when many of his bones were

* Captain Wood, at the storming of Drogheda, a subaltern in Ingoldsby's regiment, describing the massacre in St. Peter's Church, Drogheda, at which he was himself present, says : "When they (the soldiers) were to make their way up to the lofts and galleries, and up to the tower of the church, each of the assailants would take up a child, and use it as a buckler of defence, when they ascended the steps, to save themselves from being brained or shot." And he describes his own unavailing attempt to save one young woman out of the general massacre of all the women there.—*Lingard*, vol. ix, note D.

† Down to the present century the street leading to St. Peter's Street retained the name of *Bloody Street*. It is the tradition of the place that the blood of those slain in the church formed a regular torrent down the street.

broken, they cast him on the highway, where he was left to die.

FATHER PETER COSTELLO, sub-prior of the convent of Strade, was massacred by the soldiers about the same time.

REV. JAMES O'REILLY was captured near Clonmel by a troop of Cromwellian horse. Being questioned, he fearlessly answered that he was a priest and a Dominican monk. Being asked to apostatize, he boldly replied: "I am a Christian and a Roman Catholic priest; as I have lived so will I die. The will of Heaven be done!" He endured their blows and torture with great fortitude; at length he expired.

Wexford shared the same fate as Drogheda.

Stafford, who commanded for Ormond, held the garrison, which he treacherously surrendered to the enemy. Cromwell, in a letter, estimates the number butchered at two thousand, and says: "I thought it not good nor just to restrain the soldiers from their right of pillage, nor from doing execution on the enemy."

No distinction was made between the defenceless inhabitants and the armed soldiers; nor could the shrieks and prayers of three hundred females, who had gathered around the great cross in the Market Square, preserve them from the swords of the Puritan barbarians.

> "They found them there—the young, the old,
>   The maiden and the wife;
> Their guardians brave in death were cold,
>   Who dared for them the strife.
> They prayed for mercy—God on high!
>   Before Thy Cross they prayed,
> And ruthless Cromwell bade them die,
>   To glut the Saxon blade."

Father Francis Stafford, in a letter written at the time, says: "On the 11th of October, 1649, seven friars of our order (Franciscans), all men of extraordinary merit, and natives of the town, perished by the sword of the heretics. Some of them were killed kneeling before the altar, and others while hearing confessions. *

FATHER RAYMOND STAFFORD, while praying with and encouraging the citizens, both in their heroic opposition to the enemy and in their religious faith, was killed.

Dr. French, the venerable bishop of Ferns, who himself escaped with difficulty, gives the following account of the massacre, in a letter to the Internuncio, 1673: "On one day I lost, for the cause of God and the faith, all that I possessed; it was the 11th of October, 1649; on that most lamentable day my native city of Wexford, abounding in wealth, ships, and merchandise, was destroyed by the sword, and given a prey to the infuriated soldiery by Cromwell, that English pest of hell. There, before God's altar, fell many sacred victims, holy priests of the Lord; others, who were seized outside the precincts of the church, were scourged with whips; others were hanged; some were arrested and bound with chains; and others were put to death by various most cruel tortures. The best blood of the citizens was shed; the very squares were inundated with it, and there was scarcely a house that was not defiled with carnage, and full of wailing. In my own palace a

* According to an ancient and concurrent tradition, the Conventual Franciscans settled in Wexford about the middle of the thirteenth century, having been accommodated and amply assisted by the Knights Hospitallers, who were at the time in possession of an extensive establishment in that town. The Conventuals of this house adopted the more strict reformation of the Observants, A. D 1486; and it continued regularly in the hands of their successors until the 35th of Henry VIII., when this convent, with its appurtenances and eight burgesses in the town of Wexford, valued at 17s., were granted for ever, in capite, to Paul Turner and James Devereux, at the annual reht of 10d. Irish. During the storms which blew over the sixteenth and subsequent centuries, the members of this establishment remained unintimidated; affording such a display of Christian heroism, as might well become the spirit and character of primitive times.

youth hardly sixteen years of age, an amiable boy, as also my gardener and sacristan, were cruelly butchered; and the chaplain, whom I caused to remain behind me at home, was pierced with six mortal wounds."

It is no wonder that Catholicity should survive the rack and the gibbet in Ireland, when we find her priests not only fearlessly facing death for their faith, but also comforting and confessing the people on the very threshold of the grave. There is something sublimely grand in such heroism. It is the sacrifice of all that earth holds dear, to faith and religion—a sacrifice that nothing but Christianity and Catholicity could inspire.

The Rev. PHELIM O'LOUGHLIN was a very zealous priest of the County Wexford; and, despite the fate of his brethren and the certain death that awaited him from his enemies, he continued to attend to the wants of his scattered flock.

He had erected a rude altar in the ruined abbey of Tintern,* and amidst the silence of the desolated abbey and cloister, he offered up the holy sacrifice of the Mass, at-

* The abbey of Tintern, in the barony of Shelburne and county of Wexford, was founded for Cistercians by William Mareschal, the elder, earl of Pembroke, A. D. 1200. This nobleman, having been in great danger at sea, made a vow that he would erect a monastery in that place where he should first arrive in safety; which obligation he performed by the foundation of Tintern abbey, and afterwards supplied it with monks, whom he had brought from the abbey of Tintern, in Monmouthshire. Its first abbot was John Torrell; and in process of time it became amazingly enriched. In 1380 it was enacted that no mere Irishman be permitted to make his profession in this abbey. The abbots of Tintern sat as barons in Parliament, the last of whom was John Power. By an inquisition taken in the 31st of Henry VIII, the possessions were found to consist of ninety acres, being the demesne land, situated in Tintern, and two thousand two hundred acres of moor, arable, and pasture land, together with the rectories of Banne, Kilmore, Clomines, and various others. During the same year the Saltees, with the rectory of Kilmore, were granted to William St Loo; while in the 18th of Elizabeth, the abbey and sixteen townlands, with their tithes and the reversion of the premises, were granted for ever, in capite, to Anthony Colclough, at the annual rent of £26 4s

tended by groups of half-starved, half-naked peasants. At length the poor priest was hunted down, and dragged from his hiding-place and martyred, amidst the jeers and ribald oaths of a savage soldiery.

DAVID ROOTHE, bishop of Ossory, was one of the most learned and distinguished men who suffered persecution from Cromwell's soldiers. He was one of the controlling members of the Supreme Council of the Confederation, and by his wisdom, prudence, and great learning, did much to heal the unfortunate quarrels that distracted that body.

Messingham says, "that he was well versed in all sorts of learning; was an eloquent orator, a subtle philosopher, a profound divine, an eminent historian, and a sharp reprover of vice."

Perhaps he and the learned Luke Wadding have done more to preserve for us the history of the sufferings and persecutions of the Church in Ireland than all the other writers on ecclesiastical affairs of their time.

From Wexford, Cromwell advanced in a dreary season to Kilkenny, not prepared for a regular siege, but relying on the promises of an officer named Tickle, that he would betray the city of Kilkenny into his hands. The plot was discovered and the agent executed, and the custody of the city and adjacent country was entrusted to Lord Castlehaven, with a body of twelve hundred men. But the plague which had broken out obliged Castlehaven to retire, and reduced the garrison to about four hundred and fifty. Nevertheless, Sir Walter Butler made a brave defence, and repelled the assaults of the besiegers with such spirit and success that Cromwell, despairing of taking it by force, granted favorable conditions; but no sooner had the enemy possession of the city than these were violated. The Puritans profaned the churches, overturned the altars, destroyed the paintings and crosses, and profaned all things sacred. The vestments, which had been for the most part concealed, were discovered and plundered by the soldiery; the books and paintings were cast into the street, and either destroyed by fire or brought away as booty. The holy bishop, Dr. David Roothe, venerable for his years, his piety, his learning, and pure life, was flung into a dungeon, where he expired April, 1650.

Most Rev. BŒTIUS EAGAN, bishop of Ross, displayed a bravery and heroism that must endear his memory to every Irish heart.

He was a native of Duhallow, in the county of Cork; took the habit of the Franciscan monastery of Louvain; was the contemporary and friend of Colgan, Fleming, and other great men, whose names are famous in Irish literature, and returned to Ireland many years before the insurrection of 1641. The Nuncio esteemed him highly; thought him the fittest man for the see of Ross; and, despite the opposition of Muskerry and others of Lord Ormond's partisans, had him consecrated in 1648. The Ormondists were loud in their outcries against his advancement, strove to withhold from him the temporalities of his see, and did their utmost to deprive him of a seat in the assembly, on the plea that the Pope could confer no temporal barony in Ireland. All this clamor, however, was overruled by Rinuccini and the Irish bishops, and Bœtius Eagan accordingly took his place in the legislature. As matter of course, he remained unshaken in his fidelity to the Nuncio, seconded all his views, and endeavored to have them carried out in his diocese. His tenure of the episcopate was brief indeed; for when the Cromwellians had overrun Carberry, he was obliged to betake himself to the fastnesses of Kerry, where David Roche had cantoned some six or seven hundred confederate soldiers.

For his safety, the bishop kept under the protection of this force, and marched with them into the County Cork.

On the 1st of May, 1650, they were defeated near Macroon by Lord Broghill, and Bishop Eagan was made prisoner. Broghill was hastening on to join the besieging forces in front of Clonmel, but was detained by the garrison of the fort of Carrigodrohid. He offered the bishop his choice of liberty if he advised the garrison to surrender, or death if he refused. He was conducted in front of the fort for this purpose. The bishop addressed the men inside, and told them to fight to the last man against the heretics, for their religion, their country, and their king. The enraged Broghill ordered him to be strangled at once. He was then abandoned to the soldiers' fury, and, his arms being first severed from his body, he was dragged along the ground to a neighboring tree, and, being hanged from one of its branches by the reins of his own horse, happily consummated his earthly course in November, 1650.

During the siege of Clonmel, NICHOLAS MULCAHY, parish priest of Ardfinan, in the county Tipperary, a man of extraordinary zeal, was seized upon by a reconnoitering party of Cromwell's horse. He had been frequently advised to fly from the storm, but his affectionate solicitude for the people rose superior to every counsel. He was bound in irons, conducted to the camp of the besiegers and offered his pardon, provided he would but use his influence in prevailing on the inhabitants of Clonmel to surrender the town. These terms being rejected, he was brought under the walls, and, by a general order was beheaded, while in the act of praying for his flock and forgiving his enemies.

MILES MAGRATH, of the Order of Preachers, and a member of the convent of Clonmel, underwent an ordeal of sufferings and was put to death in the same town, not many days after. This excellent priest, anxious to attend the sick, had returned to Clonmel soon after the siege. Having celebrated the divine mysteries, and being in the act of attending a dying person, he was taken into custody, then put on the rack, and at length suspended from a gibbet by the orders of one of Cromwell's satellites, who at that time had command of the garrison.

JAMES LYNCH, parish priest of Kells, in the county of Meath, and RICHARD NUGENT, parish priest of Ratoath, in the same county, were both put to the torture, and died on the same day, in defence of their faith. The former, a venerable old man, nearly eighty years of age, was massacred in his bed, to which he had, through infirmity, been for a long time confined. The latter was sent, under an escort, to Drogheda; and a gibbet having been erected within sight of the walls, he ended his course with that Christian firmness which confounded his enemies, and drew forth the tears and benedictions of his disconsolate friends.

THE PURITANS IN IRELAND.

Cromwell's return to England—His bloody agents in Ireland—Ireland under the Puritans—Bishop O'Brien of Emly—His trial and martyrdom—He summons Ireton to answer for his crimes before the judgment-seat of God—Sudden death of Ireton—Fearful massacre in Limerick—Several priests put to death—St. Vincent de Paul's interest in the Catholic Church in Ireland—Fearful state of suffering and persecution of the Church.

AFTER Cromwell's brilliant but bloody campaign of nine months in Ireland, on the 20th of May, 1650, he returned to England, leaving his affairs there and the command of the army in the hands of men as bloody and remorseless as himself; and scenes of butchery, murder, and desolation followed, unparalleled in the history of any other country. The programme of extermination and confiscation seemed the only one that the Puritan soldiers and the Puritan parliament had for Ireland.

The scheme of parcelling out the lands of Ireland among the officers and soldiers of Cromwell's army, and the planters who followed in its track, and of banishing the native Irish "to hell or to Connaught," was soon carried into operation.

The commissioners appointed by the Parliament for the management of affairs in Ireland, revived the statutes passed in the reign of Elizabeth.

Twenty-eight days were allowed for the departure of all priests from the kingdom, but after that period, should any priest be detected in the country, "he incurred the guilt of high treason; he was therefore to be hanged, cut down while alive, beheaded, quartered, bowelled, and burned; the head to be set on a spike, and exposed in the most public place. Moreover, should any person entertain or harbor a priest, he shall suffer the confiscation of his property, and be put to death without the hope of mercy." Every exercise of the Catholic religion was declared a capital offence; spies and informers were to be seen in all directions scouring the country; a reward of five pounds was to be given for the apprehension of a priest, together with one-third part of the property of the person in whose house he shall be discovered.

These informers were likewise, by virtue of the edict, to be promoted to offices and dignities, as men who deserved well of the state. To this instrument of refined cruelty, the following supplement was soon after annexed: "And if any one shall know where a priest remains concealed, in caves, woods, or caverns, or if by any chance he should meet a priest on the highway, and not immediately take him into custody and present him before the next magistrate, such person is to be considered a traitor and an enemy to the republic. He is accordingly to be cast into prison, flogged through the public streets, and afterwards have his ears cut off. But should it appear that he kept up any correspondence or friendship with a priest, he is to suffer death."

Notwithstanding the threats and edicts, the commissioners and informers, the gibbets and terrors, that had for so many years been employed to overawe the nation and strip it of its faith, still the ancient religion of the country flourished as lively as ever in the hearts and affections of the people. Nor did they succeed in their scheme of extermination; numbers, no doubt, were swept away, but vast multitudes still remained shut up in the towns and villages, or scattered in countless thousands over the face of the country. This it was which filled their enemies with redoubled fury, and at length suggested the infernal design of converting the whole province of Connaught into one frightful national prison. In the year 1654, and on a given day, specified by the edict, every Catholic in the kingdom, without distinction of rank, age, or sex, was ordered to repair to Connaught. Around this province, which, from famine and the sword, had now become a desolate waste, certain boundaries were marked out, and within these precints were the wretched Catholics of Ireland enclosed, without food, raiment, or shelter — friendless, hopeless, and unpitied. "No pen can describe or mind conceive the frightful scenes of misery that now ensued. It was death to step beyond the limits; a Catholic found in any other part of the kingdom could (according to the laws of the regicides) be butchered by any private individual, without jury, or judge or magistrate. Famine, pestilence, and despair now set in; one thousand perished of hunger and disease; many cast themselves from rocks and promontories; numbers flung themselves into whirlpools and rivers; on one side they were repelled by the sea, on the other they were hemmed in by the sword of the slaughterer, while within the plantation of Connaught itself were to be seen the barren rocks, the walking spectres, and those other innumerable calamities that usually compose the awful train of the contemptible bigot, the usurper, and the tyrant."*

Such was the condition of Ireland under Cromwell's puritanical rule, which seemed to have for its aim not only the extermination of the Irish race, but also the extirpation of the Catholic faith.

Having thus given a synopsis of the state of affairs in

Morisson, p. 19.

BISHOP O'BRIEN OF EMLY.

The Right Rev. TERENCE ALBERT O'BRIEN, O. P., bishop of Emly, was a native of the city of Limerick, and a scion of the princely house of O'Brien. Brought up by pious Catholic parents, from his very boyhood he had a desire for the ministry, in which his parents encouraged him. His uncle, Maurice O'Brien, was prior of the Dominican convent of Limerick, and encouraged the pious wish of the boy, and had him received a novitiate of the Friars Preachers; thence he was sent to Toledo to finish his education. Having spent eight years there, he was ordained, and returned to his native city, and joined the Dominican house there. In 1643 he was elected provincial of the order at the Dominican chapter held in the Black Abbey,* Kilkenny, which had lately been restored to the order, and repaired by

---

* The Black Abbey in Kilkenny was founded in honor of the Holy Trinity, for Dominicans, by William Mareschal, Jr., earl of Pembroke, in the year 1225. This establishment maintained for centuries a high rank in the order; four general chapters have been held in it, namely: those of 1281, 1302, 1306, and 1346. Its last prior was Peter Cantwell; and in the 35th of Henry VIII. an inquisition was held, when the possessions, consisting of twenty-four houses, sixteen gardens, nineteen acres in Kilkenny, with one hundred and twenty acres, nine messuages, and the tithes and alterages of the same, were granted to Walter Archer, the sovereign, and to the burgesses and commonalty of Kilkenny, for ever, at the annual rent of twelve shillings and fourpence, Irish money. This ancient and beautiful abbey had been entirely demolished, with the exception of the tower and the principal south aisle of the church. About the year 1816 the abbey was repaired and beautified in a style of superior elegance; while its immense stately window of stained glass, and the other interior decorations, contrasted with the ivy-clad tower and the massive pile of mouldering ruins which surround it, have decidedly contributed to render the Black Abbey of Kilkenny one of the most venerable and magnificent remains of antiquity in the kingdom.

them; but, with the downfall of the Confederation, the abbey and its monks met the same fate.

He went to Rome the same year, to assist at a general chapter of the Dominicans. He was consecrated bishop of Emly in 1647. He found his new see in a most deplorable state, for the country had been ravaged and desolated by Inchiquin and his brutal soldiers. As a member of the Confederation, Dr. O'Brien had zealously supported the Nuncio, and approved of his excommunication of the abettors of the Ormond party. In 1650 the progress of the Cromwellian army compelled him to retire to Galway. He returned to Limerick just before its siege by Ireton, in 1651.*

Famine and the treachery of Colonel Fennell, combined, compelled a surrender of the city on the 29th of October, the articles of capitulation exempting twenty-four persons from quarter. Dr. O'Brien was one of the excluded, and, being arrested, was brought before Ireton, who ordered him to be tried before a court-martial. When asked did he want counsel, he calmly replied that he knew his doom, and only wanted a confessor. This boon was granted, and Father Hanrahan, a member of his own order, was suffered to pass the whole day and night of the 30th October with him in his prison cell.

On the following evening the finding of the court was announced to him, as he lay stripped on a pallet; and the officer charged with this duty gave him to understand that the sentence was to be carried out on the instant. On hear-

* I need not recapitulate here the well-known incidents of that heroic siege, in which the besieged suffered more by pestilence than from the efforts of the enemy. Eight thousand citizens perished by the pestilence, and the heroic missioners of St. Vincent of Paul, who were in the city, made the memory of their order dear to Catholic Ireland by their zeal in attending the sick, a task in which they were aided by Drs. Walsh, archbisop of Cashel, and O'Dwyer, bishop of Limerick, who were also in the city.

ing this he got up to dress himself, but before he had time to do so, the provost-marshal's guard pinioned his arms, and thrust him out of the cell almost in a state of nudity. It was only natural that his fine sense of delicacy should resent this cruel insult, but finding that all remonstrances were lost on the posse who surrounded him, he paused an instant, as if to collect himself, and said, in a solemn tone, that "*the time was not distant when Ireton should stand before God's tribunal to account for his bloody deeds.*" Surely they must have jeered him as a prophet of evil!*

It was a long way from the prison to the place of execution, and as the cortege proceeded it was encountered at every step by sights more appalling than that of a man going to the gallows. For two days previously Ireton's troops had been allowed to pillage and slay as they liked, and there was hardly a house that did not bear witness to their fierce licentiousness. Windows shattered, doors wrenched from the hinges, corses of men and women lying stark in the kennels, wares of every sort scattered and trodden under foot, showed that destructiveness had revelled to satiety. No living thing appeared along the route of that sad procession, and the universal stillness would have been

* It was on the 10th of November, when all this cold-blooded butchery was done, that Ireton was seized with the epidemic, which had been ravaging the whole island for nearly an entire year. In the course of a few days he grew gradually worse and more faint, and at length inflammatory fever supervened. "In his delirium," says Sir Philip Warwick, "he shouted repeatedly, 'Blood! blood! I must have more blood!'" and if we may believe other writers who had similar opportunities for informing themselves concerning the last moments of this cruel man, the Bishop of Emly was so palpably before him, that he had to turn his face to the wall to avoid the ghastly sight. In the wild outbursts of his frenzy he over and over again repeated that he was guiltless of the bishop's death, that he had no hand in it, and that the court-martial alone was responsible for the sentence and execution. Thus he raved in frightful terror until his death, which occurred eighteen days from the execution of the bishop.

unbroken were it not for the heavy tread of the doomed man's escort, and the ringing of their weapons as they clinked on the pavement. O'Brien, however, conducted himself with his accustomed firmness, and though distressed at being obliged to parade the deserted thoroughfares on that winter's evening in a state little short of absolute nakedness, his step was as steady and his bearing erect as either could have been on that memorable day when he followed the trophies of Benburb to St. Mary's Cathedral. On reaching the foot of the gibbet, he knelt and prayed till he was commanded to arise and mount the ladder. He obeyed, seized the rungs with vigorous grasp, and turned round, as if anxious to ascertain whether any of the citizens had ventured abroad to witness his death-scene. Having satisfied himself that a few of them were present, and within hearing, he exhorted them to continue true to the faith of their fathers, and hope for better days, when God would look with mercy on unhappy Ireland. A few moments more, and his soul was with the just.

Thus did Terence Albert O'Brien pass out of this life, on All Saints' Eve, 1651. As soon as life was extinct, the executioner lowered the body to the ground, and after the soldiers had discharged their muskets at it, he hacked off the head, and impaled it on the tower of St. John's gate, where it remained many a day, a ghastly evidence of Ireton's vindictiveness.*

With Bishop O'Brien perished Father JOHN COLLINS, another Dominican, who was also excluded from the terms of capitulation.

REV. JAMES WOLF, another Dominican, was also exempted and executed. He was an old man, and preacher-general, who had before been a long time in prison for the faith.

* Rev. C. P. Meehan's Memoirs of the Irish Hierarchy.

He was taken in Limerick while offering the Mass, and in a few hours afterwards was sentenced to be hung, and brought out into the market square, where he made a public profession of his faith, and exhorted the Catholics to constancy in the religion of their ancestors, and that with so much ardor that it moved his very enemies. Standing on the top step of the ladder, and about to be swung off, he joyously exclaimed: "*We are made a spectacle to God, and angels, and men—of glory to God, of joy to angels, of contempt to men.*"

O'Daly adds that he had been absent from the city during the siege, but that, when it was taken, and all the priests there either slain or driven away, zealous for the souls of the citizens, he secretly returned to administer the sacraments to them, but had hardly been there eight days when he was taken and hung.

It is probable that Father DAVID ROCHE, O. P. P., whom De Burgo mentions to have been sent as a slave to the West India tobacco plantations in this year, was taken at Limerick.

In 1646 the first Vincentians landed in Ireland, and established a house in Limerick. Abelly, in his "Life of St. Vincent de Paul," gives a feeling account of all they suffered, and all the good they did, both by precept and example, in encouraging the clergy to stick to their flocks, and in inspiring the people to withstand the persecution.

St. Vincent himself took special interest in the Church in Ireland, and sent much assistance, both in money, clothing, and church services and ornaments, to the suffering Catholics there; besides, he did a great deal for the poor, friendless priests and monks, who had to fly from the country

When the storm raged with all its fury, only three priests of the order remained in Ireland, but their labors were incessant, and an abundant spiritual harvest was their reward.

THE PURITANS IN IRELAND. 185

At that time there were twenty thousand communicants within the walls of Limerick. "The whole city assumed the garb of penance, to draw down the blessings and the grace of Heaven."

In April, 1650, St. Vincent wrote to the superior of the order, encouraging the members to meet courageously the dangers which then threatened them. In his letter he says :

"You have given yourselves to God, to remain immovably in the country where you now are, in the midst of perils, choosing rather to expose yourself to death than to be found wanting in charity to your neighbors. You have acted as true children of our most admirable Father, to whom I return infinite thanks for having produced in you that sovereign charity which is the perfection of all virtues."

As all priests and ecclesiastics were exempted from quarter, the night before the surrender of the city to Ireton, these holy men, sure that death awaited them on the morrow, passed the night in prayer and preparation.

They, however, to the number of about one hundred, escaped, in various disguises, mixed up with the garrison ; and after escaping from the city they separated.

Of the three Vincentians, one remained in the city to attend to the wants of the people, and was martyred. Father O'BRIEN went with the vicar-general of Cashel, who also escaped, while Father BARRY went towards the mountains, where he lay concealed for two months, until he succeeded in escaping to Naples.

Although these good priests escaped from that general massacre, the congregation paid its tribute to the persecution, and a lay-brother of the order, named Lee, being discovered by the heretics, was brutally put to death by them before the eyes of his own mother ; his hands and feet were first amputated, and his head was then crushed to atoms.*

Father Abelly mentions another martyr, whose name, however, is not given. He writes as follows:

"It happened that one of these heroic pastors, having gone to a missionary father (who lived in a cabin at the foot of a mountain) to make his annual retreat, was on the following night discovered in the act of administering the sacrament to some sick persons, and cut to pieces on the spot by the heretical soldiery. His glorious death crowned his innocent life, and fulfilled the great desire he had to suffer for our Lord, as he himself had declared in the preceding year at a mission given by the Vincentian Fathers in Limerick."

Here also we may hand down the names of those martyrs of charity who are known to have perished of the plague while attending the sick in this disastrous year.

Of these there are enumerated by De Burgo, of the Dominican order alone, in the year 1651: Fathers MICHAEL O'CLERY, prior of Waterford, at Waterford, and GERALD BAGOT; THADDÆUS O'CAHOLY, WILLIAM GERALDINE, and JOHN GERALDINE, of Limerick; and DONALD O'BRIEN, in County Clare; and of the Jesuits, Father FRANCIS WHITE, at Waterford.

GONER MATHEW, bishop of Clogher, while in the discharge of his duties, fell into the hands of Coote, one of Cromwell's most bloody persecutors, and was cast into Enniskillen jail, heavily laden with irons.

After several days he was executed, and embowelled; his head was cut off, and stuck on a pole in the public market.

The whole country was transformed into one scene of fearful carnage and desolation. Villages became a mass of ruins; towns and cities were stormed and plundered; in

* Acts of the order, and a letter of St. Vincent, ap. MOIAN.

short, the kingdom, from one extremity to the other, assumed the awful appearance rather of a region of death than of a land intended by Nature for the residence and happiness of human beings. The fury of the storm was particularly levelled against the altars and priesthood of the country. In rural districts, as well as in cities and towns, the churches were demolished, while the convents were converted into garrisons, in which the troops of Cromwell and his followers were quartered. Meanwhile the clergy, both secular and regular, were compelled to take refuge in the inaccessible morasses of the country, or amidst the rocks and caverns of the mountain. Some there were whom Providence protected, but a still greater number became victims; having heroically laid down their lives in testimony of the faith of their fathers.*

* Among the number of heroic exiles, we find Nicholas French, bishop of Ferns. Thomas Walsh, archbishop of Cashel, after having for a long time escaped the fury of his pursuers, by remaining concealed in that wild range of mountains which run between the counties of Tipperary and Cork, at length took shipping in one of the southern ports of the latter county, and, after a perilous voyage, arrived at Compostella, a town in the province of Gallicia, in Spain. Robert Barry, bishop of Cork and Cloyne, together with Patrick Comerford, bishop of Waterford and Lismore, proceeded to Nantz, and were received with great kindness and respect by both the clergy and people of that city. Edmund O'Dwyer, bishop of Limerick, and John Culenan, bishop of Raphoe, took refuge in Brussels. Walter Lynch, bishop of Clonfert, withdrew to Hungary. Edmund O'Dempsey, bishop of Leighlin, retired to Gallicia. Francis Kirwan, bishop of Killala, repaired to Rennes, in Brittany. Hugh Burke, bishop of Kilmacdua, was sheltered by his friends in England. Andrew Lynch, bishop of Kilfenora, found an asylum in Normandy, under the auspices of the illustrious primate, Francis de Harlai. Arthur Magennis, the venerable bishop of Down, after having been tossed about by storms for many days, and in consequence of his advanced age being but badly calculated to endure such hardship, was at length seized with a violent fever, and died on sea.

THE SWORD AND THE MITRE.

Bishop Heber MacMahon assumes the command of O'Neill's army—Brave and rash—His patriotism and execution—Coote's hostility—Governor King's kind interference—Progress of the plantation of Connaught—A large number of priests tortured and martyred—Cruel treatment of the prisoners on the island of Inisbofin—Numbers sold into slavery—Unrelenting persecution continued.

HEBER MAC MAHON.

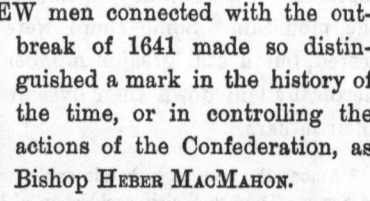

FEW men connected with the outbreak of 1641 made so distinguished a mark in the history of the time, or in controlling the actions of the Confederation, as Bishop HEBER MACMAHON.

Energetic, fearless, a devoted adherent of his religion and country, he was, in every sense, an opponent to be feared equally by the Puritans and the enemies of Ireland. Believing that both the liberties and religion of the country were identical, and that the heretics and Puritans sought the overthrow of one with the destruction of the other, he threw himself heart and soul into the cause of O'Neill. Descended from royal blood, he could not tamely submit to see the priests and people of the country hunted down with blood-hounds for adhering to the old faith; nor could he see the liberties of the people struck down by a foreign foe without raising his voice and arms in defence of both.

Heber MacMahon, son of Turlough MacMahon and Eva O'Neill, was born in Monaghan, in the year 1600. Descended from a royal and patriotic stock, young Heber was, from his very childhood, zealous in defence of the liberties of his country and the religion of his fathers. His mother was a pious lady, and used all her influence to bend his mind to an ecclesiastical life. In 1617 he entered the Irish college at Douay, which had been founded by an Irish ecclesiastic named Cusack. After his ordination he returned to Ireland, and kept alive the faith among the clansmen of the mountains.

At the commencement of the troubles of 1641, Father MacMahon informed Ormond that so great was the persecution of the Catholics of the North, that they would assuredly rise in arms unless their lives and properties were protected from the puritanical tyrants who opposed them; but this timely warning was utterly thrown away on Parsons and Borlase, whose aim was to goad the "papists" to rebellion, in order that they might share between them the remnant of property that was still in the hands of the latter. At length, however, endurance reached its extremest limit; the northern Catholics appealed to arms, and among those who were involved in the abortive attempt to seize Dublin castle and the persons of the lords-justices, was Hugh MacMahon, his near kinsman.

At the outbreak of the revolution, Father Heber exerted all his power and influence to restrain the licentiousness of the multitudes who flocked to the standard of Sir Phelim O'Neill and the other northern leaders, and such were his exertions in behalf of the Protestants, that many of them owed their lives and preservation of their property to his charitable interference. As soon, however, as the "rising" assumed the character of a general movement, he co-operated with Archbishop O'Reilly and the other prelates who assembled at Kells, and finally at Kilkenny, to direct the people in laying the foundations of the Confederacy. On all these occasions, the prelates and lay-lords gave attentive ear to his suggestion, and regarded him as one whose wisdom was only equalled by his well-known courage. At length, when the Confederacy was fully organized, and the prelates had resolved to fill those sees that were vacant, a memorial was forwarded to Rome, praying his holiness, Urban VIII., to promote MacMahon to the bishopric of Clogher, as no other could be found more deserving of such advancement, either by ancient descent or grand services rendered to the new government. The holy see granted the prayer of the petitioners, and MacMahon was consecrated at Drogheda, early in 1643, after having held the see of Down and Connor, as *bishop-elect* for two years previously.

He became the special favorite of Rinuccini, who looked upon him as his ideal of a true and energetic bishop. He was the intimate friend and adviser of Owen Roe O'Neill, who was chiefly directed and influenced by his council. It is unnecessary to follow the career and varying fortunes of this remarkable man in those stirring times. With O'Neill he shared the glory of Benburb, and labored hard to heal the unfortunate bickerings that distracted the council and armies of O'Neill and Preston.

In 1647, when the Ormond factions strove to get rid of the Nuncio, MacMahon boldly supported the latter against all the schemes and intrigues of Ormond, Muskery, Taaffe, Preston, and others. He also proved himself one of the most zealous enemies to the bloody Inchiquin, and thwarted many of his schemes and base plots.

The history of this soldier-bishop is but the history of the stirring times in which he lived. Banned, outlawed, and persecuted, he was driven, both for his own safety and the safety of his flock, to join the army under O'Neill.

After the death of the brave Owen Roe O'Neill, in November, 1649, the council of the officers of the Ulster army, convened at Belturbet, in March, 1650, and elected sturdy Bishop MacMahon as his successor. Unfortunately, the bishop's military knowledge and prudence were not equal to his zeal and bravery, and he soon frittered away the glorious Ulster army, with which the shrewd and able O'Neill threatened the safety of English rule in Ireland.

After assuming the command of the army, MacMahon returned to Ulster with his troops, storming, on his march, Dunginen, Ballycastle, and other places of no great importance. Coote's forces were fast concentrating to oppose him, and, on the 21st of June, 1650, the two armies confronted each other. MacMahon's more experienced generals urged him not to give battle to Coote, but he, with his usual determination of character, resolved to encounter the enemy.

Coote had selected a strong position on the banks of the Swilly, which the Irish troops attacked with fierce impetuosity; but after a few hours desperate fighting, they were routed with fearful slaughter. It was indeed a disastrous battle to the Irish—ill advised—and was followed by a long train of calamities.

Bishop MacMahon, accompanied by a squadron of horse, made his escape from the fatal field, but they were attacked by a detachment from the garrison of Enniskillen, which routed his escort, and carried him a prisoner to Enniskillen.

The governor of Enniskillen, John King, treated the bishop kindly, and took a great liking to him, and tried to save his life. His influence was useless, for Coote resolved that MacMahon should die. So great was King's regard for the bishop that, when he could not save his life, he rode away from Enniskillen, so that he might not witness his death.

The close of MacMahon's career was such as might have

been expected from one, a goodly portion of whose life had been divided between the church and the camp; and much as the Cromwellian troopers admired his undaunted resolution, they never were so deeply impressed by it as on that July evening when they escorted him to the ancient castle of Enniskillen—the place appointed for his execution. Marching some paces in advance of the musketeers, his bearing was calm, dignified, and martial; so much so, that a casual wayfarer might have mistaken him for the officer in command, were it not for the presence of an ecclesiastic (with whom he conversed in tones inaudible to every one else), and a small gold crucifix that he kept constantly moving between his lips and eyes. On reaching the scaffold he knelt and prayed in silence for a while, and then, turning to the troops who kept the ground, told them that he thanked God for having given him that opportunity of laying down his life in the cause of religion, king, and country. MacMahon's soul had scarcely gone to its account, when the executioner, in compliance with the barbarous usage of the times, flung the corse to the ground, hacked off the head, and spiked it on the tower of the castle, where it remained till birds of prey, rain, storm, and time destroyed every vestige of the ghastly trophy. The mutilated trunk, however, had a happier fate, for Major General King allowed some sympathizing Catholics to convey it to Devenish island, where it waits the resurrection, under the shadow of St. Laserian's oratory.*

In the year 1652 the persecution raged with fearful violence; the plantation of Connaught was fast progressing, and never did human beings labor with more zeal to exterminate noxious animals than did the planters to weed out the native Irish. The law, the gibbet, the bayonet, and the

* Rev. C. P. Meehan on the "Irish Hierarchy."

bloodhound were brought into requisition to persecute, hang, and hunt down the "mere Irish."

FATHERS LAWRENCE and BERNARD O'FARRALL, brothers, were seized about this time, while praying in the convent of Longford; the latter was killed on the spot, while the former was executed with all the cruelty and insults that characterized such murderers.

FATHER AMBROSE O'CAHILL, of the convent of Cork, was seized by a troop of horse, and by them cut to pieces.*

FATHERS WILLIAM O'CONNOR, THOMAS O'HIGGINS, and WILLIAM LYNCH, O. P. P., of the convent of Clonmel, were cruelly martyred about the same time.

FATHER VINCENT DILLON, of the convent of Athenry, who was of a noble family, died in prison from sufferings and cruelty.

In the same year, FATHER STEPHEN PETIT, of the same convent, while attending a wounded soldier, was shot down and killed.

DONATUS O'BRIEN was shot by the soldiers in Thomond for his faith about the same time.

REV. BERNARD FITZPATRICK was a most pious and holy priest of Ossory, who was driven for security to the mountains. One day, while entering his cave, he was tracked by

* The Franciscan convent of Cork, usually called Gray Abbey, was founded for Conventual Franciscans by Philip Prendergast, on the north side of the city, A. D. 1240. Henry III. and Edward I were great benefactors to this convent. A provincial chapter had been held here in 1291; and about the close of the fifteenth century, the rule of the Strict Observants had been adopted. Several illustrious members of the house of Desmond had been interred within the walls of this abbey, particularly Cormac, king of Desmond, in 1247, Dermot, in 1275, and Thadæus, in 1413. In the 8th of Elizabeth, this convent, with its appurtenances, forty acres, and seven gardens, was granted to Andrew Skydie and his heirs. Though the houses and lands of several convents were confiscated under Henry and Elizabeth, we find communities in possession at a much later period.

the soldiers, followed, and shot down.* His head was taken to Kilkenny, and spiked over the town gate.

Rev. Denis Nelan was descended from noble parents, of Limerick, and was parish priest of Kilragty. He was seized by the Puritan soldiers, and dragged to their camp at Cunon. When jeered about his religion by the soldiers, he commenced to harangue them upon the enormity of their sins and wickedness. His sermon was cut short by the soldiers, who, amidst jeers and scoffs, hung him from a temporary gallows.

Father Thadeus Carighy, of the convent of Inish, shared the same fate in 1651.

Rev. Roger Macnamara, O. S. F., of Clare, was cruelly murdered by the Cromwellian soldiers in the same year.

Among those who suffered persecution and martyrdom about this time were Daniel Clanchy, of Thomond, who was hung; Jeremiah Nerihing, Rev. Eugene O'Leman, of Donegal.

Revs. Donatus O'Kenedy, Donatus Screnan, Fulgentius Jordan, Romandus O'Maly, Thomas Tully, and Thomas Deir, of the order of Hermits of St. Augustine, were all martyred for the faith about the same time.

Rev. Francis Sullivan, O. S. F., was of the race of the chiefs of Baer and Bantry. He was appointed over the province in 1650, and governed his flock with unerring devotion. When the persecution became too warm he had to fly to the mountains of Cork and Kerry, from the fury of the heretics. Thousands of the peasantry had to

* It was no unusual thing for the persecutors to track the outlawed priests to their caves in the mountains, and then watch them until the poor peasants collected to hear Mass, when all were either shot down or smothered in the cave. In the Galtee Mountains is such a cave, called to this day *Uaibh-na-Sogart*, or the Cave of the Priests, where tradition says a poor fugitive priest and his congregation of some sixty persons, were all smothered or shot down while assisting at the sacrifice of the Mass.

seek the same shelter from their persecutors, and rallied around their poor outlawed priest. For a time he sheltered himself in the ruins of Mucross Abbey;* but even this poor retreat was denied him, and he had to fly to the mountains. He lived for some time in the lonely retreat of Gougane Barra, where he had erected a kind of rude altar and oratory of stones, with a large rustic cross raised from the centre. Here the good priest frequently celebrated Mass, surrounded by the poor outlawed Catholics of the neighborhood.

It is hard for us now to realize the feelings of this poor but pious congregation. While they knelt in prayer the bloodhounds were on their track, and human bloodhounds, more cruel still, were thirsting for their blood, and hunting out their hiding-place, to slay them.

Father Sullivan and his flock did not escape their enemies. Their retreat being discovered, a posse of soldiers was sent to hunt them down. The poor priest was saying Mass in one of the mountain caves, when he and his little flock were surrounded. Some of the soldiers who entered the cave shot the priest at the altar, and then set fire to brush piled at the mouth of the cave, and thus smothered the rest. Having done this, they closed up the entrance, thus burying their unfortunate victims in their tomb.†

* The convent of Irielagh (Mucross), in the barony of Magunihy, county of Kerry, was founded for Conventual Franciscans, by Donald M'Carthy, in the year 1440; since that period, this convent has become the general cemetery of the M'Carthy family It was rebuilt by the Catholics in the beginning of the reign of James I., but owing to the intolerance of that monarch, it soon became a heap of ruins. In the 37th of Elizabeth, a grant was made of this convent, together with the abbey of Innisfallen, to Robert Collan, to hold the same for ever, by fealty, at a trifling yearly rent.

† We have it from good antiquarian authority, that the bones found in many of the caves in Ireland are those of the victims of the persecution of the penal times, who were either smothered or shot down, while attending Mass. In some cases, rude altar service have been found with the skeletons.

Brother Anthony Broder, of the Franciscan order, was taken prisoner near Lough Derighert, County Galway. He was hunted down by Coote, and cruelly executed.

Rev. Hilary Conry, O. S. F., was a native of Roscommon, and born of noble parents. While begging for his convent at Elphin, he was seized by Coote, carried to Castle Coote, and there hanged.

Dr. Francis Kirwan, bishop of Killala, and several other clergymen, were seized about this time, and treated with great cruelty.

After the surrender of Galway to Ludlow, in March, 1652, the priests had to fly, and the fine abbey was levelled, thus rendering the monks outcasts.* The towns-people were compelled to pay a tax for the support of the Cromwellian soldiers. This pressed so heavily on them that many of them left the place. The Irish not being expelled fast enough to satisfy their enemies, in July, 1655, an order was issued, directing all the Irish inhabitants to quit the town before the 1st of November following; and, if they failed to do so, they were to be expelled at the point of the bayonet; which cruel order was fully carried out.

Colonel Stubbers was appointed military governor of Galway after its surrender. He was a pious Puritan, that loudly sang canticles to the Lord as he sentenced Catholic

* The convent of Galway had been originally the nunnery of St Mary of the Hill, and was daughter to that of the Holy Trinity of the Premonstratenses of Tuam. It continued for some time in the possession of the secular clergy until Pope Innocent VIII , at the request of the inhabitants, and by a bull dated the 4th of December, 1488, made a grant of it to the Dominicans. This convent has been justly celebrated for its learned professors; among whom may be noticed Peter French, author of the "Exposition of the Christian Faith," and Dominick Lynch, who, in 1674, became a distinguished teacher of moral and natural philosophy. The convent of Galway continued to flourish until the year 1652, when it was totally demolished by the towns-people, lest it might fall into the hands of Cromwell, and be converted into a fortress against themselves

THE SWORD AND THE MITRE.

priests and people to torture and death, or to be sent to the slaughter pens established on the islands of Arran and Inisbofin, preparatory to their transportation to the West India Islands, to be sold as slaves.

These terrible prisons were soon full of wretched victims, without regard to rank or condition. Among these were about sixty clergymen and several religious.

The hardships endured by these brave martyrs for the faith were terrible. Their only shelter from the heat, cold, and inclemency of the weather, were temporary huts and mud cabins; while they were allowed but two pence each for their daily support.

To add to their misery, squads of Stubbers' troops were daily scouring the country for new victims, whom they consigned to the already overcrowded prison-pens. It is conjectured that nearly two thousand victims were at one time huddled together on those islands, the most of whom were shipped to the West Indies to be sold as slaves.*

* Brenan, in his "Ecclesiastical History of Ireland," gives the following list of priests, who, in 1653, were confined as prisoners in Inisbofin, or shut up in the jails of Cork and Galway, namely:

Rev. James Fallen, V G ; Rev Roger Commin, secular priest ; Rev. Gerald Davock, Dominican ; Rev Brien Comy, Franciscan ; Rev. Thomas Bourke, Franciscan ; Rev. Philip Walsh, secular priest ; Rev. Thomas Grady, secular priest ; Rev Timothy Mannin, secular priest ; Rev. Miles Tully, secular priest ; Rev. Patrick Trevor, secular priest ; Rev John Kelly, secular priest ; Rev. McLeighlin Conry, secular priest ; Rev Anthony Geoghegan, abbot ; Rev. John Dillon, Dominican ; Rev. Thomas McKernan, Franciscan ; Rev. Edward Delamar, secular priest ; Rev. Terlagh Gavan, secular priest ; Rev John Russell. V. G.; Rev. W. Henessy, secular priest ; Rev William Farrell, secular priest ; Rev Redmond Roche. secular priest, Rev. Conner Keilly, secular priest, Rev. Denis Horgan, secular priest, Rev Henry Burgat, Dominican ; Rev. Timothy Donovan, Franciscan ; Rev. Connor Hurly, Franciscan ; Rev James Slevin, Rev. Thomas Roony, Rev Connor Scanlan, Franciscans ; Rev Bernard Comins, Dominican ; Rev Bonaventure Dant, Rev. Thomas Burke, Rev Francis Horan, Rev Thomas McKernan, Rev. Terence Gavan, Rev. Hugh McKeon, secular priests.

During the persecution under Stubbers, Dr. KIRWAN, bishop of Killala, lay concealed in the country in a small cabin, only issuing out at nights to visit his poor, persecuted flock, who sought shelter and protection in the mountains and caves. At length his health broke down, and for months he was confined to an humble bed of straw in the corner of the miserable cabin which he usually occupied. On one occasion his enemies came in search of him, but seeing only a poor sick old man upon a miserable bed, they did not for a moment think it was the bishop. They dragged the old "Papist Canamite" out of the bed to search it for arms. Having somewhat recovered, he returned to Galway, resolved to brave death at his post of duty. After several hair-breadth escapes, he fell into the hands of his enemies. He and several other ecclesiastics were treated in the most cruel and inhuman manner, and then sent to the island prisoners.

In 1665 he was put on board the convict ship at Galway, and, in company with the Archbishop of Tuam, and several priests and ecclesiastics, was exiled to Nantes.

REV. BONAVENTURE DE BURGO, O. S. F., was son of Oliver De Burgo, lord of Ropy, in the County Mayo. Having embraced a clerical life, he became an object of hatred to his Protestant neighbors, who persecuted him for his faith. In 1652, he and Thaddeus Connor, lord of Bealnamilly, were tried; and, having maintained their faith, were executed together.

REV. ANTHONY O'FARRELL, O. S. F., was, according to Bruodin, taken while preaching, by the Cromwellians, at Tulsk, in Roscommon, in the castle of Sir Ulysses De Burgo, and immediately hung, anno 1652.

REV. JOHN CAROLAN, S. J., was so hunted to death by the soldiers, in the mountains of Galway, that the good old man perished from cold and hunger.

Rev. Eugene O'Cahan, O. S. F., was descended from a noble family of Thomond, and entered the Franciscan convent for Irish. After his profession he proceeded to Rome, and there, in the college of St. Isidore, under the learned Fathers Luke Wadding, Anthony Hickey, James Bridges, and Thaddeus Daly, who then presided over it, he made rapid progress in learning and religion. Bruodin states that Father Eugene returned to Ireland and opened a school in the town of Quenhi,* in Thomond, which became so famous that, in 1644, under the temporary spell of Catholic toleration, it numbered over eight hundred students. Under the Commonwealth it was broken up, and Father Eugene was made guardian of the convent of Irish, which had been founded by the O'Briens. In 1651 he was seized by the soldiers, and cruelly scourged until his body became a mass of sores and wounds.

Having failed, with all their persecutions, in inducing him to recant, they hanged him on Mount Luochren, in Thomond, in the year 1651.

Father Roger Ormly was a native of Clare, and was for thirty years parish priest of Brentire. By his zeal and attention to the spiritual wants of his poor flock, he drew on himself the vengeance of the Puritan soldiers, then ravaging Clare. At length they seized him, and when he confessed himself a priest, he was hung, and so gained everlasting life, on the 12th October, 1652.

In the same year, day, and place, and by the same death, Father Hugh Carighy obtained the crown of martyrdom. He was a parish priest of Clare, and in the seventy-sixth year of his age, and the forty-fourth of his priesthood.

* Ware calls it Quinchy, where a convent of Friars Minors was founded in 1433, by Macon Macnemarra.

THE IRISH EXPELLED AND HANGED.

Persecution and martyrdom of several noble ladies and nuns—Father Fogarty martyred in Holy Cross—The tomb of the O'Fogartys—Borlase accused of the persecutions in Ireland—What Morisson says—Prendergast's Cromwellian settlement—Several priests persecuted—The Irish expelled—Persecutions slacken for want of victims.

IN the time of the Commonwealth, the Church in Ireland was reduced to the lowest ebb. Bishops, priests, and ecclesiastics of all kinds were forced to seek shelter and protection from the fierce storm of persecution, in the forests and caves of the mountains, where they were hunted by bloodhounds, and shot down in mere sport and wanton cruelty. It was justly said of this period:

"Our people trod like vermin down, all 'fenceless flung to sate,
Extortion, lust, and brutal whim, and rancorous bigot hate;
Our priesthood tracked from cave to hut, like felons chased and lashed,
And from their ministering hands the lifted chalice dashed."

The persecutions of the Catholic clergy and people of Ireland, from their commencement, under Henry, to their termination, exceeded in intensity, bitter cruelty, and devilish ingenuity of newly-devised tortures, those of the early Christians, who were strangled or tortured to death in the dungeons of Rome, or flung into the amphitheatre, the prey of hungry lions, to grace a Roman holiday, and to glut the savage hate of the enemies of Christianity.

What torture could be devised more excruciating or more horrible, than placing the victim in stocks, with his feet in long tin boots, filled with oil, and then lighting a slow fire around the boots until the oil boiled, and eat the flesh into the very bones? Just fancy the torture the poor victims endured, and it will not be wondered that shrieks and groans were often wrung from their unconquered hearts. Few of us but have either felt or witnessed the painful effects of a burn; but the pain of the worst burn is but a mere trifle to the sufferings of being thus slowly boiled alive. Yet, this was a favorite mode of torture, by the English and Puritans, for their Irish victims. Another mode, not less savage, was the rack, an instrument by which the whole frame was stretched until the very bones were torn from their sockets, and the quivering body extended several inches. The thumb-screw was another of these mild inventions, which the English imported in order to convert the Irish; by their agency the joints were compressed until the blood burst from the flesh and the very nails flew off the fingers.

It is sickening to follow the disgusting details of the fearful, racking engines of torture, which were employed by the Reformers—these meek followers of Christ—in order to root Catholicity out of Ireland. On the other hand, it is a glorious record to point back to the hundreds—aye, thousands—of martyrs, who nobly spurned life and liberty, and meekly submitted to be boiled, scourged, extended on the rack, half hung, and, while breathing, disembowelled; with their hearts and livers torn from their palpitating bodies, and all, sooner than sell their souls by denying the old, glorious Catholic religion.

In our times of freedom and toleration, we can look back with pride and sorrow upon the penal days—pride at the proud heritage and noble record left us by our ancestors; sorrow, that a Christian people should leave on the pages of history so black a record as that of the English persecutors in Ireland. With this short digression, we resume our sketches of the martyrs and confessors of the period.

Rev. Neilan Locheran, O. S. F., was a native of Ulster, and a Franciscan of the convent of Armagh, where he made his profession about his twentieth year, and made great progress in virtue. The good father was taken prisoner by the soldiers of Londonderry, and dragged to that town, with his hands tied behind his back, like a robber. After he had endured tortures, the governor ordered him to be brought before him, and offered him a wife and a good benefice if he would apostatize. Nielan, with an angelic courage, replied that he had, following the example of St. Peter the Apostle, voluntarily relinquished all, that he might gain Christ, and that he would not, by looking back, deprive himself of the reward promised in heaven; nay, he exhorted the governor to save his soul, redeemed with the blood of Christ, by abjuring heresy and embracing the Catholic faith. Furious at this audacity, the governor at once ordered him to be hanged. Joyfully did Father Locheran go to the place of execution, and was then hung, anno 1652.*

Lady Roche and Lady Fitzpatrick were among the many pious matrons, virgins, and nuns who suffered martyrdom about this period. The martyrdom of chiefs, nobles, prelates, priests, friars, and citizens could not satiate the thirst for "papist blood" that fired the ranting Cromwellians; but tender women, innocent maidens, and pious nuns alike fell victims to their savage cruelty. Lady Roche, wife of Maurice, viscount Fermoy and Roche, a chaste and holy woman, was hanged in Cork, in 1654, on a false charge of murder, brought against her by an English maid-servant, while her real crime was in being an unflinching Catholic. About the same time, Lady Fitzpatrick, wife of one of the barons of Ossory, was hanged by the Protestants of Dublin.

Though we have numerous instances of how Catholics were tortured and put to death for harboring priests, we

---

* Bruodin, lib. iv., cap. xv.

quote the following from Morisson. He tells us that a gentleman of Thomond, named Daniel Connery, was accused of harboring a priest in his house, and sentenced to death, which was commuted to perpetual exile. He left a wife and twelve children, all of whom died of starvation, except three daughters, who were shipped as slaves to Barbadoes.

Daniel Mollony was going home from Limerick, and, on his way chanced to meet at an inn a relation of his, a priest. The priest, Father Mollony, was betrayed, and because Daniel refused to give evidence against him, his ears were cut off. Morisson naively adds: "I could give a thousand such examples."

Father O'Cullinan, of the convent of Athenry,* was a most learned and pious man, and on this account was sorely persecuted. He was at length hunted down, and being carried into Limerick, he was fairly butchered by his enemies, and his head was cut off and borne about on a spear.

Father Edmund O'Bern, of the convent of Roscommon,† was seized about the same time, and actually cut in pieces by the soldiers of the garrison of Johnstown, who had captured him.

Rev. James Fogarty, a very worthy and exemplary priest, was for some time parish priest of Thurles. His piety, zeal, and religious perseverance drew down upon him the hatred of the Cromwellian soldiers and settlers, who persecuted him with their usual malignity. Being forced to fly from his parish, he wandered through the neighboring coun-

---

* The convent of Athenry, in the county of Galway, was founded in 1241, by Meyler De Bermingham, baron of Athenry. General chapters were held here in 1242 and 1311. In the 16th of Elizabeth, this convent, with thirty acres of land, was granted to the burgesses of the town of Athenry, at the yearly rent of one pound six shillings and fourpence.

† The convent of St. Mary, Roscommon, had for its founder Felim O'Conor, king of Connaught, in 1253. In 1615 this convent, with sixty-eight acres of land, was conferred on Francis, viscount Valentia.

try, ministering to the spiritual wants of the people. After some time, he and a few pious followers sought shelter in the ruins of the abbey of Holy Cross,* which had been previously despoiled. Here the poor Catholics flocked, in the silence of the night, to join the good priest in religious exercise, and to attend the holy sacrifice of the Mass before they left in the morning. Their wants were supplied by the poor worshippers from their scanty means. The priest-hunters and their bloodhounds were on their track, and soon discovered their retreat. They murdered the priest and one of his companions at the altar of the old church, and flung their mangled bodies into the Suir ; fortunately, the rest were absent at the time, and escaped. Father O'Fogarty's body was recovered, and buried in the church, where is still to be seen the tomb of the O'Fogarty's.†

* The abbey of Holy Cross, in the barony of Eliogorty and county of Tipperary, was so called on account of a piece of the *true* cross it possessed, which had been presented in the year 1100 to Muitagh, monarch of Ireland, by Pope Pascal II., and subsequently adorned with gold and precious stones, and enshrined in this abbey. It was founded in 1182, by Donald O'Brian, king of North Munster, in honor of the Holy Cross, for monks of the Cistercian Order. Its abbot was styled Earl of Holy Cross ; he was a lord of Parliament and vicar-general of the Cistercians in Ireland The last abbot was William O'Dwyre In the 5th of Elizabeth, the abbey and two hundred and twenty acres of land in Holy Cross, twenty acres in Thurles, and one hundred and eighty acres in other places, parcel of its possessions, were granted to Gerald, earl of Ormond. The architecture of this abbey was uncommonly splendid. The very ruins, which to this day occupy a considerable space, may serve to point out the former greatness of this once celebrated establishment. Its steeple, supported by an immense Gothic arch, with a display of ogives springing diagonally from the angles has been greatly admired. The choir is forty-nine feet broad and fifty-eight feet long, with lateral aisles On the south side of the choir are two chapels, intersected by a double row of Gothic arches ; and on the north side are two other chapels, finished in the same style as the former. The river Suir flows near the base of these extensive and awfully magnificent ruins.

† There is a strange tradition connected with the tomb of the O'Fogartys in Holy Cross abbey It is said that a chief of that name killed

Rev. Thaddeus Moriarty, O. P. P., prior of the convent of Tralee,* suffered much persecution. He refused to leave the country, but remained concealed in the mountains around Killarney, ministering to the wants of the scattered Catholics. At length he was seized, and hung in Killarney. On the trap he exhorted the people to faith and constancy, and advised them to suffer all things sooner than give up their religion; then, having recited the verse, "Into Thy hands, O Lord, I commend my spirit," he fearlessly, but hopefully, met his death.

Father Bernard O'Reilly, of Roscommon, after much suffering in prison, was taken to Galway and executed for the faith.

In 1653, the severest penal enactments were revived against Catholics, by which all ecclesiastics were commanded to leave the kingdom within twenty days, under penalty of being judged guilty of high treason.

It is no wonder that the persecution, if possible, increased, and that priests and people were driven wholesale from the country.

---

the son of a widow, who was celebrated for her wisdom as an herb doctress. She heard of the murder of her son while collecting herbs at a place now called Killough-hill. It is stated that, in her fright and grief, she flung down the herbs she had collected, from which sprung every herb known to grow in Ireland, and since the hill is called the garden of Ireland. This widow cursed the O'Fogartys, and prayed that some visible mark of Divine wrath would follow them for seven generations After O Fogarty's death, water commenced to fall from the dry roof of the abbey upon his tomb, and never ceased, winter or summer, until the seventh generation became extinct. This, in course of time, wore a hole some three inches deep in the stone, which is yet to be seen. Persons still living are said to have witnessed the falling of the water, which has been called in Irish the *Braon Sensear Mhuantire Fhogartaugh* (the ancestral drop of the O'Fogartys)

* The convent of Tralee, in Kerry, under the invocation of the Holy Cross, was founded by Lord John Fitz-Thomas, in 1243. It became the general cemetery of the Desmond family.

Borlase, the Protestant historian, estimates the number of Irish transported in the year 1654 at twenty-seven thousand. A contemporary document states that no less than twenty thousand Irish took refuge in the Hebrides and other Scottish islands. Dr. Burgatt, agent of the Irish clergy in Rome, afterwards archbishop of Cashel, in a relation presented to the Sacred Congregation in 1667, says:

"In the year 1649, there were in Ireland twenty-seven bishops, four of whom were metropolitans. In each cathedral there were dignitaries and canons; each parish had its pastors; there were, moreover, a large number of other priests, and innumerable convents of the regular clergy. But when Cromwell persecuted the clergy, all were scattered. More than three hundred were put to death by the sword or on the scaffold, among whom were three bishops; more than a thousand were sent into exile, and among these all the surviving bishops, with one only exception, the Bishop of Kilmore, who, weighed down by age and infirmities, as he was unfit to discharge the episcopal functions, so too was he unable to seek safety by flight. And thus for some years our island remained deprived of its bishops, a thing never known during the many centuries since we first received the light of Catholic faith."

At this time the Catholic church of Ireland was reduced to a most deplorable condition. "Neither the Israelites," says Morisson, "were more cruelly persecuted by Pharaoh, nor the infants by Herod, nor the Christians by Nero, Diocletian, or any other pagan tyrant, than were the Roman Catholics of Ireland at that juncture." Never did the host of hell put forth half such violence, even in Ireland; never did any religion, in any country, survive so bloody a persecution, or withstand such infernal machinery, as were then levelled against the Irish Church. The clergy of every grade and order were driven by the law into perpetual banishment; and if they dared to remain in the kingdom, or return to it again, after the 1st February, 1653, they were condemned to be hanged till half dead, then cut down alive and beheaded, their heads put upon poles on the highways, and their hearts and entrails publicly burned.

Nuns and religious ladies did not escape the fury of the persecutors, for many of them were tortured and put to death with a cruelty that even savages would not inflict upon their victims.

We read that Lady HONORIA DE BURGO, who had become a professed nun, was so persecuted that she fled, accompanied by SISTER HONORIA MAGAEN, to Holy Island, for shelter and protection. Her retreat was discovered, and her savage persecutors first despoiled her of everything, even to her clothes, though it was in the depth of winter, and then flung her into a boat, breaking her ribs by their violence. Thinking her dead they left, when her servant carried her to the church of Burishool, where she died, praying before the altar of the Blessed Virgin.

Sister Magaen was taken prisoner by the same party of soldiers, and stripped almost naked. Fearing even greater violence, she managed to escape, and hide herself in the trunk of a hollow tree, which she dared not leave for fear of falling into their hands. On the following day she was found dead of cold, with her hands raised to heaven. The martyred sisters were buried in one tomb.

REV. HUGH MACGOELLY, O. P. P., was master of the novices of the convent of Rathbran, county of Mayo. With pious zeal he proceeded to visit the Catholics in Waterford. He was soon arrested, and sentenced to be hanged. Standing under the gallows, he exhorted the people to adhere to their religion, despite persecution and death. He was martyred in the year 1654.

Dr. Moran, in his work on the state of the Catholic church

in Ireland, says: "We lived for the most part in the mountains and forests; and often, too, in the midst of bogs, to escape the cavalry of the heretics. One priest, advanced in years, Father JOHN CAROLAN, was so diligently sought for, and so closely watched, being surrounded on all sides, and yet not discovered, that he died of starvation. Another, Father CHRISTOPHER NETTERVILLE, like St. Athanasius, for an entire year and more lay hid in his father's sepulchre. One was concealed in a deep pit, from which, at intervals, he went forth on some mission of charity." He then enumerates the hardships, trials, and sufferings of several priests, who were either persecuted or martyred for the faith.

FATHER TOBIN, of Kilkenny, was a most pious and exemplary priest. Despite the grievous persecution, he remained, administering to the wants of the Catholics in the diocese of Ossory. He was tracked and banned by those worthless minions of the law, the "priest-hunters," who made their living by tracking priests and receiving five pounds for their head or capture. He, for some time, took refuge in the splendid ruins of the priory of Kells.* Even here he was not safe. His quiet and solemn retreat was discovered, and he was forced to fly. He next visited Cal-

---

* The priory of Kells, in the barony of Kells and county of Kilkenny, was founded, under the invocation of the Blessed Virgin Mary, by Geoffry Fitz-Robert, for Canons Regular of St. Augustin, in 1193. This foundation was confirmed by Felix O'Dullany, bishop of Ossory, and by various charters during the reigns of Richard II, Henry IV, and other monarchs. The prior of Kells sat as a baron in Parliament. Its last prior was Philip Holegan, under whom, in the 31st of Henry VIII, its possessions had been surrendered, viz: forty-five messuages and two hundred and ten acres of arable land in Kells, together with thirty-three messuages, three water-mills, and eleven hundred acres of wood and arable land in Desert, Grange, and other parts of the county of Kilkenny, and the rectories of Kells, Knoctopher, Kilmaganey, Burnchurch, and twelve others, all situated in the said county. This priory, and six carucates of land, with the rectory of Kells, were granted, in capite, to James, earl of Ormond.

lan,* and was concealed for some time by the good Catholics of the place. He next sought shelter there in the ruined priory, but was ruthlessly dragged from it by his enemies. He was thrown into prison while suffering from violent fever, and left to sleep upon the bare floor. Whether he died of the fever, or was martyred, is not related.

After the suppression of the Franciscan convent of Carrick-on-Suir,† members of the order occasionally resorted to its ruins, with the vain hope that persecution would cease, and that the confiscated property would be restored to the order.

About the year 1656, two of the brothers, named WHITE and POWER, who frequented the abbey and made it their retreat, were seized by the Cromwellian soldiers, and cruelly put to death.

It would be but a repetition of the bloody catalogue to narrate the sufferings, persecutions, and, in numerous cases, the martyrdom of the thousands who suffered for the faith

* The convent of Callan, in the barony of Kells, county of Kilkenny, had for its founder James, earl of Ormond, about the year 1487. The last prior was William O'Fogarty. On the 13th of December, 1557, this convent, with four acres in Callan, three gardens, and three messuages, together with the abbey of Athassel, in the county of Tipperary, was granted for ever to Thomas, earl of Ormond.

† The convent of Carrick-on-Suir, in the barony of Upper-third, county of Waterford, was founded in 1336 by James, earl of Ormond, for Conventual Franciscans, John Glynn, the celebrated annalist, from the convent of Kilkenny, having been the first guardian. The last superior was William Cormac, in 31st of Henry VIII, when this convent, with the appurtenances, twelve messuages, ten gardens, and one hundred and fifty acres of land, in the vicinity of Carrick, was granted to Thomas, earl of Ormond. The elegance and ancient splendor of this venerable establishment may be readily collected from the very ruins which happened to escape the ravages of time and of persecution. Some fragments of the church still remain, while the steeple, rising from a single stone, like ah inverted pyramid, stands at this day an existing monument of the taste and architectural skill of ancient times.—*Brenan*.

about this time. Those who were not executed were thrown into prison, and exiled or transported to the West India Islands, where they were sold as slaves. In 1653 two English merchants, named Sellick and Leader, signed a contract with the government for a consignment of two hundred and fifty women and three hundred men, to be captured in the neighborhood of Cork, Youghal, Kinsale, Waterford, and Wexford. Lord Broghill deemed it unnecessary to have such a hunt for a cargo of "mere Irish," and engaged to supply the whole number from the County Cork alone. In November, 1655, all the Irish of Lackagh, County Kildare, were seized by the government. Of these, four were hanged, and the rest, including two priests, were sent as slaves to Barbadoes. In the same year the commissioners wrote to the governor of Barbadoes, informing him of the approach of a ship, with a cargo of proprietors, deprived of their lands, and seized for not transplanting.

Among the priests who suffered martyrdom about this time were Father JOHN FLANERTY, O. P. P., of the convent of Coleraine, who was stoned to death by the soldiers, and Father JAMES O'REILLY, of the same order and convent.

REV. JOHN O'LAIGHLIN, of Derry*, was strangled in prison, and his head cut off and stuck on a pole.

It is sickening to follow the catalogue of bishops, priests, and people put to death or exiled for the faith. The un-

* The monastery of Derry was founded by St. Columbkill, about the year 546. This abbey became a constant scene of plunder during the ravages of the Danes, and particularly under the government of the abbot Gilla O'Brenain, and of his successor, Gill Chiist O'Keainich, when the noted Rotsel Pitun was defeated by the O'Neils, and his troops routed with dreadful slaughter. By a decree passed at the Council of Brigh-Macthighe, in the county of Meath, in 1158, the abbot of Derry had supreme jurisdiction over all the abbeys of the Columbian order in the kingdom; and its superiors continued in regular succession until the sixteenth century, when its possessions, of which we have no exact account, became involved in the general confiscation.

shaken fortitude of the bishops and priests martyred seemed but to confirm the faith of the people, and the government changed their tactics, and, instead of executing them, either exiled them or sent them to be sold as slaves in the West Indies.

From the year 1641 to 1660 the persecution had nearly exterminated the Catholics, till the persecutors slackened, rather from diminution of victims than from want of animosity. In 1641, according to Sir William Petty, the Catholics in Ireland were about 1,240,000; in 1659, there were only 413,984 persons of Irish descent in Ireland, which therefore must have been the maximum number of Catholics left, or, in other words, in these eight years 826,000 Irish Catholics had perished, or been exiled, or sold as slaves to the West Indies.

Prendergast, in his "Cromwellian Settlement," cites numerous instances of the severity of the persecution, and gives the names of several persons who received pay for either murdering or betraying priests. In one place he says:

"August 10th, five pounds, on the certificate of Major Stanley, to Thomas Greyson, Evan Powell, and Samuel Ally, being three soldiers of Colonel Abbott's regiment of dragoons, for the arrest of DONOGH HAGERTY, a popish priest, by them taken, and now secured in the county jail of Clonmel. To Arthur Spunner, Robert Pierce, and John Bruen, five pounds, for the good service by them performed in apprehending and bringing before the Chief-Justice Papys, on the 21st January, 1657, one Edmund Duin, a popish priest. On 13th April, 1657, to Sergeant Humphrey Gibbs and Corporal Thomas Hill, ten pounds, for apprehending two popish priests, namely, Maurice Prendergast and Edmund Fahy, who were secured in the jail of Waterford, and, being afterward arraigned, were both of them adjudged to be, and were accordingly, transported into foreign parts.

IRELAND UNDER CHARLES II.

The reign of Charles II.—The persecution of the Catholics abated—What the various orders had suffered by death, exile, and persecution—Sufferings of Dr. Lynch, bishop of Tuam—Persecution of Dr. De Burgo and Bishop Talbot—Talbot's influence with the king—Charles becomes a Catholic, and dies one—The Puritans fearing the influence of Dr. Talbot, get up a strong persecution against him—Sufferings and persecution of Dr. Forstall, bishop of Kildare, and De Burgo, bishop of Elphin.

WITH the restoration of Charles II., in 1660, the persecution of the Catholics considerably abated. Though several noble victims suffered in his reign for the cause, we no longer find the hecatombs of martyrs and daily sacrifices that disgrace previous reigns and the Commonwealth.

We find that in 1654, three bishops and over three hundred priests had been put to death for the faith, while all the surviving bishops, and upwards of one thousand priests, were banished for ever from the country, under pain of death if they returned.

The friars of all orders were expelled from their convents. Of six hundred Dominicans, very few remained. The more numerous Franciscans and Augustinians shared the same fate, and had to fly or were cruelly butchered; aye, even the very nuns were turned out of their convents—some of them put to death, and more exiled to the West Indies, where they were sold as slaves. History tells us how numbers of them perished by their own hands sooner than sacrifice their virtue to the lust of brutal planters. A large number of the members of the various orders braved the storm of persecution, and died at their posts. They not only refused to leave, but craved martyrdom, and all the horrid cruelty and devilish tortures inflicted by their persecutors, until the latter became sick of their fiendish work, and found that the blood they so freely shed was the seed from which sprang fresh victims and aspirants for immortal glory.

There remained also a portion of the parochial clergy, who, whenever their functions were to be exercised, nobly braved the axe and gibbet, and who, when the sinner was reconciled to God, or the departing soul prepared for heaven, sought a hiding-place in the forest, and sheltered themselves in caverns and morasses from the blood-hunt of spies and priest-catchers. They did not, however, always escape. Even after the restoration of Charles II., when persecution relaxed its fury, not less than one hundred and twenty of these heroic confessors were sometimes crowded into the same loathsome jail, to pine away and starve together. In this state did things continue till 1661, and with very little change until 1669.

Though few of the clergy were put to death in the reign of Charles, many of them were incarcerated, exiled, or sold into slavery. As we are writing the lives of those who actually suffered death, we can give but a passing notice to the no less deserving victims who underwent fierce persecutions, but did not attain the crown of martyrdom.

REV. DR. LYNCH was consecrated archbishop of Tuam in 1669. A certain apostate Augustinian monk, named Martin French, who had been reprimanded by the archbishop, denounced him to the authorities, and had him accused, under the statute of præmunire, of exercising foreign jurisdiction in the British dominions. In consequence of these accusations, the archbishop was detained many months in prison, and for some time was in great danger of being led to the scaffold. Archbishop Plunket, on the 24th April, 1671, thus refers to his sufferings :

"The good Archbishop of Tuam was imprisoned anew, during the past Lent, on the accusation of Martin French, and was found guilty of præmunire—that is, of exercising foreign jurisdiction ; but now, having given security, he is allowed to be at liberty till the next session of August ; but Nicholas Plunket, who is the best lawyer in the kingdom, and the only defender that the poor ecclesiastics have in such circumstances, writes that he should appeal from the courts of Galway to the supreme jurisdiction of Dublin, in which there is greater equity."

On the trial being sent to Dublin, French did not appear to prosecute, and soon afterwards, touched with repentance, he petitioned the primate to pardon him his guilt, and re-admit him to the bosom of the Holy Church. Bishop Lynch was released, and restored to his diocese.

RIGHT REV. DR. JOHN DE BURGO, vicar-apostolic of Killala, suffered grievously for his devotion and steadfast faith. Of him might be said that he was a "minister of Christ in labors more abundant, in stripes above measure, in prisons more frequent, in deaths often ; in perils of waters, in perils of robbers, in perils by mine own countrymen, in perils by the heathen, in perils in the city, in perils in the wilderness, in perils in the sea." In his youth he had served for some years as an officer in the Austrian army of Northern Italy ; but, renouncing the world, he dedicated himself to the service of the altar, and was appointed Abbot of Clare. From 1647 till the bishop's death, in 1650, he acted as Vicar-General of Killaloe, and we find him three years later arrested by Cromwell, and sent, in company with eighteen other priests, into banishment. He devoted himself to the ministry in France and Italy ; in 1671 he received a brief from Rome appointing him to the see of Killala. Before the close of 1674 he was arrested by order of the crown, accused of "bringing Protestants to the Catholic faith, contrary to the statutes of the kingdom, exercising foreign jurisdiction, preaching perverse doctrines, and remaining in the kingdom despite the act of Parliament of 28th March, 1674," etc. For two years he was detained in prison, with irons on his hands and feet. At the assizes he publicly declared that the Pope, as Vicar of Christ, was head of the Catholic Church. He rejected with scorn a private offer that was made to him of being promoted to a Protestant bishopric, should he conform to the Established Church. Conducted from Ballinrobe to Dublin, he there displayed great firmness, and was at length sentenced to the confiscation of his goods and perpetual imprisonment, but was released through the influence of the Earl of Clanricard, who was his relative. In fulfilment of a vow he had made, he visited Jerusalem; and, on his return, was captured by pirates and sold into slavery, but finally escaped. He retired to Rome, where he spent the closing years of his life.

MOST REV. PETER TALBOT, archbishop of Dublin, was of the noble family of the Earls of Wexford and Waterford, and son to Sir William Talbot, of Malahide. Talbot, duke of Tirconnell, and lord-lieutenant of Ireland, was the prelate's younger brother. A pure and religious impulse inspired him to renounce the wealth, honor, and position which the world flatteringly held forth to him, to embrace a life of poverty, mortification, and persecution, as a minister of a persecuted faith. He was educated in Portugal, and ordained in Rome.

While Talbot was enjoying the peace and quiet of college life, the Puritans were spreading death and desolation over both England and Ireland. When Charles fled to the Spanish Court, to enlist its favor in his cause, he became acquainted with Talbot, who possessed considerable influence with many of the Spanish ministers. Talbot was of incalculable service to Charles in his distress, and frequently visited him at Cologne. Charles was a Catholic at heart, and was, without doubt, received into the bosom of the Catholic church by Talbot; but he kept his renunciation secret, as it would interfere with his chances of restoration.

Charles was not a man to sacrifice a crown for his religious convictions: and when, after his restoration, his Protestant supporters called on him to make an open profession of his faith, he, with characteristic inconstancy, dissembled, equivocated, and finally announced himself a Protestant.*

Dr. Talbot was consecrated Archbishop of Dublin in the year 1669. He lost no time in visiting his diocese, and set to work to effect some necessary and salutary changes in its administration.

Dr. Talbot's appointment to the see of Dublin, his supposed influence with the king, and his great zeal in behalf of Catholicity, got up a fierce spirit of Protestant hostility against him.

The Protestants, who had by plunder and spoliation secured both the power and wealth of the country, began to tremble for their safety, and resolved on the ruin of Bishop Talbot. An address was accordingly presented to the king, requiring, among other things, that "Peter Talbot, pretended archbishop of Dublin, for his notorious disloyalty, and disobedience and contempt of the laws, be com-

---

* Charles II., though a weak man, was sincere in his conversion, for there is no doubt but he died a Catholic; and, if he dared, would have proved that sincerity through life which he evinced at his death When the earthly crown could no longer be held, Charles made an anxious effort to seize on a crown in heaven. He sent for Father Huddlestone, to receive him again into the Church, and to prepare him for eternity He needed but little instruction; Talbot had supplied that want His repentance had every appearance of being intense and fervent; he received the last sacraments with piety, and died a Catholic.

manded by proclamation to depart forthwith out of Ireland and all his majesty's dominions, or otherwise to be prosecuted according to law," etc. In consequence of this edict, Dr. Talbot was banished the kingdom, about the beginning of 1673. He went to England, and resided in Poole Hall, Cheshire. His health rapidly failing, through the interest of his brother, he was allowed to return to Ireland, as he said, "to die." Shortly after his arrival in Ireland, though he was so weak that he had to be moved about in a chair, he was accused of being concerned in the "popish plot," and thrown into prison in Dublin castle, where he was detained for over two years, without, as Harris says, a single charge against him, until he died in prison, in 1680.

To add to the sufferings of this amaible prelate, he saw his own brother, Colonel Talbot, and Father Ryan, superior of the Jesuits, first cast into the same prison, and then, when the horrors of the jail became insupportable, ordered out of the country. And he knew well, if he was deprived of the happiness of sharing in their exile, it was only because the attempt to remove him in his present exhausted state would instantly cause death.

Richard Arsdekin, S. J., a contemporary of his, pays the following tribute to the merits and sufferings of this good bishop. He says :

"After a short time, when the storm of persecution had abated somewhat rather than subsided, Dr. Talbot returned to Ireland, where he labored to restore church discipline, to encourage the Catholics, and to elude the machinations of heretics. But his enemies could not long bear the light. They were incensed at his zeal, and jealous of his influence with the people ; and, as is usually the case, they resolved to destroy what they feared. Secret accusations were made before a heretical tribunal, suspicions created, and all other means craftily employed to oppress the just man, opposed to their wicked designs, and whose worst crime was to have the name, the office, and authority of a priest. At length the excellent prelate was seized on suddenly by wicked officials, and cast into a public prison, without being guilty of the least offence. There this faithful soldier of Christ was shut up in close imprisonment for some time; but neither keepers, nor prison walls, nor chains could restrain that freedom of spirit which animated the true pastor, and made him more careful of the salvation of others than of his own life. While he patiently awaited the usual inhuman sentence of that heretical tribunal, his feeble body, no longer a fit tenement for the noble spirit, was broken down by heavy sickness. Still the soldier of Christ struggled on against disease and the filth of a loathsome dungeon, destitute of almost all human aid, with nothing to console him but a firm resolution and conscious innocence. At length, after enduring various and repeated tortures, he suffered death, not, indeed, beneath the axe of the executioner, but immured in a filthy prison; and he passed to that better world where God has promised a crown of justice to those who strive lawfully. But this most illustrious prelate shall ever live in the memory of men; he shall ever live in the society of holy confessors; from him the injustice of man, the cunning and envy of heretics, shall never take away the laurels won in a glorious fight. O blind Tyranny! thou art deceived: whatever thou dost, whatever thou proposest, the blood of martyrs has been, and ever will be, the seed of Christians! Of this truth Ireland, ever faithful to her God and to her king, has given for ages, and will continue to give, a noble example."

RIGHT REV. DR. FORSTALL, bishop of Kildare, unjustly suffered severe persecution about the same time. Towards the close of the year 1679 he was cast into prison. After his liberation, the fury of the persecution against him was so great that he had to seek safety in the woods and mountains until his death, in 1683, which took place in the diocese of Cashel.

RIGHT REV. DOMINICK DE BURGO, O. P. P., bishop of Elphin, suffered fearful persecution about this time. Having devoted himself to the Church, he embarked for Spain, but was seized by the English and flung into prison at Kinsale. Having made his escape, and received fresh supplies from his friends, he took shipping at Galway, and safely arrived in Spain. After holding many high offices in the Church in Spain, he was consecrated, in 1671, Bishop of Elphin, and immediately returned to his native land. O'Heyn, who was his frequent companion, has left us a life of him, in which he says:

"It were long to tell all he suffered in the bitter persecution which was got up against the Catholics in England and Ireland in 1680. A reward of two hundred pounds was offered for his apprehension by the viceroy and council, for which reason he always travelled by night while that persecution lasted. For four months he lay hid in a solitary house, and never even put his foot outside the door; but when the time came for consecrating the holy oils (Maundy-Thursday), he travelled by night forty miles from that place. I was his companion all that year, until the illustrious archbishop of Armagh, Dr. Oliver Plunket, was taken prisoner. He often, from his prison in Dublin, warned the Bishop of Elphin of the plans of the Supreme Council for his apprehension, and by this means much aided him to escape their snares. Had he fallen into their hands, no doubt his fate would have been the same as that of the primate, who was hung, beheaded, and quartered." He was driven into exile again, after the surrender of Galway to the Williamite troops, and died in the convent of Louvain, in the year 1704.

NEW PLOTS AND PERSECUTIONS.

The Puritans aroused—The Titus-Oates plot—Intrigues of Lord Shaftesbury and others—New persecutions aimed at the Catholics—Life of Dr. Plunket—His arrest—His accusers fail to appear against him at Diogheda—His acquittal—His enemies succeed in having him tried in London—The perjured witnesses—His trial and condemnation—He declares his innocence—His death.

OLIVER PLUNKET.

AS we have stated, the restoration of Charles II. filled the Catholics of Ireland with the hope that a more liberal spirit of toleration would restore peace and harmony to the nation, and tranquillity to the Church; and, to a great extent, their hopes were realized. Charles II., a Catholic at heart, would fain restore to the Church all its ancient rights and privileges, as also much of its temporal possessions, if he only felt safe in doing so; but he was surrounded by a court that had grown rich upon the spoliations of the Church, and therefore wanted to keep alive the persecution which gave them wealth and power.

The king leaning towards Catholicity alarmed the Puritans and church-spoilers; they felt that something should be done to alarm the king, and to induce him to sanction fresh persecutions.

Under the mild administration of Lord Berkley, many of the Irish prelates had returned to their sees; places of worship were again opened, and the religious fervor of the

Catholics seemed to revive with new ardor. This pleasing state of things did not last long, for the bigoted Lords Shaftesbury and Buckingham, and their adherents, succeeded in hatching the "Popish plot" in England; and also in implicating in it, by perjured witnesses, many of the Irish prelates and priests.

It is now admitted by all impartial writers that Oates and the other perjured scoundrels who figured in this plot, were but the secret tools of the Protestant ascendant party, who wanted to revive the persecution of the Catholics.

They so far worked upon the timid and vacillating mind of the king, as to frighten him into the belief that the "Popish plot" was organized with the design of killing him, and that Oates was the agent of the conspirators, including Bishop Plunket.

Oliver Plunket was born at Loughcrew, in the county of Meath, in the year 1629. He was a near relative of Dr. Patrick Plunket, who successively ruled the dioceses of Ardagh and Meath, as also of Dr. Peter Talbot, archbishop of Dublin. He was also related to the Earls of Fingall and Roscommon, and to the Barons of Dunsany and Louth. From an early age he evinced a desire to devote himself to the sacred ministry, and his education was entrusted to his relative, Dr. Patrick Plunket, then titular abbot of St. Mary's, Dublin, until the age of sixteen, when he proceeded to Rome, there to pursue his studies. In 1643 Father Peter Francis Scarampo, an Oratorian, had been sent by the Holy See on a special mission to Ireland; in 1645 he returned to Rome, and young Plunket accompanied him. He completed his course of ecclesiastical studies in the Ludovisian college at Rome, graduated a doctor in divinity, and afterwards became a distinguished professor of theology in the college De Propaganda Fide, the duties of which office he continued to discharge for more than twelve years.

His exemplary life, as well as his learning, had recommended him to the notice of the sovereign pontiff; accordingly, on the decease of Edmund O'Reilly, archbishop of Armagh, he was nominated by Clement IX. and promoted to the vacant see in the year 1669. He lost no time in hastening to his diocese, where he held two synods and two ordinations, and in less than two months administered confirmation to over ten thousand people.

This good and zealous bishop labored zealously to reform abuses, and to restore his diocese to the purity and correct discipline it enjoyed before it was disordered by fierce persecutions. So great was his zeal, so forgetful was he of his personal comforts, that while laboring to dispel the religious ignorance that long persecution had engendered, and the want of pastors had fostered, he all the time resided in a mud cabin at Ballybarrack, County Louth. From this humble abode he sallied forth to administer the sacraments, to visit the various parishes in his diocese, and to correct abuses and to reform errors of discipline among his people and clergy.

Plunket became a great favorite, even among the liberal Protestants; for his candor, his charity, and peaceful submission to the laws, disarmed rancor and gained him the respect and esteem of all classes and denominations. Despite all this, he was soon to be immolated to the spirit of fanaticism and treason.

The Puritans and fanatics of England had nursed several treasonable plots to subvert the monarchy, and to exclude James from the throne. Having failed in this, they resolved to force the Irish Catholics into another rebellion, so as to enrich themselves by fresh confiscations, and to create a spirit of distrust in the minds of the king and his brother, the Duke of York.

Ormond, who had been succeeded by Lord Berkley and

Lord Essex, as viceroy, was restored through the influence of Shaftesbury and Buckingham, in 1677.* About this time the persecution began to rage again, and Dr. Plunket, with Dr. Brennan, bishop of Waterford, were forced to conceal themselves in a thatched cabin, through the roof of which the rain poured down in torrents.

The convents were again ransacked and despoiled, the monks scattered, and the bishops and priests obliged to fly to the mountains and woods for safety and shelter.

In 1678 fresh edicts were issued, and bishops and priests were sought for more rigorously than ever. The infamous conspiracy against the lives of Catholics was set on foot this year in England, and the Viceroy, the Duke of Ormond, although his private letters show he was well aware of the falseness of the story, fostered the delusion, and issued fresh edicts against the Catholics: all bishops, Jesuits, regulars, and priests were ordered to leave the kingdom; all chapels, or Mass-houses as they were called, were closed or pulled down.

In the month of November, 1679, Dr. Plunket left his place of concealment in the secluded parts of his own diocese, and came to Dublin to assist, in his last moments, his relative, the aged Bishop of Meath. Ten days later he was arrested in the city of Dublin, by a body of militia headed by Hetherington, and by order of the Viceroy he was com-

* Whether Ormond was in league with the *Cabal*, or was simply their dupe, is hard to determine. One thing is certain—that he was an unprincipled, deceitful man; treacherous to his friends, a coward and sycophant to his enemies. After apostatizing from the Catholic faith, like the Vicar of Bray, his religion always chimed in with his interests and the wishes of the king. Indeed, it is generally conceded that he was an infidel in religion; still, he never lost a safe opportunity of persecuting the Catholics, and of throwing all possible obstacles in the way of the tolerant measures of Charles. In fact, the only interval of respite the Catholic Church got from persecution in this reign, was during the nine years that he was withdrawn from the vice-royalty.

mitted a close prisoner to Dublin castle. This was on the 6th December, 1679. For six weeks no communication with him was allowed ; but after that term, nothing treasonable having been discovered in his papers, he was treated with more leniency, and permitted to receive visits from his friends. The only crime of which he was at first accused, was that of remaining in the kingdom, notwithstanding the proclamation, and of exercising the functions of his sacred ministry. Thus his relative, the Rev. William Plunket, wrote on the 20th March, 1680, to the Propaganda : "I hastened thither (to the castle), and having heard and learned for certain that he had been imprisoned only for being a Catholic bishop, and for not having abandoned the flock of our Lord in obedience to the edict published by Parliament, I was somewhat consoled, it being his and our glory that he should suffer in such a cause."

So on his trial the primate declared, "I was a prisoner six months, only for my religion, and there was not a word of treason spoken of against me for so many years." And the attorney-general himself avowed that he was arrested "for being an over-zealous papist."

It was not till the month of June, 1680, that the witnesses had fully matured their plans. Armed with commendatory letters from the English court, they now returned to Ireland, assured of success. Among the many precautions taken by the apostate friar MacMoyer, one was to have a government order sent from London to the Viceroy that no Catholic should be a member of the jury. "Orders had been transmitted to Ireland," says the primate on his trial, "that I should be tried in Ireland, and that no Roman Catholic should be on the jury ; and so it was in both the grand jury and the other jury ; yet there, when I came to my trial, after I was arraigned, not one appeared."

It was at first thought that his trial would take place

NEW PLOTS AND PERSECUTIONS. 225

before the Court of King's Bench, at Dublin. The Viceroy, however, decreed that the trial should be held in Dundalk, the scene of the reputed treasonable crimes. This alone sufficed to derange all the plans of the witnesses, for they were conscious that their characters were well known in that quarter, and that evidence could be without difficulty procured there of their malignity, and evil designs, and perjuries. Dr. Plunket, writing to the Internuncio on the 25th of July, 1680, the day after his return from Dundalk, gives the following detailed account of the proceedings of this trial:

"Your letter of the 17th July consoled me in my tribulations and miseries. The friar MacMoyer, as well in the criminal sessions of Dundalk as after these sessions, presented a memorial that the trial should not be held in Dundalk, where he was too well known, and that it should be deferred till September or March next, but the Viceroy refused.

"I was brought with a guard to Dundalk on the 21st of July. Dundalk is thirty-six miles from Dublin. I was there consigned to the king's lieutenant in that district, who treated me with great courtesy; on the 23d and 24th of July I was presented for trial. A long process was read, but on the 24th MacMoyer did not appear to confirm his depositions and hear my defence. I had thirty-two witnesses, priests, friars, and seculars, prepared to falsify all that the friar had sworn, forsooth, that *I had seventy thousand Catholics prepared to murder all the Protestants, and to establish here the Romish religion and popish superstition;* that I had *sent numerous agents to different kingdoms to obtain aid; that I had visited and explored all the fortresses and maritime ports of the kingdom;* and that I held a provincial council in 1678, *to introduce the French.* He also accused, in his depositions, Monsignor Tyrrell; Rev. Luke Plunket, the ordinary of

Derry; and Edward Dromgole, an eminent preacher. Murphy (the second witness) no sooner heard that the sessions and trial would be held in Dundalk, than he fled out of the kingdom; and hence, MacMoyer alleged that he himself could not appear, as he awaited the return of Murphy; and so these sessions terminated, and, according to the laws of this country, I must present myself at three criminal sessions before I can be absolved; and, as there will be no sessions in Dundalk till the end of March, my counsel and friends recommended me to present a memorial to have the cause adjudged in Dublin at the next criminal sessions of All Saints, and that the jury of Dundalk should be brought to Dublin, which perhaps I may obtain. The manner of proceeding here in criminal cases seems very strange to me. The person accused knows nothing of the accusation till the day of trial; he is allowed no counsel to plead his cause; the oath is not given to his witnesses, and one witness suffices for the crown. They receive, however, the evidence of the witnesses of the accused, although they do not administer the oath to them. The sessions being over, I was reconducted, by order of the Viceroy, to the Royal Castle of Dublin."

A new and more fatal plot was concocted for his ruin and execution. In superintending the concerns of his diocese, he had occasion to censure the immorality of some few individuals among his clergy, persons whose abandoned lives had already afforded notorious scandal to the country, and had long since loudly demanded reproof and punishment. The names of these men were MacMoyer, Duffy, and Maclean, three Franciscans, and Murphy, a secular priest, chanter of Armagh, and a noted rapparee. Filled with rage truly diabolical, these depraved wretches had now conceived the design of taking away the life of their venerable unsuspecting prelate; the dark-laid conspiracy was readily formed, and in this bond of iniquity they were soon after joined by four laymen, MacMoyer, Hanson, and two miscreants who were a disgrace to the honorable name of O'Neal. The charges which these wretches had brought against their primate were : that on his advancement to the see of Armagh, he had entered into a correspondence with the French court, for the purpose of effecting an invasion of Ireland ; that he engaged to raise a force of seventy thousand Irishmen ; that he was to put Dublin and all the seaports into the hands of the French ; and that he was to cause money to be collected among the Irish clergy, in order to meet the expenses of this invasion.

Ireland, however, was not the theatre for his enemies to carry out their villainous scheme with success. There, their infamous characters were too well known, as well as the innocence of the accused, to afford them the least chance of success. His enemies succeeded in having the trial transferred to London, where the primate was conveyed under a strong escort.* So bad was the character of his accusers that the jury of the King's Bench refused to find bills of indictment against him.

The conspirators were not to be thus foiled They had him arrested on a new and more formidable series of charges. He was brought to trial on the 8th of May, 1681. The charges contained in these indictments amounted to

* This was under a most iniquitous and unconstitutional act of the English Parliament, and its application in Dr Plunket's case was peculiarly outrageous. To send him to be tried by a London jury of that day was to hand over the good prelate to enemies thirsting for his blood ; it was to procure credence for his perjured accusers, removing them from the country where their crimes and perjuries were known, and where Protestant juries had already refused credence to their sworn testimony It was also, in the existing circumstances, to deprive the accused of the probability of defence, and to oblige him to answer the highest charge against the crown before a court where there could be no witnesses in his favor, no evidence of his innocence.—*Moran*, p. 322.

seven heads, and are thus recapitulated by the dying prelate in the powerful appeal which he delivered from the scaffold on the morning of his execution :

"First, that he had sent letters by one Neal O'Neal to Monsieur Baldesche, the Pope's secretary; also to the Bishop of Aix and Principe Colonna, that they might solicit foreign powers to invade Ireland. Secondly, that he employed Captain Con O'Neal to solicit the French king for succor. Thirdly, that he exacted money from the clergy of Ireland, for the purpose of introducing the French and maintaining seventy thousand men. Fourthly, that he had this force in readiness, and that he had given directions to a friar named Duffy to raise two hundred and fifty men in the parish of Foghart and county of Louth. Fifthly, that he was to surround all the forts and harbors of Ireland, and that he fixed upon Carlingford as a fit harbor for the invasion. Sixthly, that he had held several meetings, where money was collected for this purpose. Seventhly, that there was a meeting in the county of Monaghan, at which three hundred gentlemen of three several counties had attended, and whom he exhorted to take up arms for the recovery of their estates."*

Never has there been witnessed a more flagrant act of injustice than that which had been perpetrated during the course of these proceedings. The witnesses and documents so indispensable for the case were all in Ireland; the accused primate, therefore, prayed the court that time might be granted him for summoning his witnesses, collecting his papers, and making the arrangements necessary for his defence.† Five weeks were allowed him by the chief justice; but by reason of contrary winds, and the uncertainty of the seas, they had not arrived at the termination of that period. He accordingly prayed that a further allowance

* Archbishop Plunket's speech † Archdekin, p 760.

of twelve days might be granted him, but this request was refused, and the judges proceeded on the trial.*

To any person acquainted with the state of Ireland and the circumstances of the accused, the charges by which this innocent prelate's life was now threatened must appear at once visionary and incredible. "In his defence (observes a Protestant writer), the primate alleged the improbability of all that was sworn against him; which was apparent enough. He stated that the Irish clergy were so poor, that he himself, who was the head of a whole province, lived in a little thatched house, with only one servant, having never above sixty pounds yearly income; so that neither he nor they could be thought very likely to carry on a design of this nature."† But a band of blood-stained and perjured wretches were now arrayed against him; in the face of Heaven they sealed their eternal infamy: a verdict of guilty was returned by an ignorant jury, and sentence of death pronounced by a partial, temporizing judge. As soon as the verdict was returned, the innocent and injured prelate bowed in humble submission to the court; and raising his eyes to heaven, in the spirit of a martyr, he exclaimed: "The Lord be thanked!" He was recommended by the chief justice to become an approver, but the primate assured him that his salvation was dearer to him than a thousand lives.

"If (he adds), I were a man that had no care of my conscience, I might have saved my life; for I was offered it by divers people here, if I would but confess my guilt and accuse others. But, my lord, I had rather die ten thousand deaths, than wrongfully take away one farthing of any man's goods, one day of his liberty, or one moment of his life."‡

* Archdekin, p 761. † Baker's Chronicle, p. 710.
‡ Memoirs of Missionary Priests, part ii., p. 467.

The Lord Chief-Justice,* in passing sentence of death, said: "Well, however, the judgment which we give you is that which the law says and speaks. And therefore you must go from hence to the place from whence you came—that is, to Newgate; and from thence you shall be drawn through the city of London to Tyburn: there you shall be hanged by the neck, but cut down before you are dead; your bowels shall be taken out and burnt before your face; your head shall be cut off, and your body be divided into four quarters, to be disposed of as his majesty pleases. And I pray to God have mercy on your soul."

Plunket replied: "God Almighty bless your lordship. And now, my lord, as I am a dead man to this world, and as I hope for mercy in the other world, I was never guilty of any of the treasons laid to my charge, as you will hear in time; and my character you may receive from my Lord-Chancellor of Ireland, my Lord Berkley, my Lord Essex, and the Duke of Ormond.

---

* The judges on the trial were the Lord Chief-Justice Sir Francis Pemberton and Judges Dolbein and Jones. According to the truly barbarous policy of the law in the seventeenth century (and indeed the same law was in force till a very late period), no person accused of treason was allowed the assistance of counsel, unless in the case that some purely legal question should arise during the trial. Hence Dr Plunket now stood alone at the bar, to plead his cause before judges who seemed to vie with each other in their partiality for the perjured witnesses, and in their animosity against the accused, while at the same time the jury had naught to guide them in their decision but the long-concocted, and nevertheless occasionally conflicting, evidence of these perjurers. One instance will show the bias of the judges. When, at the close of the first witness's evidence, Dr. Plunket asked him why, if all he had said were true, he had never, during the past seven years, given any notice to the government of the plot, the Chief-Justice, seeing this witness somewhat perplexed, suggested to him an answer, saying, "Of what religion were you then?" and the witness replying, "A Roman Catholic," Justice Dolbein at once added, "Therefore it will be no wonder you did not discover the plot."—*Moran*, p 324.

Eachard, in his "History of England," states that the Earl of Essex was so sensible of the primate's innocence that he appealed to the king for his pardon, and told his majesty that the witnesses must needs be perjured, for these things sworn against him could not possibly be true. Upon which the king, in a passion, said: *"Why did you not attest this at his trial? It would have done him good then. I dare not pardon any one."* And so concluded with the same kind of answer he had given another person formerly: *"His blood be upon your head, and not upon mine."* *

At length, on the 1st of July, 1681, the day destined for the carrying out of the fatal sentence, the keeper of the prison, imagining that the apprehension of approaching death, and horror of the atrocious punishment, would have made some impression on that soul hitherto so resolute, went early in the morning to visit him, and, if necessary, to give him courage and comfort him; but he was yet more surprised and filled with astonishment on finding that the prelate, on being awakened, was as little moved by the approach of sufferings as though his body was insensible to pain, while, nevertheless, he was of an ardent and delicate temperament. In a little while the announcement was made that everything was in order, wherefore he was taken from prison, and stretched, with his face uppermost, and tied with cords upon a wooden hurdle, and thus drawn by a horse to Tyburn. "At this awful moment," observes Father Corker, his bosom friend and fellow-prisoner, "there appeared in him something beyond expression — something more than human. The most hard-hearted people were melted into tears at the sight. Many Protestants, in my hearing, wished their souls in the same state with his. All believed him innocent, and he made Catholics, even the most timorous, in love with death." When he had reached

---

* Eachard, vol. iii., p. 631

the place of execution, he addressed the immense multitude in the following speech, which has been handed down as an affecting memorial of his sufferings:

"I have some few days past abided my trial in the King's Bench, and must very soon appear at the bench of the King of kings, and before a Judge who cannot be deceived by false witnesses or corrupted allegations, whereas He knoweth the secrets of all hearts. Neither can He deceive any, or give an unjust sentence, being all goodness, and a most just Judge. Therefore will He infallibly decree an eternal reward for all good works, and condign punishment for the smallest transgression of His commandments. This being the case, it would be a wicked act, and contrary to my eternal welfare, should I now, by declaring anything contrary to truth, commit a detestable sin, for which, within a very short time, I must receive sentence of everlasting damnation. I protest, therefore, upon the word of a dying man, and, as I hope for salvation at the hands of the Supreme Judge, that I will declare the truth with all sincerity; and this I do, in order that the circumstances of my case may be known to all the world.

"It is to be observed that I have been accused in Ireland of treason and præmunire; the prosecutors, however, knowing that I had witnesses who would clearly establish my innocence, came to this city, and procured that I should be brought thither, where the crimes objected to me were not committed, and where the jury were unacquainted with me, and with the character of my accusers. Here, after six months' close imprisonment, I was brought to the bar on the 3d of May. But, whereas, my witnesses and records were in Ireland, the Lord Chief-Justice gave me five weeks to procure them. However, by reason of the seas, and other impediments, this was found impossible. I therefore begged for twelve days more, that I might be in readiness for my trial, which the Lord Chief-Justice refused."

At this point in his address, the Archbishop enumerated the several heads of the accusation, as already stated, and refuted each in a strain of reasoning the most convincing; and, after having appealed to Heaven in testimony of his innocence, he thus proceeds:

"You see, therefore, the circumstances in which I am placed; you have heard what protestations of innocence I have made; but that you may be the more induced to give me credit, I do also assure you that a great peer sent me notice *that I could save my life if I would accuse others.* My answer was: *that I never knew of any conspirators in Ireland, except those who were publicly known as outlaws, and that, to save my life, I would not falsely accuse any person, or prejudice my own soul.* To take away any man's life or goods wrongfully ill becometh any Christian, especially a man of my calling, being a clergyman of the Catholic Church, and also an unworthy prelate, which I do openly confess. Neither will I deny to have exercised in Ireland the functions of a Catholic prelate, as long as there was any toleration; and to have endeavored to bring the clergy, of whom I had the care, to a due comportment according to their calling; and, although in this I did nothing but my duty, yet some who would not amend had a prejudice for me, and especially my accusers, to whom I did endeavor to do good. Those to whom I allude are the clergymen; as to the four laymen who appeared against me, I was never acquainted with any of them. This wicked act of theirs ought, however, not to reflect on religion; whereas, it is well known that there was a Judas amongst the twelve apostles, and a wicked man named Nicholas amongst the seven deacons. And even as one of the said deacons, holy Stephen, did pray for those who stoned him to death, so do I pray for those who took my life, saying, as St. Stephen did, *O Lord, lay not this sin to them.**

"Now that I have declared how innocent I am of any plot or conspiracy, I would I were able with the like truth to clear myself of high crimes committed against the Divine Majesty's commandments, often transgressed by me, for which I am sorry with all my heart; and if I should or could live a thousand years, I have a firm resolution and a strong purpose, by your grace, O my God, never to offend you; and I beseech your Divine Majesty, by the merits of Christ, and by the intercession of His Blessed Mother, and of all the holy angels and saints, to forgive me my sins, and to grant my soul eternal rest."

Having concluded this appeal amidst the tears of a numerous audience, he continued for some time in prayer, and then resigned himself into the hands of his executioners. He was suffered to hang until he expired, and was then cut down, beheaded, bowelled, and quartered; after which his heart and bowels were cast into the fire. The head, adorned with silvery-colored locks, is still preserved in the convent of the Dominican nuns at Drogheda.† His body, which was begged of the king, was interred in St. Giles' churchyard. On his breast was placed a copper plate, with the following inscription:

---

* It is recorded that Duffy, one of his perjured murderers, writhing under the vengeance of an angry conscience, had some time after presented himself before a successor of Archbishop Plunket, exclaiming in a tone of awful desperation: "Am I never to have peace? is there no mercy for me?" The good prelate before whom he stood observed for a time an awful silence; then producing a glass case and placing it before him, he said, in a voice deep and solemn, "Look here, thou unfortunate wretch!" It contained the head of his innocent victim. The wretched man, unable to bear the sight, swooned away. It is said that he spent the remainder of his days in making public atonement, and died a great penitent.—*Stewart's Memoirs of Armagh*, p. 363.

† Hib. Dom.

"In this tomb resteth the body of the Most Rev. Oliver Plunket, late Archbishop of Armagh, and Primate of All Ireland, who, when accused of high treason, through hatred of the faith, by false brethren, and condemned to death, being hanged at Tyburn, and his bowels being taken out and cast into the fire, suffered martyrdom with constancy, in the reign of Charles II., King of Great Britain, on the 1st day of July, 1681."

Having been raised about four years after, his body was found entire, and conveyed to the Benedictine monastery at Lambspring, in Germany, where, with great solemnity, it was re-intombed. In 1693, the holy Abbot Corker caused a magnificent monument to be erected over the remains, with the following inscription :*

"Reliquiæ, Sanctæ Memoriæ, OLIVERI PLUNKET, Archiepiscopi Armachani, HIBERNIÆ Primatis, qui in odium Catholicæ fidei laqueo suspensus, extractis visceribus et in ignem projectis, celebris martyr occubuit LONDINI, primo dei Julii (stylo veteri), anno salutis, 1681."

* Memoirs of Missionary Priests. Amplest details of the life and death of the Most Rev. Dr. Plunket will be found in the Rev. Dr. Moran's Memoir of that martyr-prelate.

THE DAWN OF TOLERATION.

The downfall of Dr. Plunket's enemies—Narrow escape of Bishop Creagh—Heaven's judgment upon his perjured enemies—Persecution of Archbishop Russell—Fresh penal laws—The priest-hunters and their bloodhounds—Spies pretending to be priests, in order to betray their victims A poor priest and several of his flock killed—A cry for toleration—The Catholic churches of Dublin thrown open by order of the Viceroy, on Patrick's Day, 1745.

REV. DR. PLUNKET was the last bishop who fell a victim to the intolerant spirit and anti-Catholic fury of the times. The disgrace of Shaftesbury, that arch-enemy of Catholicity, brought relief to the Catholics. It is a remarkable fact that his ruin was caused by the perjured witnesses whom he had fostered and trained to swear away the life of Plunket and others. The death and well-known innocence of the Primate sent a shudder of horror and detestation throughout all Europe; and even Englishmen began to fear that the intolerant persecution of the Catholics would bring on a coalition of the Catholic powers of Europe to revenge such bloody enactments; and though persecution did not cease, it greatly abated; and as if Dr. Plunket's blood satiated the fanatical thirst of the Puritans, very few ecclesiastics were martyred, though numbers still suffered the tortures of prison or banishment.

The Right Rev. PETER CREAGH, bishop of Cork, narrowly escaped sharing the same fate as the pious primate of Armagh. When the Titus-Oates plot was hatched in England, it was thought advisable to implicate in the scheme the

Catholic hierarchy of Ireland. In consequence of false evidence, connecting him with it, the venerable Archbishop Talbot, of Dublin, was flung into prison, where he died. Bishop Creagh was also accused, and escaped for some time, but was finally taken prisoner, and cast into Limerick prison. Dr. Renehen, in his collections, tells us that—

"He there continued for three months, and then an order came from the English Parliament that he should be transmitted to London, along with the Rev. Oliver Plunket, archbishop of Armagh. He was conveyed to Dublin for that purpose, but, being there seized with a violent fit of sickness, occasioned by the hardships he suffered in jail, they would not transmit him to London along with the Archbishop of Armagh, and consequently our holy prelate was by this means robbed of the crown of martyrdom, which the blessed Primate of Armagh received there, and which his granduncle, Richard Creagh, of Armagh, received there before from Queen Elizabeth. For the space of two years our bishop was kept a prisoner in Limerick and Dublin, during which time the eyes of King Charles II. began to be opened. He put to death many of those who before accused innocent Catholics; he committed Oates to perpetual imprisonment; and restored to liberty the imprisoned Catholics, both priests and prelates.

"Yet this could not be done without acquitting them, according to the formality of the laws. Our prelate, Pierse Creagh, was therefore conveyed to Cork to stand his trial. The judge was intent upon acquitting him, and one of the witnesses against him repented of his crime; but there was another witness who was hardened in wickedness, and was resolved to prosecute him with all his might. Our poor prelate was as a criminal seated at the bar, patiently listening to many lies and calumnies which the wicked fellow was laying to his charge. But just as this villain had kissed the book, and called for the vengeance of Heaven to fall down upon him, if what he swore to was not true, the whole floor of the court-house gave way, and, with all the people upon it, tumbled down into the cellar, and the rogue was crushed to death in the ruins. The other false witnesses who were at hand immediately fled, and none escaped falling down with the floor except the judge, whose chair happened to be placed on a beam which did not give way, and there he continued sitting, as it were, in the air. The judge cried out that Heaven itself acquitted him, and therefore dismissed him with great honors. But, that perjured villains should not go unpunished, the judge next day got them apprehended, and was going to put the penal laws in force against them for their perjury; but our holy bishop prostrated himself on his knees before him, and, with tears in his eyes, begged the judge to pardon them; and it was with great difficulty that the judge, who was greatly incensed against them, condescended to his charitable request."

During the Williamite and Jacobite revolts in Ireland, the Catholics selected Bishop Creagh as ambassador to Louis XIV. to beseech his assistance. Having completed his mission, he was detained by King James at St. Germains, who wished to keep him about his person. He also presented him with the archbishopric of Dublin; but Bishop Creagh never returned to Ireland, but accompanied his friend, the Bishop of Strasburg, with whom he remained exercising all his episcopal functions and duties until his death, in the month of July, 1705.

During the bloody struggle for the crown of England, between William and James, the clergy suffered fearfully, and many were cruelly put to death by the Williamite soldiers. It would fill volumes to follow closely the history of the sufferings and persecutions of the clergy, as well as those of the people, during these trying and bloody times. The triumph of the Williamite cause gave power to the enemies of Catholicity, and new persecutions followed.

Not one of the Irish prelates felt the consequence of this change more bitterly than the Most Rev. PATRICK RUSSELL, archbishop of Dublin. It was probably remembered for him that he was the friend of King James. He was accordingly seized, in the very beginning of William's reign, and cast into prison, where he remained almost without interruption to the time of his death. In an interesting letter from Francis, archbishop of Rhodi, and Nuncio at Paris, to Cardinal Spada, December 31, 1690, it is stated that King James was then at Brest, "examining the state of all those who had already come over from Ireland, amounting to about fifteen thousand, of whom about seven hundred were women, and four or five hundred children. Among the exiles are the Archbishops of Armagh and Tuam, and the Bishops of 'Cluan' and Elphin. The Archbishop of Cashel and the Bishop of Kildare, both of whom were at Limerick, and the Bishop of Ossory, are supposed to be still in Ireland. *So is also the Archbishop of Dublin, now a long time in jail.*"

Dr. Russell died in July, 1692, after suffering much affliction and torture in prison.

Though the Treaty of Limerick guaranteed to the Irish Catholics then in arms liberty of conscience, this was, however, soon violated by the enactment of the penal laws. The first of these was enacted in 1697, after the Peace of Ryswick had freed William from the embarrassment of a continental war. In this year an act was passed "for banishing all papists exercising any ecclesiastical jurisdiction whatever in Ireland before the 1st May, 1698, and if found there after that date to be imprisoned during pleasure without bail, and then transported for life; that in the meantime no archbishop, bishop, vicar, etc., should ever land in

Ireland from abroad, after the 29th December, 1697, under pain of a year's incarceration, and then perpetual banishment ; and that if any archbishop, etc., should in either case return from banishment, he should be judged guilty of high treason, and die the death of a traitor." Moreover, harboring or concealing them was punishable by a fine of twenty pounds for the first offence, forty pounds for the second, and confiscation of all estates and chattels for the third, the fines to be divided, one half to the informer, and one half to the king.

Under these inhuman laws, nearly every bishop, and most of the regular clergy in Ireland, were either deported out of the country or obliged to seek safety in flight. Among these were Dr. Dominick Maguire, archbishop of Armagh, the Archbishops of Dublin and Tuam, and the Bishops of Ossory and Elphin. Though the persecutions were continued, still, few ecclesiastics were put to death, but either cast into prison or banished out of the kingdom.

In 1704, all the secular priests in Ireland, not bishops or other dignitaries, were ordered to register themselves, and were promised protection if they complied. In 1709, an act had been passed, offering a reward of fifty pounds for the arrest of a bishop or vicar-general, and twenty pounds for a friar. What rendered this bribe peculiarly grievous, was that the money was to be levied on the Catholics of the county in which the ecclesiastic was convicted. In 1710 the real object of the Registration Act of 1704 was made manifest ; for it was enacted that before the 25th March, 1710, every *registered* priest should present himself at the quarter sessions and take the oath of abjuration, under the penalty of transportation for life, and of a traitor's death if he returned. By the oath of abjuration the priest was ordered to swear that the sacrifice of the Mass and the invocation of the saints were damnable and idolatrous. In other words, the priest, who had been induced to register under the promise of protection, was called upon to apostatize, under the penalty of transportation for life, and a bribe of thirty pounds a year for life was offered to any priest who would apostatize. The *priest-hunters* were now called into full activity, and for some thirty years pursued their infernal trade in full force. Each of these wretches had under him an infamous corps, designated *priest-hounds*, whose duty was to track, with the untiring scent of the bloodhound, the humble priest from refuge to refuge. In cities and towns the Catholic clergy were concealed in cellars or garrets, and and in the country districts they were hid in the unfrequented caves, in the lonely woods, or in the huts of the faithful Irish peasantry. De Burgo tells us that this persecution and hunting after priests was most bitter towards the close of the reign of Anne and the commencement of George I.; and he says that none would have escaped were it not for the horror in which *priest-catchers* were held by the people, Protestants as well as Catholics.*

All these threats and enactments were no idle boast, for we find soon afterwards the Franciscan nuns were expelled from Galway and elsewhere; and in 1717 the Dominicans suffered the same fate. As an instance of how the *priesthunters* did their work, De Burgo tells us—

"In this year (1718), as I well remember, seven priests were taken prisoners together in Dublin, by means of a Portuguese Jew named Gorsia, who pretended to be a priest, in order to discover the true priests. Among them were Father Antony Maguire, Irish provincial of the Dominicans, two Jesuits, one Friar Minor, and the other three secular priests. They were sent into exile, and threatened with death if they returned. Nevertheless, they all returned under feigned names, and escaped detection."

* Cogan, Diocese of Meath.

In this liberal and enlightened age of religious toleration, we can form but a poor conception of the sufferings, hardships, persecutions, and tortures endured by those brave soldiers of the cross, the priesthood of Ireland, in order to preserve the faith alive in the hearts of the people. Outlawed, persecuted, banned, with a price set on their heads, and with either the gibbet or all the horrors of a long imprisonment looming before them, they travelled from place to place, from cabin to cabin, distributing graces to the oppressed poor, instructing them in their religious duties, recommending patience and perseverance, and administering the sacraments. We must, in justice, state that many noble and generous Protestants afforded both shelter, food, and protection to the poor outlawed priest.

This state of things continued until 1744, when such a sensation was created by the falling in of an old house in Cook Street, Dublin, in which a poor, outlawed Meath priest was saying Mass, and by which both the priest and several of the congregation perished, that a cry of toleration was raised, even by respectable Protestants themselves ; and by order of the Viceroy all the chapels in Dublin were thrown open for free worship on Patrick's Day, 1745.

EXECUTION OF FATHER SHEEHY.

Persecutions in the eighteenth century—Contest between the people and the Cromwellian settlers—The Whiteboys—Their depredations—Father Nicholas Sheehy—His sympathy for the people and opposition to their oppressors—They plot his ruin—His trial and acquittal in Dublin—Arrested for the murder of John Bridge—How the Orange landlords of Tipperary managed his trial and procured perjured witnesses—His sentence and execution—Horrible fate of the jurors and witnesses—The execution of Ned Sheehy and others.

FATHER SHEEHY.

FROM 1745 the Catholics of Ireland heard Mass and received the sacraments in safety. Bishops and priests were restored to their missions, the severity of the penal laws relaxed, the axe had become blunted with use, and the gibbet clogged with the blood of its victims. The martyrs had fought the good fight and conquered, and the fruit of their victory was the immortal crown they had earned for themselves; and this victory and triumph they had secured for the Church.

Though no more blood was shed, persecutions did not cease, and over-zealous bigots and intolerant fanatics kept alive the penal laws, in order to wreak their vengeance upon o jectionable Catholics. The same thirst for papist blood that persecuted Dr. Plunket to death, betimes cried out for new victims, and was sure to devise new plots and conspiracies, in order to entrap them. The same trumped-up charges of high treason, supported by perjured witnesses, that sent the martyred bishop to the gibbet in 1681 were to send a good and true priest of Tipperary to the gallows in 1766.

The broad, fertile lands of Tipperary had become the spoil of the Cromwellian planters and soldiers, and its landed gentry had been driven "to hell or Connaught," to make room for the conquerors. Many of these old proprietors settled down among the peasantry, who were the clansmen or retainers of their fathers, cherishing the fond hope that the "Wild Geese" would return, and that they would have their own again. Clinging to their hereditary rights, they kept up the feud with the Cromwellian settlers, and the peasantry warmly enlisted themselves in their cause.

The Cromwellians were mostly men of as much pluck as their fathers, and did not tamely submit to the exactions of outlawed chiefs, backed by a daring peasantry; and, having the administration of the civil laws, and the disposal of the military in their hands, they proved themselves more than a match for their enemies. They mercilessly used all the means in their power to accomplish their ends. If a poor priest rendered himself obnoxious by sympathizing with his flock, and thus gave umbrage to the Protestant ascendancy party, the penal laws, which had partly fallen into disuse, were at once revived, and he was forced to fly or was flung into jail. If, on the other hand, it was necessary to make a wholesale sweep of their enemies, a popish plot, which had in view a French invasion and the restoration of the exiled Stuarts, was easily manufactured.

Such petty tyranny as this has at all times driven the peasantry to band together in illegal societies; and from such persecution, aided by rack-rents, tithe-proctors, and wholesale extermination, sprang that terrible organization called the "Whiteboys," which caused such terror in Tipperary towards the close of the last century. They fairly overran the country at night, dressed in white shirts, from which they took their name; levelled the fences with which the landlords had enclosed the public commons for their own use; dug up the fields which had been sown in grass, and from which, most likely, some of the Whiteboys themselves had been evicted; cut down trees, and, in fact, had carried on such a harassing war of destruction that the landlords were at their wit's end. But they were equal to the occasion, and laid their plot with terrible effect. In the first place, in order to enlist the aid and sympathy of the government, they got plenty witnesses to swear that there was a treasonable conspiracy on foot for the restoration of the Stuarts and Catholicity. In the next place, they resolved to strike terror into the hearts of the people by inflicting summary vengeance upon some of the priests.

Their well-digested plot succeeded admirably, for the Earl of Drogheda was ordered to Clogheen with his command, and with instructions to act in conjunction with the magistrates and country gentlemen. Thus strengthened and emboldened, they proceeded to carry out the rest of their programme, and Father NICHOLAS SHEEHY was selected as their victim. He was a bold, fearless man, who could not be awed into tame submission by the petty tyrants around him: he felt for the sufferings of the poor; he sympathized with them in their distresses and afflictions, and did all in his power to soften the wrath or stay the persecution of their oppressors.

Father Sheehy was just such a man as the Irish, the *Celtic* heart, most loves; warm, generous, and utterly unselfish—sympathizing with the oppressed wherever found, and fearless in denouncing the oppressor. His very faults endeared him the more to the people by whom he was surrounded, and to their posterity in our own day; for they, indeed, "lean'd to virtue's side," and sprang, to some extent, from his real virtues. He was rash, and, it might be, reckless in exposing himself to danger; guileless he was, and unsuspecting, and, therefore, incautiously regardless of the plans and plots of his powerful enemies.

The Rev. Nicholas Sheehy was born in the parish of Fethard, in the year 1728, his parents being of an old respectable Catholic family of the farmer class. At an early age, having manifested a desire for the ministry, he was sent to France, where he remained until after his ordination, when he returned to Ireland, and commenced his mission in Clogheen, and soon afterwards assumed the ministration as parish priest of the joint parishes of Shandraghan, Ballysheehan, and Templeheny.

At a time when priests were barely tolerated in Ireland, it is no wonder that a man of Father Sheehy's independence and hatred of oppression, should be marked out for destruction. The consequence was that his enemies swore that he was not only the leader of the Whiteboys, but also a secret agent in the service of France, and accordingly laid their plans for bringing him within the grasp of the law. In addition to the grievous taxation, tithes, and rack-rents that ground down the peasantry, the Protestant ministers levied a fine of five shillings upon every Catholic marriage. Such an odious tax irritated the people more than heavier ones, and was opposed by Father Sheehy, who denounced such an insolent demand.

This opposition drove the rector of Clogheen, Parson Hewitson, and others of his cloth, into alliance with the Bagwells, Maudes, Jacobs, Bunburys, Bagnells, and others who sought the priests' destruction.

As an instance of Father Sheehy's opposition to the lawlessness of the peasantry, though sympathizing in their sufferings and wrongs, the night that the soldiers arrived in Clogheen, wearied and fatigued after a long march, the

EXECUTION OF FATHER SHEEHY.

Whiteboys had assembled to attack them, and would have done so only for the interference of Father Sheehy and Father Doyle. This very act was used against him by his enemies, as connecting him with the Whiteboys as their leader.

In 1762 his enemies bolstered up a charge, by suborned witnesses and informers, against Father Sheehy and others, for having assaulted one William Ross at Scarlop, and for having sworn him not to prosecute persons under bail, charged with levelling his fences at Drumlemmon. Not having succeeded in their accusation, in the following year they had him indicted, with others, for assaulting one John Bridge for turning informer against the Whiteboys.

Bridge was bound over to prosecute certain parties at the following assizes; he was a half simpleton, who had been tortured by the magistrates until he became an informer.

A few months after he had sworn his informations, John Bridge disappeared, and the priest's enemies at once circulated the report that Bridge had been murdered at his instigation. Here was a chance for the landlords, if they could only secure witnesses to prove the priest's connection with the murder. Parson Hewitson made himself quite active in hunting them up; and finally, by promises and bribes, succeeded in enlisting in his service a disreputable woman named Mary Bradley, alias "Moll Dunlea," whom Father Sheehy had expelled from his chapel for her wicked, immoral life; one Toohey, a noted horse-thief, who was brought out of the jail of Kilkenny for this purpose; and a vagabond, strolling boy, named Lonergan. On the information of these immaculate witnesses a warrant was issued for the arrest of the priest, and three hundred pounds offered for his apprehension.

Father Sheehy, knowing full well that if he were brought

to trial at Clonmel, he had not the least chance of escape from his relentless enemies, concealed himself for several months, and was even sheltered by several Protestants, particularly by a farmer named Griffith, at Shandraghan. After much suffering and many escapes, Father Sheehy wrote a letter to Secretary Waite at Dublin Castle, offering to surrender if tried in Dublin, stating that so bitter were the Tipperary magistrates against him, that he could not have a fair trial at Clonmel.

His offer was accepted. Father Sheehy at once delivered himself up to Mr. O'Callaghan, a just magistrate, and ancestor to the present Lord Donoghmore, who not only received him kindly, but sent to Clogheen for a troop of horse to escort him to Dublin, fearing to deliver him to the Orange constables, whom his brother magistrates had in their service.

On the 10th of February, 1766, he was arraigned at the bar of the Court of Queen's Bench, before Chief Justice Gore and Judges Robinson and Scott. So contemptible were the charges preferred against him, and so unworthy of credence appeared his prosecutors that he was immediately acquitted.

It is remarkable that on his trial in Dublin he was only accused of treasonable practices, but not for the murder of Bridge. The fact is, the Tipperary magistrates wanted him in Clonmel, where they could have the trial to order. While in Dublin, a friend of his, named O'Brien, knowing the relentless nature of his persecutors, urged him to fly to France; but Father Sheehy, conscious of his innocence, refused to do so, little thinking how terribly the odds were against him.

His relentless enemies had followed him to Dublin, and no sooner was the verdict of "not guilty" pronounced, than Bagwell demanded his committal on the charge of being accessory to the wilful murder of John Bridge. The Chief Justice, with great reluctance, remanded him to prison. Father Sheehy, in reply, said :

"My Lord Chief-Justice : This new accusation—terrible as it is—does not at all surprise me. Knowing the men from whom it comes, and their persevering enmity towards me, I had every reason to expect that they would be prepared to follow up my acquittal here—if acquitted I should be—with some other charge. Such a charge as this, no one who knows me could have anticipated, but God's will be done! I accept this grievous humiliation as coming from His paternal hand, and will only pray Him to turn the hearts of those who persecute me. I am thankful to this worshipful court, my lord, and to the gentlemen of the jury for the impartiality with which my trial has been conducted, and will ever pray that the righteous Judge of all may deal mercifully by those who have not shrunk from doing justice to an oppressed and persecuted man. I am now ready to submit to whatever fate awaits me, always declaring that if John Bridge were indeed murdered!—which God forbid!—I have had neither act nor part in, nor knowledge of, that execrable deed. I am well aware that this declaration avails nothing before a court of justice, but I owe it to my reputation as a man, and still more as a priest of the Most High God, and that God, who seeth the heart, knoweth that I do not prevaricate. I have done, my lords!"

"Mr. Sheehy," replied the humane Chief Justice, "it is not for me to express an opinion of any sort in this matter; but this I will say : that I have seldom performed a more painful duty than that of remanding you to prison. Mr. Sheriff," he added, addressing that functionary, "you will take the prisoner at the bar again into custody, until such time as he be brought up for trial."

No sooner had the prisoner quitted the dock and the

judges withdrawn from the bench, than the fierce shout was heard: "A groan for Maude, Hewitson, and Bagwell!—the priest-hunting, blood-thirsty magistrates of Clogheen!— there goes one of them, boys—let him hear how well the Dublin lads can hoot such rascals!" The groan, or rather a series of groans and hisses which followed, made Bagwell right glad to escape to his carriage, which was in waiting, while his black heart overflowed with venom to hear the wild and oft-renewed cheer which ascended from many thousand voices at the mention of Father Sheehy's name.

But Bagwell had his revenge, for he succeeded in having Father Sheehy sent back to Clonmel for trial; and, in order to heap indignities upon him, on his way back, his hands were manacled and his feet tied under the horse's belly, until the cords eat through the very flesh into the bones.

On the 12th of March, 1766, he was brought to trial at Clonmel, with Edmund Meehan, or Meighan, of Grange, charged with the murder of John Bridge, at Shanbally, on the 28th of October, 1764. So great was the terror in which the Tipperary magistrates were held that he could not get a lawyer to take up his case, except a Dublin attorney, named Sparrow, who knew little of its merits, or the characters of the priest's enemies, and who had to steal out of the town at night, owing to the threats of the Orange faction.

Toohy, who had been brought out of jail to swear away the life of the priest, stated that he was present with a party of Whiteboys when Sheehy tendered an oath to Bridge, binding him to deny his informations at the coming trial. Bridge refused to take it, and then one Pierce Byrne struck at him with a slane, and Edmund Meehan struck him with a bill-hook on the head, killing him instantly. Father Sheehy then swore all present to keep the murder secret, and to be true to the king of France. The body was then removed two miles from the scene of the murder, and interred in a lonely place.

The boy Lonergan swore that he met the party on their way to bury the body, and that Father Sheehy gave him three half crowns not to inform on them.

Moll Dunlea was the next witness; and, as she had an old spite against the priest, for hunting her out of the parish on account of her debauchery, she did some strong swearing. She swore that she lived with her mother at Clogheen; that Michael Kearney was at their house, and that, the night of the murder, Father Sheehy called for him. She followed them to Shanbally, when she saw themselves and Ned Meehan, Thomas Magrath, and others carrying the dead body of Bridge, which they buried at a place called the Bawn. She was also present when the body was removed from there and buried at Ballysheehan. The priest swore all present to secrecy on both occasions.

The above is the leading testimony upon which several persons were hanged. Is there anything more improbable than that a body of men contemplating murder would let a notorious thief and scoundrel, a strolling boy, and an unprincipled prostitute into the secret?

Ann Hullan, Moll Dunlea's mother, swore that Moll slept in the same bed with her the night of the murder, and several nights before and after, and that Michael Kearney was not in their house that year at all.

George Flannery, Thomas Gorman, Harry Keating, and others proved that Michael Kearney had left the country before the time of the murder; and a farmer, named Hendrekin, swore that Edmund Meehan spent all the night in his house, in which it was said Bridge was killed.

In any other country but Ireland such an impeachment of the prosecutors would immediately acquit the prisoners; but the ascendancy party had the judge and jury in their hands, and were resolved to hang their victims. Father Sheehy had several respectable witnesses to testify on his behalf, but his relentless enemies laid snares for them, and had some arrested, as Whiteboys and others, for murder.

A Mr. Herbert, a respectable farmer, was arrested on the charge of being a Whiteboy, on his way to court, and was so terrified by threats of execution that he subsequently turned a witness for the prosecution.

Mr. Keating, of Tubrid, a highly respectable Catholic gentleman, testified that, during the entire night of the supposed murder, Father Sheehy was in his house at Tubrid, and could not have left it without his knowledge.

At this stage of the proceedings, Parson Hewitson rose in court, with a paper in his hand, and said: "I find in this list Mr. Keating's name among those concerned in the late murder of a sergeant and corporal at Newmarket." Mr. Keating was at once removed and committed to jail, and his testimony expunged.*

This ruse showed how well the magistrates had laid their devilish plots, and struck terror into several in court, who might have given important evidence; but they saw that by so doing they would get themselves flung into jail, without doing any good to the doomed priest.

Dr. Egan, the Catholic bishop, had important testimony to give, but it is to be presumed that he refrained from attending the trial through fear of the Orange faction.

The high sheriff of the county, Daniel Toler, ancestor of the notorious and bloody Lord Norbury, made himself very active intimidating witnesses from appearing on behalf of the prisoners.

---

* Mr. Keating succeeded in having his trial removed to Kilkenny, out of reach of the Tipperary Orange magistrates, and was honorably acquitted. The jury scouted the evidence brought against him, which was partly the same as convicted Father Sheehy.

EXECUTION OF FATHER SHEEHY.

Father Sheehy saw how deeply the plot had been laid for his ruin, and as he saw Mr. Keating removed a prisoner from the witness stand, he knew that his fate was sealed. It availed little that several witnesses proved that they had seen Bridge after the night on which it was said he had been murdered; and that he stated to them that he was about leaving the country for good, in order to avoid swearing at the trials of some Whiteboys.* All this availed little, for the jury found Edmund Meehan guilty of the murder of John Bridge, and the same jury found Nicholas Sheehy *guilty of the murder of John Bridge, that is to say, as having aided and abetted Edward Meehan therein.*†

* It is strange that there was nothing said about the body of Bridge during the trial. The impression at the time, and which still exists in Tipperary, was that Bridge had fled the country to avoid both the Orange faction, who were using him as an informer, and the Whiteboys, whom he feared on account of his testimony against them. It is also stated that he was afterwards identified by several parties in St. John's, Newfoundland. On the other hand, Major Sirr, of Dublin Castle, father of the notorious Major Sirr, of '98, held a letter purporting to be from Father Sheehy, in which he stated that Bridge was killed, but that he knew nothing of the murder until a dying man accused himself of the crime. Though Dr. Curry, Dr. Egan, and other eminent authorities accept this letter as genuine, we doubt it, and look on it as a forgery, for if the witnesses saw Bridge murdered, and saw the body buried, as they testified, they could have pointed out the place to the authorities, who would, most certainly, have made the most of such a strong proof in their favor; but the fact is, neither the body nor the grave were ever found. Furthermore, Father Sheehy's reply to the judge confirms the belief that the document was a forgery concocted to mitigate the atrocity of Father Sheehy's foul murder.

† It is a remarkable fact that not one of the jurors who tried Father Sheehy, died by a natural death. Sir Thomas Maude died a raving maniac, crying out that Father Sheehy was dragging him down to hell. Bagwell, of Kilmore, became an idiot; and his eldest son shot himself in a packet on his way to England, and that branch of the family soon became extinct. Jacob was seized with fits, in which he barked like a dog, and could scarcely be kept from eating the flesh off himself. Cook, of Kiltinan, was drowned. Parson Hewitson died suddenly. Barker had no

Again was the voice of wailing, loud and deep, heard echoing through the building : sighs and loud groans gave note that many a heart, even in that packed assemblage, sympathized with the unfortunate victim of injustice. But the prisoner himself only raised his eyes to heaven and said, "Even *this*, my God! even *this* can I bear! All things, whatsoever Thou wilt, whether they be good or evil! so long as Thou keepest me in the state of grace, I can cheerfully submit to Thy holy will."

On the following morning the prisoners were brought up for sentence. Poor Meehan received his death sentence heir, and died in fits. Tuthill cut his throat. Another juror, named Shaw, was choked to death. Alexander Hoops was drowned. Ferris died mad. Another dropped dead at his own door. Another died in a privy. Dumvill was killed by his horse. Minchin died in beggary. The Pennefeather family was reduced to poverty, and many of them died idiots. The Barker and Jacob families are also extinct, in a direct line. The same might be said of the families of nearly all the jurors who tried Father Sheehy. Though I cannot give the fate of each of the jurors, it is remarkable that a curse seemed to blight each and every one of them, and even their descendants.

To finish the catalogue : Moll Dunlea was killed by falling into a cellar, in Cork, while drunk ; Lonergan died of a loathesome disease, in Dublin ; and Toohey died of the leprosy. On the other hand, the descendants of Mr. Callaghan, who showed justice and mercy to the poor persecuted priest, have become nobles in the land.

The following verses, taken from an old Irish song, allude to the fate of Father Sheehy's jury, and are attributed to his sister, who went half crazy, and watched his head for twenty years, until it was given up to her :—

"And where are they, dear head! that once reviled thee?—
Who spiked thee high, and with filthy pitch defiled thee?—
All prayers for pity spurn'd, scoff'd, and slighted—
They crush'd my heart, and left me old and blighted.

"Sure of their doom, some died in madness, yelling
Of Sheehy's quarter'd corpse, of Hell's dark dwelling ;
And some, O righteous God! impious and daring,
Pour'd forth their cursed lives, and died despairing."

with great composure, but the sobs and cries of his aged father and distracted wife were pitiful to hear. Father Sheehy was then put forward.

"Nicholas Sheehy," said the judge, "have you any reason to offer why sentence of death should not be passed upon you?"

"My good lord," said the priest, with a simple earnestness of manner that touched every heart that was not steeled by prejudice, "my good lord! I am aware that your question is a mere form, and that anything I can or could say would have no effect; still, as the opportunity is afforded me, I must say that I am entirely innocent of the crime—the heinous crime—of which I have been convicted. Not only am I innocent thereof, but, to the best of my belief, no such murder has been committed. I am almost fully persuaded that this very John Bridge is still living, for we have the clearest evidence that some days subsequent to the date of the supposed murder the man was seen alive and in good health, and took leave of his friends to go either to Cork or Kinsale, to embark for some foreign country."

Here he was interrupted by the judge, who desired him to confine himself to his own case.

"My lord! it appears to me that I speak to the purpose; surely I do when myself and another are to be put to death for a crime which *never was* committed by any one. Knowing, or at least believing, this to be the case, I protest against the entire proceedings, as regards Meehan and myself, and *will* protest until my latest moment against the shameful injustice, the gross perjury, the deadly malice of which we are the victims. In conclusion, I must declare that notwithstanding all this, I bear these unhappy men who persecute me even to death, not the slightest ill-will; I leave them in the hands of a just God, knowing that He will deal with them according to their deserts! That is all I have to say! I leave God to distinguish between the innocent and the guilty!"

The judge, after a few remarks, passed sentence in the following words :—

"You shall be hanged, drawn, and quartered, on Saturday next, the 15th inst., and may God have mercy on your soul, and grant you a sight of the enormity of your crime!"

"I thank your lordship for your good wishes," replied the poor priest; "doubtless I have much to answer for before God, since we are all sinful creatures at the very best, but He knows that of this crime, or aught like unto it, I am wholly innocent. To His justice I fearlessly and with all confidence give myself up. Praise, however, and glory to His holy name, now and for ever more, and may His will be done on earth as it is in heaven!"

On the 15th of March, two days after receiving their sentence, Father Sheehy and Ned Meehan were executed in Clonmel.* An immense concourse of the afflicted peasantry had assembled on the melancholy occasion. Women and children wept bitterly as they knelt in prayer; strong men knit their brows in vexation, for they saw their faithful *Soggarth Aroon* going to be strangled to death for their sakes, and they powerless to help him, for that strong force of cavalry and infantry that surrounded the gallows, looked

---

* Some authorities state that Father Sheehy was executed in Clogheen. This opinion gained credence from the fact that his cousin, Ned Sheehy, and his companions, were hanged there. Dr. Madden and tradition agree in stating that he was executed in Clonmel. After the most diligent research I have come to the conclusion that he was hanged on Gallows Hill, now a most beautiful suburban retreat of the Malcomson family. Tradition also states that as the headless trunks were borne through the street, Father Sheehy's sister collected the blood that dripped from the body in the palm of her hand, and smeared it over Bishop Egan's door. As it is very hard to remove the stains of blood from wood, this gave rise to the belief that the doctor's door was mysteriously covered with blood which never could be eradicated.

threateningly on, as if they would desire nothing better than a pretence to fall on the people and butcher them. The sobs and moans of the multitude were hushed, as the victims were led forth to the scaffold. A wail of agony went up from that living mass, accompanied by a deep-muttered curse against their persecutors. The priest and his fellow martyr bent their heads in prayer, as they eagerly profitted by the ministrations of Father Doyle, their spiritual attendant and their warm friend.

At length, having reached the place of execution, the troops formed in a ring around the gallows, with the sobbing multitude outside them. The rope having been placed around Father Sheehy's neck, he turned to the weeping crowd, and said :

"May the Almighty God, before whose judgment seat I am about to appear, bless and protect you all, and may he grant to each of you the graces of which you stand most in need! May He preserve you steadfastly in the true faith by which alone salvation is to be obtained. I need scarcely tell you, my good people, that I die entirely innocent of the foul crime laid to my charge. As for those who have persecuted me even to death, and the jury who condemned me on such evidence, I forgive and pity them all, and would not change place with any one of them for all the riches of the earth. The care of my reputation I leave to my God—He will re-establish it in His own good time. In conclusion, I pray you all to retire quietly to your homes, and make no disturbance, for that would only give a pretext for fresh persecution."

As he concluded, a wail of woe rang to heaven from the afflicted crowd, and a shriek, loud and piercing, ascended from the foot of the gallows. It was a wail of anguish from three broken-hearted women, who had forced their way through the soldiers, namely, Father Sheehy's two sisters,

Mrs. Green and Mrs. Burke, and the stricken young wife of Ned Meehan.

The tears rushed to the eyes of the dying men, and Meehan, stretching forth his hands to his poor wife, exclaimed: "O Biddy, Biddy dear, may God pity and protect you and our children, my poor wife." Father Sheehy held his hands over the prostrate women, whom the soldiers were removing from the foot of the gallows, and exclaimed: "May God pity and comfort ye, poor stricken people!" He then embraced his old friend, Father Doyle, and, calmly turning around, gave the signal to the hangman, and was immediately launched into eternity, as a wild, heart-piercing wail went up from the horror-stricken crowd.*

As soon as life was extinct, the bodies were cut down and the heads severed from the trunks. The latter were deliv-

---

* The death of Father Sheehy did not satisfy the Orange landlords In the following month, his cousin, Ned Sheehy; a respectable farmer, James Buxton, and James Farrell were also tried for the murder of Bridge, for swearing Toohy to be true to *Shaun Meskill* (a name given to the Whiteboys, after one of their leaders) and her children, and other charges. The swearing against them was reckless and savage, being the same as hung the priest. They were, of course, sentenced to death, and executed at Clogheen. When their heads were chopped off, a young girl named Ann Mary Butler snatched up the head of Ned Sheehy, and made off with it. The pitying soldiers made way for her, and closed up on the hangman, who pursued her. The head was decently interred with the body, while the other two were spiked at Clonmel. These men declared, just before their execution, that they were offered their liberty by the Rev. Lawrence Broderick, Rev. John Hewitson, Sir William Barker's son, Matthew Bumbury, Bagnell, Toler, and Bagnall, if they would swear against Bishop Creagh, Lord Dunboyne's brother, Robert Keating, several other gentlemen, and some priests, charging them with being engaged in a conspiracy with the French government to raise an insurrection in Ireland; but, above all, if they would declare that Father Sheehy was guilty, and that he "had died with a lie in his mouth." These brave men withstood all, and died with remarkable fortitude, declaring their innocence to the last. Ned Sheehy was the grandfather of the celebrated Countess of Blessington, one of his daughters being married to Edmund Power, of Curragheen.

ered to their friends, for interment, but the heads were spiked over the old jail, where they, and the heads of Buxton and Farrell, remained for years, ghastly spectacles of the savagery and ruffianism of the Orange landlords of Tipperary.

Just twenty years afterwards, in 1786, Father Sheehy's sister was allowed to take away his head, and inter it with his body, in Shandraghan graveyard.

Beside the ruins of the Old Church sleeps the remains of Father Sheehy. A beaten path leads to the grave, for many a pilgrim has trod over it. The white headstone that marks this hallowed spot bears the following inscription :

"Here lieth the remains of the Rev. Nicholas Sheehy, parish priest of Shandraghan, Ballysheehan, and Templeheny. He died March 15, 1766, aged 38 years. Erected by his sister, Catherine Burke, *alias* Sheehy."

The tyrannical power and religious intolerance that trampled down the people's rights in the name of liberty, that despoiled their altars and churches, and tortured and martyred their priests, in the name of religion, are no more. Brighter days have dawned upon Ireland, and we can pityingly look back upon the past, thanking God that that noble heritage of Ireland, her Catholic faith, has been preserved pure and undefiled by the sacrifices of the long and noble array of martyrs and confessors, whose blood has fructified into such a rich harvest, and has brought forth such noble fruit, not only in Ireland, but also in America and other countries.

The lives, sufferings, and deaths of such men as Bishop Plunket and Father Sheehy kept warm the spirit of freedom and religion in the hearts of the people.

Religion and liberty have ever been associated in the minds of the Irish people. Like twin sisters, they have gone hand in hand ; and now, when the shackles that manacled the fair form of the one have been broken and flung in the dust, may the other soon stand forth as pure and as free.

A kinder feeling and a more generous spirit pervades the land; the dark past is buried with its bloody record, and a brighter future—a future of peace and happiness—seems to dawn upon long-suffering Ireland. The dark cloud that St. Patrick, in his vision, saw overspread the length and breadth of Ireland, has been dispelled by the light of faith and the teachings of the Gospel; and though tyrants have desolated her by their bitter hate, and bedewed her soil with streams of martyrs' blood, still she has gloriously risen from long ages of darkness and sorrow, and proudly stands forth to-day, the uncrowned queen of nations, the hallowed Isle of Saints and Martyrs.

We have now concluded these sad memorials of a dark and troublous period in the history of Ireland, and though the sad volume is written in the blood of the best and most pious of Ireland's persecuted children, still, it is a record that we can look back upon with the conscious pride that no other country can produce a parallel, where a whole nation made such terrible sacrifices to preserve unsullied their religion and their national independence. Speaking of these cruel penal times, we select, as a fitting conclusion to our work, the following expressive poem on the subject, from the pen of an anonymous writer. Short as it is since the poem first appeared, the intolerance that the poet deplores has passed away, and the Catholic religion is to-day free and disenthralled in Ireland. Let us trust that a few years more shall crown the victory with the priceless boon of national liberty.

THE PENAL DAYS.

In that dark time of cruel wrong, when on our country's breast,
A dreary load, a ruthless code, with wasting terrors press'd—
Our gentry stripp'd of land and clan, sent exiles o'er the main,
To turn the scales on foreign fields for foreign monarchs' gain;
Our people trod like vermin down, all 'fenceless, flung to sate
Extortion, lust, and brutal whim, and rancorous bigot hate;
Our priesthood tracked from cave to hut, like felons chased and lashed,
And from their ministering hands the lifted chalice dashed—
In that black time of law-wrought crime, of stifling woe and thrall,
There stood supreme one foul device, one engine worse than all;
Him whom they wished to keep a slave, they sought to make a brute;
They banned the light of heaven, they bade instruction's voice be mute.

God's second priest, the Teacher, sent to feed men's mind with lore—
They marked a price upon his head, as on the priest's before.
Well, well they knew that never, face to face, beneath the sky,
Could tyranny and knowledge meet, but one of them should die;
That lettered slaves will link their might until their murmurs grow
To that imperious thunder-peal which despots quail to know;
That men who learn will learn their strength, the weakness of their
   lords,
Till all the bonds that gird them round are snapped like Samson's cords.
This well they knew, and called the power of ignorance to aid.
So might, they deemed, an abject race of soulless serfs be made—
When Irish memories, hopes, and thoughts, were withered, branch and
   stem,
A race of abject, soulless serfs, to hew and draw for them.

Ah, God is good and nature strong; they let not thus decay
The seeds that, deep in Irish breasts, of Irish feeling, lay;
Still sun and rain made emerald green the loveliest fields on earth,
And gave the type of deathless hope, the little shamrock, birth;
Still faithful to their Holy Church, her direst straits among,
To one another faithful still, the priests and people clung,
And Christ was worshipped, and received with trembling haste and fear,
In field and shed, with posted scouts, to warn of bloodhounds near;

Still, crouching 'neath the sheltering hedge, or stretched on mountain
    fern,
The teacher and his pupils met, feloniously—to learn;
Still round the peasant's heart of hearts his darling music twined,
A fount of Irish sobs or smiles in every note enshrined;
And still beside the smouldering turf were fond traditions told
Of heavenly saints and princely chiefs, the power and faith of old.

Deep lay the seeds, yet rankest weeds sprang mingled—could they fail?
For what were freedom's blessed worth, if slavery wrought not bale?
As thrall, and want, and ignorance, still deep and deeper grew,
What marvel weakness, gloom, and strife fell dark amongst us too;
And servile thoughts, that measure not the inborn wealth of man,
And servile cringe, and subterfuge, to 'scape our master's ban;
And drunkenness, our sense of woe a little while to steep;
And aimless feud, and murderous plot—oh, one could pause and weep!
'Mid all the darkness, faith in Heaven still shone, a saving ray,
And Heaven o'er our redemption watched, and chose its own good day.
Two men were sent us; one for years, with Titan strength of soul,
To beard our foes, to peal our wrongs, to band us and control.
The other, at a later time, on gentler mission came,
To make our noblest glory spring from out our saddest shame!
On all our wondrous, upward course hath Heaven its finger set,
And we—but, oh, my countrymen, there's much before us yet!

How sorrowful the useless powers our glorious Island yields—
Our countless havens desolate, our waste of barren fields;
The all unused mechanic might our rushing streams afford,
The buried treasures of our mines, our sea's unvalued hoard!
But, oh, there is one piteous waste, whence all the rest have grown,
One worst neglect, the mind of man left desert and unsown.
Send Knowledge forth to scatter wide, and deep to cast its seeds,
The nurse of energy and hope, of manly thoughts and deeds.
Let it go forth: right soon will spring those forces in its train
That vanquish Nature's stubborn strength, that rifle earth and main;
Itself a nobler harvest far than Autumn tints with gold,
A higher wealth, a surer gain than wave and mine enfold.
Let it go forth unstained, and purged from Pride's unholy leaven,
With fearless forehead raised to man, but humbly bent to Heaven.

Deep let it sink in Irish hearts—the story of their isle,
And waken thoughts of tenderest love and burning wrath the while;
And press upon us, one by one, the fruits of English sway,
And blend the wrongs of bygone times with this our fight to-day;
And show our Father's constancy by truest instinct led,
To loathe and battle with the power that on their substance fed;
And let it place beside our own the world's vast page, to tell
That never lived the nation yet could rule another well.
Thus, thus our cause shall gather strength; no feeling vague and blind,
But stamped by passion on the heart, by reason on the mind.
Let it go forth—a mightier foe to England's power than all
The rifles of America, the armaments of Gaul!
It *shall* go forth, and woe to them that bar or thwart its way;
'Tis God's own light, all heavenly bright, we care not who says nay.